SOCIAL POLICY AND SOCIAL WORK

Social Policy and Social Work

DAVID DENNEY

CLARENDON PRESS · OXFORD

1998

Oxford University Press, Great Clarendon Street, Oxford OX2 6DP
Oxford New York
Athens Auckland Bangkok Bogota Bombay Buenos Aires
Calcutta Cape Town Dar es Salaam Delhi Florence Hong Kong Istanbul
Karachi Kuala Lumpur Madras Madrid Melbourne Mexico City
Nairobi Paris Singapore Taipei Tokyo Toronto Warsaw
and associated companies in
Berlin Ibadan

Oxford is a registered trade mark of Oxford University Press

Published in the United States
by Oxford University Press Inc., New York

British Library Cataloguing in Publication Data
Data available

Library of Congress Cataloging in Publication Data
David, Denney.
Social policy and social work / David Denney.
Includes bibliographical references.
1. Social service. 2. Social policy. I. Title
HV41.D23 1998 361.6′1—dc21 98–17440
ISBN 0–19–878150–4
ISBN 0–19–878149–0 (Pbk)

1 3 5 7 9 10 8 6 4 2

Typeset by BookMan Services, Ilfracombe
Printed in Great Britain
on acid-free paper by
Bookcraft (Bath) Ltd
Midsomer Norton, Somerset

To Shirin, Joe, and Eve

ACKNOWLEDGEMENTS

It would have been impossible to write a book of this eclectic nature without support and encouragement. Bob Broad offered detailed comments on Chapter 14. Helen Cosis-Brown read and commented helpfully on Chapter 13. Paul Daniel and Claire Wendelken, both always a source of sensitive encouragement, helped as I struggled with Chapter 12. Lorraine Radford despite a heavy research schedule read the chapter on women and constructively pointed out many omissions. I am grateful for the clarity and encouragement of Vic George. His close critical reading of my work made me rethink. Mark Doel, Derek Kirton, and Mike Oliver painstakingly read the book in its entirety and provided comments which were enormously helpful. I would also like to thank the anonymous readers from Oxford University Press and Tim Barton, a calm and supportive editor. I must take sole responsibility for any remaining inaccuracies.

D.D.

CONTENTS

LIST OF FIGURES

LIST OF TABLES

ABBREVIATIONS

ADP	anti-discriminatory practice
ASW	approved social worker
CCETSW	Central Council for Education and Training in Social Work
COS	Charity Organisation Society
CPA	care programme approach
CQSW	Certificate of Qualification in Social Work
Dip. SW	Diploma in Social Work
D.o.E. and E.	Department of Education and Employment
D.o.H.	Department of Health
DSS	Department of Social Security
FGC	family group conference
NAPO	National Association of Probation Officers
NCVO	National Council for Voluntary Organisations
NVQ	National Vocational Qualification
PACE	Police and Criminal Evidence Act 1984
PC	political correctness
PSSRU	Personal Social Services Research Unit (University of Kent at Canterbury)
SSA	Standard Spending Assessment

Introduction

Aims of the Book

Readers who remember the BBC's *Mastermind* might recall that contestants were well advised to choose their specialist areas of knowledge with great specificity, e.g. 'The Life of Giovanni Boccaccio at the Papal Court of Avignon between 1354 and 1365', rather than elect an area like 'European History since 1945'. Although this book focuses on the UK it still reflects the latter approach. It covers a wide corpus of literature and research which presents an array of complexities to the student approaching this area for the first time. Since there is no A level in social work, care management, or social policy, students can experience difficulties in grasping basic theoretical ideas and linkages with practice.

Social work grew out of a mid-nineteenth-century concern for those who suffered distress or those who created distress in others (Howe 1996: 81). The emergence of market testing in the 1980s, and internal markets and care management in the 1990s, have questioned the basis upon which the state becomes involved in distressing situations. Moreover, in the late 1990s prophecies of deprofessionalization and the possible demise of social work itself are being expressed (Parton 1996, Dominelli 1996). Following the election of a Labour government in 1997, the consensus amongst all the major political parties about the appropriateness of market forces within the delivery of state welfare appears to be even clearer.

This book is intended to introduce some of the fundamental debates which link social work and social policy and is based upon two propositions.

- A critical appreciation of how ideas about the formation of the welfare state have developed is a necessary part of social work and care management education.
- Social work and social policy should not simply reflect pragmatic institutional requirements and current ideology, but should be self-critical.

The book will be of assistance to social work practitioners, to those currently on social work and care management training courses, and to social policy students. It will also provide an introduction to the social services for students on social policy degree programmes.

An introductory text of this kind cannot provide new and original insights in all the areas it seeks to address, nor can it make reference to all available research materials. The intention is to suggest how issues, ideas, and debates in social work are rooted in the development of social policy.

A note on structure

The book is divided into three parts. The first part provides an overview of the development of social work and an introduction to the basic concepts which link history and social theory with social work and social policy goals. Part II will examine social policy in relation to social work with specific user groups—disabled people, people experiencing mental health problems, children, and offenders—in greater detail. In the third and final part wider issues emerging from social care will be given detailed attention. Community care, the emerging role of the care manager, the mixed economy of welfare, and the future of social work will be examined.

Many individuals are subjected to the negative impact of racism, ageism, and sexism. Dividing people on the basis of organizational structures should not be seen as diminishing the impact of multiple oppression (see Chapters 5, 7, 8, 9, 15, 16, and 18).

All chapters contain a summary of the main points at the beginning, exercises, and guided further reading. The exercises aim for flexibility, and can be used by individuals working alone or by groups of students. An example of how an exercise might be tackled is given at the end of Chapter 2. There is no specific chapter on older people in Part II, which examines specific user groups. Chapter 6 is intended to emphasize the importance of work with older people. Here an extended case analysis relates ideological perspectives to social work practice with older people. References to older people are also made in Chapter 18.

It should be noted that this book was almost completed when a Labour government was elected in May 1997 after almost two decades of Conservative government. Much of the book is concerned with the impact of policy on practices during that eighteen-year period. With the exception of some ideological differences noted in Chapter 6, early signs would indicate that New Labour will build upon many of the social policy changes made by the Conservative government during the 1980s and 1990s.

PART I

Concepts, Context, and Ideas

CHAPTER 1

Historical Developments

- The idea of the welfare state
- Tracing the roots of welfare
- The impact of industrialization
- The influence of war
- Principles of the welfare state
- The development of social work
- Criticisms of the Seebohm Report
- Defining social work
- The probation service: policy and practice

In this chapter the origins of the welfare state will be briefly discussed. A chronological approach will be taken with regard to both the development and history of social work and social policy.

The idea of the welfare state

The term 'welfare state' is probably not English in its origins but derives from the German word *Wohlfahrsstaat*, a term of abuse used by right-wing critics of the German Social Democratic Weimar Republic of the 1920s (Glennerster 1995). In this sense it denoted a form of consensual state activity which underplayed the importance of Germanic militarism and nationalism. Briggs (1961) has defined welfare states as having three characteristics which modify the play of market forces:

- the guarantee of a minimum income;
- state intervention to assist people in meeting particular social contingencies like old age and unemployment;

- the management of the economy in such a way as to reduce inequalities in income (A. Briggs, quoted in Lowe 1993: 13).

Tracing the roots of welfare

Many millions of words have been written on the historical origins and development of the welfare state. What will be described here is a framework for understanding the main landmarks.

There is nothing new or unusual about local government being involved in the alleviation of need. In 1601 the Elizabethan Poor Law made each parish responsible for its own poor. An overseer of the poor was appointed who collected a poor rate from each landowner, and who was also responsible for apprenticing pauper children, providing money, food, and protection for elderly and disabled people, and providing them with accommodation.

It is in the Elizabethan Poor Law that we see the origins of employment benefit, since the overseer of the poor provided work or money to the unemployed poor. In 1662 the Act of Settlement gave the overseer of the poor the right to remove from a parish settlers who could not give an assurance that they could find work within forty days. These provisions broke down, since the overseers were lax in the administration of their duties, whilst the industrial revolution led to the growth of new towns which were not included within the provisions of the Poor Law. Farm labourers moved into the towns, and common land disappeared as a result of the enclosure of land during the eighteenth century.

The Speenhamland system emerged in 1795 with the breakdown of the Elizabethan Poor Law and the Act of Settlement. The system was devised by the magistrates of Speenhamland in Berkshire who constructed a scale of relief based on wage level, marital status, the number of children in a family, and the current price of bread. Problems immediately arose, since employers tended to lower wages whilst large families and marriage were encouraged. The system also became corrupt (Fraser 1984).

The workhouse system had developed in the late eighteenth century and in 1782 Gilbert's Act allowed parishes to build workhouses. In 1832 a Poor Law Commission was set up to investigate the existing system, since the cost of the system had been increasing, whilst the Speenhamland system was thought to be demoralizing rural workers.

The 1834 Poor Law Amendment Act required parishes to form unions to build workhouses with regimes which were to become strict and segregated, in order to discourage people from entering them. This became known as the less eligibility principle. Unions of workhouses were to be controlled by boards of guardians elected by ratepayers and a Poor Law Commission was set up in London to control the system (Woodroofe 1971).

Edwin Chadwick, a secretary to and disciple of Jeremy Bentham, became the secretary to the Commission. His insistence on the Benthamite principle of utility led to him being thought excessively harsh (Rose 1970). There was no central control of the boards of guardians, who were financially independent, whilst bitter opposition to the Poor Law developed, particularly in the north of England (Checkland and Checkland 1974). The 1834 Poor Law Amendment Act was chiefly motivated by a desire to maximize the labour force and reduce government expenditure in order to stimulate economic growth. Thus, in the words of the time, the Act would stimulate industry and not idleness (Fraser 1984). From its inception social policy was inextricably linked to economic policies and a preoccupation with cutting public expenditure. The principle of less eligibility for state benefit bears a resemblance to the new right approach which came to dominate social policy in the 1980s. Of all the legislation for social reform which was produced in the early nineteenth century, few Acts aroused such hostility as did the new 1834 Poor Law. The 1834 Act, like much of the legislation which followed the election of Margaret Thatcher in 1979, assumed that those who were destitute were to a large degree responsible for their own fate. The notion that there might be any social causation related to pauperism was anathema. Social policy-makers considered poverty to be a moral condition in both 1834 and 1979. There was continuous agitation against the Poor Law from its inception in 1834 to the demise of the boards of guardians in 1929.

In 1847 the Poor Law Commission became the Poor Law Board responsible to Parliament, and by 1871 it was part of local government. It was not until 1905 that a Poor Law Commission estimated that up to 300,000 children were receiving outdoor relief, whilst some 14,000 children were living in workhouses. The Poor Law Commission produced a majority report arguing that the Poor Law should be replaced by a Public Assistance Committee (Evans 1978).

The impact of industrialization

Changes which took place between 1760 and 1830 saw rapid advances in technology initially within the woollen and cotton industries of East Anglia, the south-west of England, and the West Riding, and the Lancashire cotton industry. The invention and use of machinery overcame the shortage of labour and heralded the demise of the old domestic system of labour, and the development of the factory system.

The social impact of industrialization cannot be overemphasized, marking a fundamental transformation in life for many millions of people (Hobsbawm 1969). Industrialization was relatively slow to develop but after 1760 rapidly gathered momentum. Developments in the iron and steel industry, steam power, and technological developments in mining and engineering enabled Britain to gain a position of global influence. This process was accentuated by the development of more efficient communications, particularly the railways, which developed in the 1830s.

Industrial capitalism led to the creation and redistribution of populations towards the urban centres, and rural depopulation. Appalling unregulated conditions in factories and mines were endured, particularly by women and children. This gave rise to the creation of a new capitalist industrialist class and the development of working-class movements (Thompson 1968, Perkin 1969).

What we are most interested in is the consequences of industrialization in terms of the development of state response to the social problems. Slowly, possibly out of fear of mass revolt, the state began to develop social policies in a number of important areas. During the nineteenth century public health, education, the regulation of working conditions, and income maintenance became priorities. The growth of the national economy led to the regulation of transport, money, and business.

The accumulation of large numbers of industrial workers living close to the workplace in deplorable conditions had created a form of working-class consciousness which demanded better working and living conditions. The Chartist Movement, which gained prominence between 1837 and 1848, called for the reform of a corrupt Parliament, universal suffrage, annual Parliaments, vote by ballot, equal electoral districts, reform of the Poor Law, and improvements in state education and factory regulations (Wilson 1970). Trade unions and friendly societies had developed throughout the eighteenth and nineteenth centuries despite legislation in 1799 which sought to outlaw trade unions. Gradually, after many years of struggle, a collective responsibility began to develop in a number of obvious areas. Government itself was reorganized in order to create an administrative structure for the development of social policy

The influence of war

Another major factor influencing the development of welfare states in the twentieth century was war. Some argue that the fight against a collective enemy in both wars to some extent temporarily transcended class and gender divisions, creating an expectation that something would have to be done to relieve poverty when the war was over. Second World War emergencies, including the blitz and mass evacuation, combined with memories of the great inter-war depression to expose hitherto concealed social evils. Such a view of the importance of the Second World War has been supported by Titmus, who argued that the circumstances of the war created an unprecedented sense of solidarity, preparing the way for more egalitarian policies (Titmus 1958, 1968).

Although the Second World War was a significant factor in the development of the welfare state, its importance should not be overemphasized. Despite the presence of particular individuals like Keynes, who was an economic adviser to the war cabinet, and Beveridge during this period, little conscious central planning of post-war economic and social policy was discernible when the war was at its height. A low priority was given to social issues by the wartime cabinet. Thane (1982) has argued that most politicians and civil servants regarded the growth of government intervention during the war as a regrettable necessity, blocking many attempts made by such people as Beveridge to reconstruct after the war. Yet the characteristic governmental cry after the First World War was for a return to the status quo ante.

The aftermath of the Second World War produced a number of wide-ranging plans based upon more egalitarian values. Beveridge formulated ideas for a comprehensive welfare system which integrated hospital and personal social services. His reforms were designed to tackle the five evils of ignorance, idleness, squalor, disease, and want, through a system which would provide a minimum standard of subsistence and care for the entire population. He believed that the establishment of such a universal system based on the principle of social insurance could be financed through single weekly contributions from employer and employee, plus a contribution from the exchequer. The system for employed people was to be augmented by a means-tested, government-financed system of public assistance. Benefits would be calculated on Rowntree's Human Needs scale of 1936 plus rent (Thane 1982).

The Beveridge Report which contained these principles and assumptions was published in December 1942. It was seen by the Ministry of Information as being a way of boosting wartime morale. More than any other wartime plan for reconstruction it caught the imagination of the public. Although, as after the First World War, the advocates of a welfare state faced some opposition, in 1945 those opposed to Beveridge's plan were more prepared to make concessions.

Principles of the welfare state

The basic principles of the welfare state have been well summarized by Glennerster (1995).

- Full employment, which incorporated the idea that the national budget should be used to seek high levels of stable employment. This reflected the ideas of John Maynard Keynes and had preoccupied Beveridge's thinking between 1903 and 1908 (Silburn 1995).

- A national minimum wage. Beveridge believed that a national minimum was impossible unless unemployment was eradicated. The state would take on the responsibility for a national minimum wage, and the development of mass leisure.

- Equal and free access to co-ordinated health care and education services.

- A central form of administrative control; this was necessary in order for the above goals to be achieved. Local authorities would effectively become agents of central government.

- Provision to be made by the state, unlike the insurance provisions which had been made following the 1911 National Insurance Act (Glennerster 1995).

The new services were initiated on 5 July 1948, three years after the election of the post-war Labour government. The welfare state was not created by the Labour government of 1945. It was as connected to long-term political, economic, and social forces as it was to the Second World War or the ideas of Beveridge and Keynes.

The creation of a welfare state was a pragmatic necessity brought about according to Lowe by two fundamental factors. First, the introduction of universal suffrage in 1918 and 1928 had created a constant electoral pressure to 'match equal political status with equal opportunities' and equal distribution of resources. Secondly, the structural needs of an advanced industrial capitalist society working within a highly competitive international marketplace required intervention to manage the economy. During the post-war period across a number of industrialized countries government policies transformed the fundamental nature of the relationship between the state and its citizens (Lowe 1993). None of the proposals made by Beveridge or Keynes was ever implemented in full, since the central priority of the government after both wars was the achievement of a sound economic base and not social equality.

Unlike the aftermath of the first world war measures were taken to reconstruct the economy, in the short term by the maintenance of wartime controls, in the longer term by the nationalisation of essential but unprofitable industries, railways, coal and electricity. (Thane 1982: 2)

The development of social work

Table 1.1 indicates some of the major landmarks in the history of social work and social work policy. Social work emerged in the industrialized countries during the latter half of the nineteenth century and played a dual role in Victorian society. Whilst it ameliorated and defused discontent amongst poverty-stricken people, acting as a 'social sedative', it was also a 'social regenerator'. The task of the Victorian caseworker was to rescue character and 'Ferret out, beneath the surface of dependence, apathy, and hopelessness, some elements of character and willpower' (Woodroofe 1971).

Frequently at this period such a transformation was thought to be linked to divine intervention. Police 'court missionaries', the precursor to the probation officer, were as interested in saving recalcitrant souls as in providing relief to the usually deserving poor (May 1991).

The Charity Organisation Society (COS), founded in 1869 in London to co-ordinate forms of charitable good works, also aimed at attacking pauperism by increasing co-operation with other charities and the Poor Law, in order to eliminate the indiscriminate administration of relief. The COS also had the job of investigating and assessing applications for relief. The COS assessed need in order to establish whether the client was deserving or undeserving. Educated women volunteers were recruited to develop assistance plans, and offered advice to those in need. These activities were based on the belief that the source of distress and hardship often lay within the individual.

Table 1.1. **Some major landmarks in the development of policy and practice**

Practice	Legislation and government reports	Policy
Purchasing and co-ordinating packages of care. Negotiating with a variety of agencies to create new resources assessing need.	1990 NHS and Community Care Act.	Mixed economy of welfare. Priority to informal care. Deinstitutionalization.
Development of financial assessment skills and contracting skills.	1989 Griffiths Report.	Local authorities to take the lead in providing community care. Provide an independent sector to work alongside state sector.
	1988 Wagner Report.	Service users to be consumers. Range of alternative forms of care. More information required for users to make choices.
Counselling. Assessment skills.	1989 Children Act.	Parental responsibility. Duty of local authorities to return child to family unless this is against child's best interest. Continued contact with natural parents.
Specialist knowledge (approved social worker status).	1983 Mental Health Act.	Sectioning of those in need of institutional care with the development of community mental health service.
Counselling. Linking service plan with individual needs.	1982 Barclay Report.	Social care planning. Decentralized social care.
Innovative practice to complement services provided by the state.	1974 Wolfenden Report.	Partnership between state and voluntary sector.
More task-centred casework—Reid and Epstein (1977). Systems approach—Pincus and Minahan (1973).	1970 Chronically Sick and Disabled Persons Act.	Extension of state social work, managed at local authority level to meet needs.
Community work. Groupwork.	1970 Local Authority Social Services Act.	
Casework.	1969 Children and Young Persons Act. 1968 Seebohm Report.	Unified local authority social service departments. Simplifying functions.
Generic casework.	1959 Mental Health Act. 1959 Younghusband Report.	
Influence of psychology/psycho-analysis US casework, e.g. Hollis (1964). 'Friendly visiting'.	1954 First generic social work course. 1948 National Assistance Act. 1948 Children Act. 1942 Beveridge Report. 1925 Criminal Justice Act. 1907 Probation of Offenders Act. 1869 Charity Organisation Society.	

The nineteenth-century model of visiting was initially set up on a parochial basis. Whereas in the nineteenth century district visiting had been more concerned with assessing and establishing eligibility for relief, after 1869 volunteers concentrated on assessing the needs of families (Midgeley 1995, Lewis 1995).

The 1907 Probation of Offenders Act first gave magistrates the right to appoint probation officers, but it was not until 1925 with the Criminal Justice Act that specific probation areas were created. Throughout the 1930s and 1940s social work and probation went through a 'phase of diagnosis' with an emphasis on quasi-scientism of assessment and the 'treatment of the individual' (May 1991: 15).

The impact of legislation following the Beveridge Report laid the foundations and provided shape for social work tasks in post-war Britain. The Children Act of 1948 made local authorities responsible for children whose parents were unfit or unable to care for them, whilst also supervising adoption services. Since the adoption legalization of 1926, proliferating services had remained unsupervised. Local authorities were also given the primary duty to place children in foster care (Thane 1984). Throughout the nineteenth century and as late as 1930, the major objective of policy in this area had been to set apprentices and orphans to work. The 1948 Children Act changed the approach to social work with children, placing the best interests of the child at the forefront of practice. The legislation failed to take account of the need for preventive services in child care. Part III of the 1948 National Assistance Act placed a duty on local authorities to provide residential accommodation and welfare services for people aged 18 or over or those who were in need by virtue of age, disability, or illness. Any service beyond residential care or home help was provided at the discretion of the local authorities, who were not generally inclined to develop services beyond minimal levels.

As the 1950s progressed casework became increasingly psychodynamic in its orientation, often utilizing American concepts and quasi-Freudian ideas (Yelloly 1987). In 1954 the first generic social work course was introduced at the London School of Economics. Lewis argues that

The LSE generic course represented an attempt to universalise the casework method across social work settings relying on conceptualisation of casework as a professional relationship between client and worker that was no longer class related. This also involved a bid to make social work something more than a residual activity defined in relation to state social services. (Lewis 1995: 115)

Eileen Younghusband, who developed the course, had advocated in her 1959 report to the Ministry of Health the development of genericism with a concomitant increase in the number of social workers nationally.

The 1959 Mental Health Act followed the findings of the Royal Commission on the Law Relating to Mental Health and Mental Health in the Community. The Commission recommended that care in the community provided a cheaper and more humane alternative to institutional care. The Act also introduced more informal admission procedures to mental hospitals (Allsop 1995).

The Act came under increasing attack due to the unclear role of the social worker in the admissions process, and the abuses of a system which allowed relatives to put pressure on mentally ill people to become voluntary psychiatric patients. Social workers were uneasy about their role in mental health admissions and poorly trained in the sectioning process.

The 1983 Mental Health Act in response to some of those criticisms created the 'approved social worker' status which required social workers specializing in mental health to undergo specialist training and assessment in the process of compulsory admission to mental hospitals (see Chapter 13). The 1983 Act emphasizes patients' rights whilst recognizing that social workers and other health professionals are fallible. The social worker treads a delicate tightrope, protecting the interests of both the patient and the community while also being strong enough to withstand any pressure to admit from relatives, GPs, or local authorities (Rashid and Ball 1984).

The creation of local authority children departments in 1948 laid the foundations for a movement to create a broader professionalized generic base for social work which was later encapsulated in the Seebohm Report of 1968. Seebohm recommended that each local authority should have an enlarged social service department, which would incorporate the generic principle and more effectively co-ordinate social work activity. Centralization would simplify services by performing tasks previously undertaken separately by children, welfare, health, housing, and education departments. The latter two were never incorporated in the 1970 Local Authority Social Services Act, which created single social service departments with a single local authority social services committee. Directors of social services were to be appointed initially with the approval of the Secretary of State for Health and Social Security. Thus a network of services would develop within the community, enhanced by the activities of the voluntary social services.

The Seebohm Report also recommended that generic social work training should be developed. The Central Council for Education and Training in Social Work was set up to regulate the first unified generic social work training qualification, the Certificate of Qualification in Social Work (CQSW), by statutory instrument in 1971. This led to the establishment of numerous social work departments within institutions of higher education and the gradual academization of social work education.

Criticisms of the Seebohm Report

Whilst the Seebohm Report proved to be most influential, having had a lasting effect until the present day, it has been like the Beveridge Report, heavily criticized for a number of reasons.

- It provided no justification for social work, which enabled critics to argue that social work had no clear definition or purpose (Brewer and Lait 1980).
- It failed to give guidance as to how priorities for social work action were to be established.

- It gave no indication as to the cost of the measures recommended.
- The wishes of consumers were not sufficiently taken into consideration.
- It was a lost opportunity in that it gave the impression of tidying up anomalies rather than creating a wholly new structure for the delivery of personal social services (Townsend 1976).
- The report was riven with basic contradictions. Whilst arguing for centralization it recommended the construction of local area teams (Bolger, Corrigan, Docking, and Frost 1981).
- It failed to recognize the discrimination suffered by women, black people, and other oppressed groups.

The 1969 Children and Young Persons Act provided a strengthened role for the social worker, by emphasizing the importance of providing care for children in trouble rather than punishment. This legislation reflected the notion that there was little difference between the needs of the 'delinquent' child and the child destined for care, marking an ideological shift in the way in which children were to be treated.

The incoming Labour government of 1964 had intended to set up a family social work service which would minimize the distinction between young offenders and those who were in need of care and protection, but this did not materialize. The Seebohm Report and subsequent legislation had made little reference to disabled people. The 1970 Chronically Sick and Disabled Persons Act required all local authorities to register disabled people and to publicize available services. However, like section 29 of the 1948 National Assistance Act which gave local authorities the power to make arrangements for promoting the welfare of disabled people, the 1970 Act has been severely criticized, most vociferously by disabled people (Oliver 1990). The Act perpetuated the view that people who have disabilities are 'helpless' and unable to make choices about their requirements for independent living (Shearer 1981).

The period from the late 1970s to the mid-1980s was one of stagnation within the social services (Langan 1990). It is often argued that the political climate in which social work operated changed with the election of Margaret Thatcher. The continuity in post-war social policies had been broken earlier in 1976, when public spending came under the partial control of a team from the International Monetary Fund, who were called in by the Labour government to give financial help. Between 1981 and 1990 Mrs Thatcher claimed to have brought about a profound change in the direction of policy which constituted a break with the post-war consensus (Thatcher 1993). However, as Glennerster argues,

Mrs Thatcher's first two administrations did not produce revolutionary change in social policy. Her Government first returned to the principles established in the 1940s: containing public spending, shifting the finance of services away from direct taxation, targeting social security, enforcing tenants' rights to buy their council houses. Structural change came later, not least because spending proved so difficult to check. (Glennerster 1995: 178)

Significantly for social work, the election of the first Thatcher government created a climate in which a number of critics of social work, many of whom had been waiting for the moment during the late 1970s, could allow their voices to be heard unbounded.

Brewer and Lait (1980) thought the time propitious to argue that social work failed to make any measurable difference to the lives of those whom they were professionally charged to assist. Appalled by Marxist critiques of social work practice which temporarily appeared in the 1970s to be gaining some limited ascendancy within social work training (Corrigan and Leonard 1978), they claimed that predominant forms of state social work were an untested and self-indulgent waste of taxpayers' money. In some instances social workers made situations worse for clients. The case for a separate social work profession had not been made and social workers should be regarded as occupying a subordinate status within health care provision or alternatively should become residually involved with practical bureaucratic tasks. Brewer and Lait's attack was tantamount to a justification for abolishing state social work as it had developed post-Beveridge. The impact of this attack within the profession, however rhetorical, was, like Thatcherism itself, more attributable to the historical moment than to intellectual rigour. Aldridge has argued that the work of Brewer and Lait was the nearest social work came to the 'Black Papers' in education. There seems little doubt that the case made by Brewer and Lait, which was reported widely, was pressed upon Conservative politicians (Aldridge 1994).

Other fundamental critiques of casework came from more serious academic voices within the social work establishment. Sheldon for instance claimed that too little attention had been paid to measuring the effects of social work intervention, whilst there had been a failure to consult consumers on their reaction to social work practice. Sheldon advocated positivist principles in the evaluation of the social work process, whilst also emphasizing the importance of specificity of goals and the establishment of baselines for the measurement of problem behaviour prior to intervention (Sheldon 1982). All this was some distance from the psychodynamic casework which had been advocated and reflected in social policy during the 1950s and 1960s.

Brewer and Lait failed to recognize the softer forms of behaviourism which had developed with the emergence of task-centred casework (Reid and Epstein 1977). This form of practice advocated the prioritization of client need and contractual agreements between social worker and client. By the mid-1970s task-centred casework was a popular method of focused intervention which was taught widely on social work training courses, and used extensively in practice.

Despite this in 1980 the Secretary of State directed the National Institute of Social Work to set up a working party to examine the role and tasks of social workers. The Barclay Report delineated some fundamental aspects of social work. Counselling denoted activities which involved direct relationships with clients but did not constitute the basis of social work. The report's findings combined the notions of community work, social care, and decentralized social planning as being the way forward for social work (Webb and Wistow 1987).

In 1988 the Wagner Committee focused attention on the provision of residential care. The findings of this report appeared to be on the same conceptual trajectory as Barclay, since it recommended deinstitutionalization, and the idea that services should whenever possible be provided for people in their own homes. More choice for consumers of services was advocated whilst retaining good-quality residential provision as one of a number of options. The report also recommended that service users should have more information relating to the range of services available. This report also suggested that local authorities should play a leading role in the provision of welfare (Wagner Report 1988).

The 1989 Children Act was a major milestone in social policy legislation which had an impact on social work practice. It followed a number of major child care scandals including the Maria Colwell case of 1973, and the cluster of intensely covered cases in the mid-1980s—Jasmine Beckford, Kimberley Carlile, Tyra Henry, and the Rochdale, Cleveland, and Orkney cases. The resulting official inquiries and media coverage, while rightly drawing attention to many weaknesses in child care practice, appeared to produce an insoluble practice dilemma. On the one hand social workers were being blamed for not taking precautions quickly enough in order to avoid child abuse and in some cases murder of children. In other cases they were seen as being over-zealous in their attempts to protect children from abuse (Butler-Sloss 1988, Bloom-Cooper 1985). The 1989 Act sought to protect children from both these aspects of danger, both over-emphasis on social work intervention and the abuse which can be inflicted by families. The Act shifted emphasis from parental rights to parental responsibilities. The latter term encompassed all the rights, powers, and duties of parents in relation to the child and any property belonging to the child (D.o.H. 1989b). The 1989 Children Act gives single mothers and married parents parental responsibility whilst unmarried fathers and those who have been looking after a child can apply for parental responsibility. In cases in which parents are living apart neither party has sole power. There are instead other forms of jurisdiction, e.g. residence orders, contact orders, specific issue orders, and prohibited steps orders, which are meant to settle disputes.

The principle of partnership is central to social work practice under the 1989 Children Act although the word is not used in the Act. The Act stresses that whenever possible a child should stay within the family, and in cases where a local authority does take responsibility for the child that this should be done with the consent of the parents and the care of the child should be a partnership between local authority and parent (Asquith 1993, D.o.H. 1989b). The Act also formalizes child care practice between voluntary and statutory sectors (Kaganas, King, and Piper 1995).

The 1990 National Health Service and Community Care Act represented the beginnings of structural change which had been promised by the rhetoric of the new right in the early 1980s. The genesis of this legislation can be seen in four official documents. The 1985 House of Commons Select Committee Report *Community Care with Special Reference to Adult Mentally Ill and Mentally Handicapped People* argued that the plans to close hospital resources for the mentally ill were not being matched by the provision of community resources. These concerns were further emphasized in 1986 by an Audit Commission Report *Making a Reality of Community Care* (HMSO 1986) which also stressed the need for a new, more flexible form of community care. Lady Wagner had chaired a committee which reported in 1986 and evidenced low morale in the residential care sector. The Wagner Report arrived at the conclusion that residential care must be seen in the context of the community care provision. People should not be forced to enter residential accommodation if appropriate service could be delivered in the community. Residential care should become one of a number of alternatives. The government responded to this report by setting up an inquiry headed by Roy Griffiths, which produced the Griffiths Report *Community Care: Agenda for Change* (HMSO 1988). Here it was argued that the local authority should take the lead in providing community care. The 1989 White Paper 'Caring for People', on which the 1990 Act is based, contained most of the Griffiths and Wagner proposals. The White Paper recommended that whenever possible people should live in their own homes, which firmly enshrined deinstitutionalization into the legislation. Practical support for carers was to be a priority for a service which was 'needs led'. The White Paper also called for the development of an independent sector to work alongside public services and the consequent creation of a new funding structure. The National Health Service and Community Care Act was published days after the publication of 'Caring for People' and passed through Parliament in 1990. The legislation extended the powers of local authorities to make arrangements with private and voluntary accommodation for the care of those in need. Local authorities were also required, in consultation with district health authorities, family health services, and voluntary organizations, to produce and publish a plan for community services in the area. The concept of care management was introduced (it will be considered in greater depth in Part III), which in essence involved publishing information about the availability of community care, assessing need, care planning, implementing, monitoring, and reviewing individualized care plans (D.o.H. 1991*a*).

Although the 1984 Registered Homes Act safeguarded the interests of residents in homes, the White Paper suggested that inspection units should be set up within local authorities to ensure a good quality of life for people in homes run by the voluntary and state sectors.

Defining social work

CCETSW to some extent has had to 'move with the grain' in defining social work. In 1991 social work was described by CCETSW in the following terms:

An accountable professional activity which enables individuals, families, and groups to identify personal social and environmental differences adversely affecting them. Social work enables

17

them to support those difficulties through supportive, rehabilitative, protective or corrective action. Social work promotes social welfare and responds to wider social needs promoting equal opportunities for every age, gender, sexual preference, class, disability, race, culture and creed. Social work has a responsibility to protect the vulnerable and exercise authority under statute. (CCETSW 1991a: 8)

In 1995 CCETSW under their new requirements for the Dip. SW described the purpose of social work in the following manner:

The purpose of social work is to enable children, adults, families, groups, and communities to function, participate and develop in society. Social workers practice in a society of complexity, change and diversity, and the majority of people to whom they provide services are amongst the most vulnerable and disadvantaged in society. (CCETSW 1995: 16)

The two statements represent more than just a change in emphasis. The first statement makes reference to the shortcomings of a society in which needs are experienced, whilst integrating an appreciation of the difficulties faced by particular groups. The second, altogether less critical of society, exhorts social workers to enable service users to become more integrated into society as it exists. Such a definition accommodates recent changes in policy towards the mixed economy of welfare, whilst making no reference to the role of the social worker as a potential agent of change towards a more equitable society. Thus it can be argued that ideology is an important concept in understanding the relationship between social policies and social work practice since it provides a conceptual link between abstract philosophical judgements which deal with concepts such as need, justice, equality, and freedom, and institutional policies of welfare as exemplified in the creation and implementation of party political programmes (Clarke, Cochrane, and Smart 1987).

The probation service: policy and practice

Although the 1907 Probation of Offenders Act gave magistrates the right to appoint probation officers it was the Criminal Justice Act of 1925, and the Criminal Justice Amendment Act of 1926, which laid the foundations for the modern probation service. Probation was slow to take off since sentencers, particularly magistrates, were unable to see it as an alternative to custody. It was not until 1925 with the Criminal Justice Act that probation areas were created. May has argued that underlying the Victorian system of penology was the notion of the responsible subject. This contrasted according to May with the development of criminology, which emphasized causal factors which pushed people into criminal behaviour. The compromise was to introduce measures which made the subject become an object for assessment by the expert. Between 1895 and 1914 the number of criminal sanctions increased rapidly due to the 'Reforming zeal and evangelical spirit of the middle class entrepreneurial philosophy, [and] legislation provided a focus for the puritan combination of a "consciousness of sin" . . . with a generalised compassion towards the "disadvantaged" ' (May 1991: 7).

Throughout the 1930s and 1940s the probation service went through the 'phase of diagnosis' with an emphasis on scientific assessment and treatment of the individual. This provided the probation officer with a professional status and refocused work from the divine redemption of the Methodist missionaries towards the quasi-psychiatric assessment and treatment of the inadequate individual. Newburn describes a mood of scepticism during the inter-war years. The Criminal Justice Bill introduced in 1938 included new restrictions on the use of custody and would have created residential hostels. However, the Bill never progressed through the House due to the onset of the war (Newburn 1995). The late 1950s and early 1960s saw the numbers of probation officers increasing as duties expanded. The role of the probation officer was extended to matrimonial proceedings in 1958. In 1966 the probation service took on the after care duties from the National Association of Discharged Prisoners Aid Societies. In 1967 the Criminal Justice Act further extended the role of the probation officer to cover parole. In 1971, following the implementation of the Seebohm Report, probation training became more closely linked to generic social work, as CCETSW took responsibility for the training of probation officers, under the aegis of generic social work training.

Probation thus became integrated into the rehabilitative orthodoxy of the day. Although probation students constituted a relatively small number of all social work students, they were regarded by CCETSW and the Home Office as undergoing professional social work and not specifically probation training. Despite this apparent integration probation students were funded independently by Home Office sponsorships, and were expected by the Home Office to apply for vacancies within the service on completion of training, although this expectation was not legally binding. Considerable numbers of recruits to the probation service were not sponsored by the Home Office. Following the move towards generic training and practice in the 1970s, social work with offenders in England and Wales still retained a certain separateness. No separate probation service exists in Scotland, since social work with offenders is integrated into generic social work. The debate surrounding the implementation of the 1991 Criminal Justice Act and the policy of 'Punishment in the Community' marked the point at which overt questioning of CCETSW-based training of probation officers became significant and overt. Official policy for the training of probation officers was moving away from the Seebohm model, and there was a call from the Home Office for specialized training more suited and relevant to the task of being a probation officer (Nellis 1996).

Probation was also expected to become more market based and punitive in its approach to working with offenders (Home Office 1990a, 1991a, 1991b). The accumulative results of all these developments is that since the retreat from the 1991 Criminal Justice Act the probation service has been propelled towards a more correctional, regulated service controlled by the Home Office. There has been a growing acceptance of the idea that social work training and generic social work stemming from rehabilitative values did not equip probation officers to deal with the probation task.

One of the most symbolic recent developments in keeping with this trend has been the dominance of the employment-based requirements. Probation training in 1995 despite considerable protest from the National Association of Probation Officers was separated not only from generic social work but from higher education. This is a significant development not only for the future of probation training, but also for the future development in practice. The influence of the NCVQ in the area of the training of probation officers and generic social workers marks an important development. The emergence of the NCVQ must be seen in the political context of government policy to subordinate education and training in general to the need to commercialize the probation service (Nellis 1996). The probation service will be more geared to the pragmatic servicing of the requirements of the courts and Home Office. At the same time the extent of control which can be centrally exerted will be increased.

Conclusion

Social work developed in response to an increasingly collectivist approach to social policy which emerged after the Second World War. During the 1950s and 1960s social work became increasingly specialized and professionalized. Throughout the 1980s and 1990s the professional principles upon which social work was established have been challenged by developments in social policy. The professional edifice created by Seebohm is now the subject of increased government scrutiny and its future as a template for practice is in some doubt.

Exercise

Critically assess the impact of one of the following on the development of social work:

Edwin Chadwick;

the Charity Organisation Society;

William Beveridge;

Joseph Chamberlain;

Aneurin Bevan;

the Seebohm Report;

the Wagner Report (see also Part III);

the Griffiths Report (see also Part III).

FURTHER READING

R. Lowe (1993), *The Welfare State in Britain since 1945* (London, Macmillan) offers an excellent and full account of theoretical perspectives within policy-making, and the nature of policy-making in relation to employment, health education, housing, and the personal social services. H. Glennerster (1995), *British Social Policy since 1945* (Oxford, Blackwell) provides an extremely readable assessment of the development of the welfare state since the war, and is particularly useful on the impact of new right ideology in the 1980s. N. Timmins (1995), *The Five Giants* (London, HarperCollins) has produced a full account of social policy over the last fifty years— a *tour de force*. K. Jones (1991), *The Making of Social Policy in Britain 1830–1990* (London, Athlone Press) is a well-written account of policy which covers a wider historical period than some of the other texts. Fraser's carefully written account of the evolution of the welfare state (D. Fraser (1984), *The Evolution of the British Welfare State* (2nd edn., London, Longman)) and P. Thane (1982), *The Foundations of the Welfare State* (London, Longman) provide invaluable introductions to the historical development of the welfare state. Jane Lewis traces the development of ideas and practices of social work, examining the meaning of voluntary personal social services which became statutory social work from the late nineteenth to the twentieth century: J. Lewis (1995), *The Voluntary Sector: The State and Social Work in Britain* (London, Edward Elgar). Pete Alcock's (1996) *Social Policy in Britain* (London, Macmillan) provides a well-written introduction to current issues within social policy.

CHAPTER 2

Ideology, Social Policy, and Social Work

- Ideology: policy and practice
- Criticisms of social policy and social work analyses based upon ideology
- Social work and postmodernity

Although ideology is only one of many factors affecting social policy it is central in attempting to understand the relationship between policies and practice. This chapter will

- explore some of the meanings which are ascribed to the term 'ideology' in understanding the construction, transmission, and ordering of ideas, which constitute the active components of social policy and social work practice;
- examine some of the problems which are created by basing analyses of social policy and social work on ideology.

Chapter 6 takes up some of these themes with respect to a specific practice example.

Ideology: policy and practice

The term ideology was probably first used to counter the dominance of religion and superstition in the immediate aftermath of the French Revolution of 1789. Here ideology was used to denote the science of ideas which provided a rational methodology for the collection of evidence which would be used to guide government decisions (George and Wilding 1995). Such a tension between ideology as objective rationality and bias has influenced the way in which social science has developed. Although there are many ways in which ideology can be conceptualized, three central elements appear to be present which will be referred to as ideas, order/transmission, and action.

Ideas

Ideologies are based upon ideas which relate to all aspects of social life. Ideologies represent 'The interrelated sets of ideas and values which shape the way that problems are understood and acted upon' (Spicker 1995: 72). For Beveridge in the 1940s the problems which social policy needed to address were ignorance, idleness, squalor, disease, and want. The creation of a welfare state which provided welfare services from the cradle to the grave, free and universal at the point of delivery, provided a solution to the problems. For the incoming Thatcher government in 1979 the problem was defined as the welfare system itself which had developed since Beveridge's report. The solution for the Thatcher government was to restructure the problematic system which Beveridge had envisaged as marking the way forward. Ideas relating to social policy and social work are generated by political parties, managers of welfare services, civil servants, government advisers, populist forms of entertainment, the various arms of the media, and to an ever lessening extent practitioners and academics. Few opportunities exist for the ideas of service users to be heard or acted upon (Coote 1992, Broad and Denney 1996).

The ordering and transmission of ideas

Ideologies are ordered into a form which is accessible and understandable to large numbers of people. Political parties, organized religion, the media, popular entertainment, and the education system play fundamentally important roles in the process of ideological presentation.

Action

Ideology conceptually links ideas to social action as suggested in Fig. 2.1. It is possible to describe the main concerns of social policy and social work within the same conceptual framework. The content of social policy is directly related to the ideas which constitute a particular ideology. Ideology becomes fundamentally important to the study of social policy and social work because it provides the possibility of understanding the processes whereby ideas become ordered into transmittable form and are acted upon (see Fig. 2.1).

Professional social work training transmits ideas which form the basis for social action. The Beveridge Report incorporated a collectivized approach to tackle the five giants—disease, ignorance, idleness, squalor, and want. This was achieved principally through state-run welfare services, universally available at the point of delivery and paid for through social insurance. These ideas were ordered into a comprehensible form through the Beveridge Report, which recommended specific actions to be taken which reflected these collectivist ideas. The series of associated legislative measures which

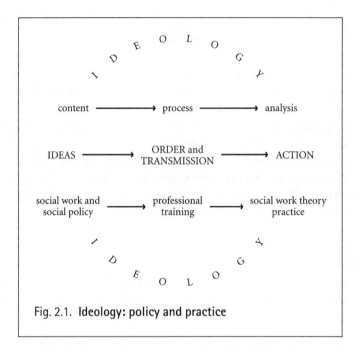

Fig. 2.1. **Ideology: policy and practice**

passed through Parliament in the period immediately following the Second World War formed a basis for what became known later as the welfare state.

Ideologies relating to welfare appear to gain a credence and mass acceptance at specific historical moments when social and political conditions are favourable. Similarly, ideas about the nature, purpose, and techniques thought by government to be most suitable for social workers are affected by current thinking in social policy which is grounded within a particular ideological current. Mrs Thatcher came to power with an agenda to cut public spending, curb the power of the trade unions, encourage people to buy their own homes, create choice in education, and take firm action against crime. Although the policies were not new and resembled those advocated by other post-war Tory politicians, her message enabled her to win three general elections. She was, in Glennerster's words, 'Moving with the grain' (Glennerster 1995) as Beveridge had done in 1945.

Criticisms of social policy and
social work analyses based upon ideology

Accounts of social work which emphasize the importance of ideology have been criticized from a number of perspectives. It has been argued that George and Wilding were wrong to assume that the only form of collectivism can be socialist. Neither Beveridge nor Keynes were socialists, but enthusiastic collectivists (Pinker 1979).

Others have argued that early attempts to analyse policy in relation to class and ideology have failed to incorporate an appropriate analysis of the structured nature of subordination, particularly with regard to race and gender (Williams 1989, Dominelli 1988).

Analyses of social policy built upon a narrow range of ideological positions can become oversimplistic (Spicker 1988). The relationship between welfare ideologies and political programmes is a complex one. There are numerous examples of social policy failing fully to reflect particular ideological positions. According to some Marxist writers the radical right created a discourse emphasizing the need for law and order, economic discipline, and authority. This was in the face of a crisis which was constructed in terms of a conspiracy and the onset of social anarchy as evidenced by the 1979 'winter of discontent'. An unqualified respect for authority was exemplified in the 1982 Criminal Justice Act which symbolized a move from treatment towards an uncompromising 'short, sharp, shock' for young offenders. While it is right to emphasize the authoritarian populism which characterized the early Thatcher years, such an approach to law and order is not without precedent. The 1948 Criminal Justice Act, which was introduced by a Labour government at the point where state welfare services were being constructed, represented a drift into a law and order society (Hall 1979). The Act introduced punitive detention centres which were designed to create a disciplined environment. The idea of abolishing the death penalty was abandoned during the same period, whilst the minimum age thought suitable for imprisonment was reduced from 16 to 15 (Gilroy and Sim 1985, Brake and Hale 1992).

Similarly the notion of giving more control to an increasing number of Labour-controlled local authorities under the 1990 NHS and Community Care Act was anathema to the Conservative government. According to Glennerster (1995), this bitter pill was sugared for Mrs Thatcher through the simultaneous introduction of an internal market which ensured that a great bulk of welfare expenditure would occur in the private sector. There is no simple, direct causal link between ideology and policy, and indirectly practice.

By the beginning of the 1960s waning faith in the old belief systems like fascism and communism was thought by some writers to herald the end of ideology, seriously questioning the existence of a dominant ruling-class ideology (Bell 1960, Abercrombie, Hill, and Turner 1980). Political changes in eastern Europe, the collapse of the Soviet empire, and the end of the cold war indicate that democracy and capitalism have triumphed over all other socialist alternative forms of government. The future global ideology will be one reflecting the end point of ideological evolution (Fukuyama 1992). Explanations incorporating Marxist and neo-Marxist notions of false consciousness and ideology are reductionist and over-determined. In a withering theoretical attack on reductionism in social work theory and practice, Sibeon argues that the claim that individuals possess structurally given (objective) but unacknowledged interests that exist by virtue of location within the social structure, or membership of a particular group, is a claim that is 'irremediably flawed in both a theoretical and empirical sense' (Sibeon 1991: 19). This applies according to Sibeon not only to class, but also to other categories such as race and gender. The radical social work texts of the 1970s and 1980s relied too heavily on the ideas that the problems facing users of social work services were structural in location. For the Marxist writers of the 1970s and early 1980s the overemphasis on the affects of capitalist ideology, capital accumulation, and the role of the state within capitalist societies reduced all social relations to a contradiction between those who own the means of production and those who do not—the proletariat (Corrigan and Leonard 1978). Put crudely, from this perspective service users and social workers become dupes absorbing coded messages through a state-controlled media and education system. Social workers are seen as a part of a ruling-class conspiracy, the ideological state apparatus, their function being to inculcate dominant ideologies, which will ultimately serve to perpetuate ruling-class dominance.

Explanations of the transmission and construction of new right ideology cannot be based upon the productive relation alone, and such an approach leads to a crude, exclusive focus upon the mode of production (Jessop, Bonnet, Bromley, and Long 1984).

Social work and postmodernity

Marxist certainties have increasingly given way to analyses built upon the idea of postmodernity. In the seventeenth century the Enlightenment represented a point at which divine ordination was increasingly challenged by human reason and scientific discovery. This period of modernity was marked by an increasing belief in the ability of human beings to shape the world in which they live. Social work can be viewed as a product of the modern age of industrialization in which modern 'rational' systems can repair and reform dysfunctional and damaged human beings, enabling them to behave in ways which are appropriate to the modern world. For Howe 'Social work therefore formed and was thoroughly immersed in one of modernity's key projects—to bring discipline and order, progress and improvement to the human condition' (Howe 1996: 81).

Postmodernity raises doubts as to whether the social world is understandable through scientific enquiry and rationality, casting doubt on the possibility of universal truths. 'Truth' is a concept which is moving relative to time and place, arising from endless linguistic variations and differences in possible interpretation.

Postmodern theorists thus focus on the nature of professional knowledge itself. Rojek, Peacock, and Collins (1988) have argued that social workers use words and forms of impression management which correspond to specialist systems of knowledge. The deconstruction of official discourse could provide an alternative analysis of the way in which social workers exercise power to define service users' need. 'There is no single professional discourse dominating social work practice but rather a variety of negotiated discourses emerging from particular encounters between individual social workers' (Rodger 1991: 77).

Attention is focused on sites at which social workers appear to exert most power in professional assessments, and the form of discourse that social workers use in official reports and other forms of formal explanation (Stenson 1993, Stanley 1991). Social workers tend not to utilize social work theory learned on professional courses in their daily work, preferring to make highly subjective judgements based upon professional convention and institutional requirements (Denney 1992). From a postmodern perspective the overarching nature of ideology represents an intellectual straitjacket which removes the possibility of alternative forms of analysis. It is a rational attempt to understand what is a fragmented, contradictory, complex social world of social interactions.

Conclusion

Movements in analytical method present a number of possibilities for understanding both social work practice and social policy which could enhance social work practice. Social workers have been rightly criticized for being theoretically circumspect and restricted (Sibeon 1991). A similar conceptual straitjacket to some extent has dominated the social policy literature (Cahill 1994).

Disagreements as to what constitutes good policy or social work practice are rooted in differing values, ideas, and problem definitions. Attempts to penetrate dominant ideas are important in that they force social policy analysts and social work practitioners to ask fundamental questions about possible future developments. New forms of analysis must be developed in order for social policy and social work practice to develop. Latterly, attempts to understand the nature of ideological debates within social work have been overshadowed by an unquestioning, some would argue creeping anti-intellectual, approach to social work (Jones 1996). In many respects social work is fighting for its intellectual life within higher education.

Exercise

There is no 'right' answer to any of the exercises in this book. What follows is a possible way of tackling an exercise, drawing on the material in this chapter and Chapters 15, 16, and 18.

N. Poulantzas (1975) describes the effects of ideology in terms of: masking, displacing, fragmenting, separating, imaginary coherence.

How is it possible to demonstrate that these aspects of ideology impinge upon social policy and social work?

Possible answer

We can illustrate this account of ideology with reference to the marketization of welfare.

Masking and displacing. In a Treasury policy document entitled 'Competing for Quality' it was simply asserted that 'Competition is the best guarantee of quality and value for money' (Treasury 1992: 1). Here a central idea (competition) is introduced in such a way as to suggest that it is no longer necessary to justify or clarify the link between competition and quality services. Such an assertion presented in an official document masks the serious doubts that many have expressed over the applicability of market principles to public welfare services. However, competition is presented in such a way as to suggest that its introduction into welfare and social work practice is so obvious and self-evident as not to warrant any serious discussion. Criticism and doubts relating to the practicality of a market system which have been discussed in the previous chapter, including cash limits, the possible increased costs of the resulting bureaucracy, duplication of services, and the proliferation of managers, are masked by an overwhelming confidence in what is an untried radical transformation of the financing and organization of welfare and services. An assertion about the imaginary relationship between marketization and quality of public services therefore becomes a reality for service users and social workers which displaced the previous arrangements for the provision of state welfare.

Fragmenting and separating. The introduction of market principles into the delivery of welfare services fragments welfare service centrally into providers and purchasers. Following the 1990 NHS and Community Care Act, social services departments now 'purchase services' from a range of sources including on occasions themselves. Programme-planning is an individualized process which separates user from user. The sectors of care become fragmented to include now the statutory sector, the voluntary sector, the private sector (basically comprising commercial companies operating on a fee-paying basis), and the independent sector, which is a term now used to denote services offered by both the voluntary and private sectors. It has been argued that evidence for collaboration between agencies, most notably health and personal services, is patchy.

An imaginary coherence. Despite the uncertainties and vicissitudes of any market there is an underlying invisible hand which ultimately brings a coherence to the forces of supply and demand. Providers, always having an eye to the market habits of other purchasers, will adapt their fees so as not to price themselves out of the market, which will lead to savings for local authority purchasers and ultimately more money available to buy more services for those in need. The market is more equitable in that it destroys supernormal profits and democratic since it responds more effectively to stated needs.

Exercise

Lynn is 19 years old and lives with her parents and 6-month-old son Adam. Lynn now has no contact with the father of her child. Tensions have been building up for some time particularly between Lynn and her father. Lynn claims that her father has been violent towards her and she has approached the social services office for help. She has already made an unsuccessful application to the local housing department, who say that the best they might be able to offer is bed and breakfast accommodation.

1. In what ways can ideology assist in understanding the situation faced by Lynn?
2. What action should be taken by social services in this case (see Chapters 9 and 12)?
3. In what ways are the plans for intervention affected by prevailing ideologies?

FURTHER READING

F. Williams (1989), *Social Policy: A Critical Introduction* (London, Polity Press) is an important introduction to social policy which examines ideological perspectives in great detail with particular emphasis on gender and race. V. George and P. Wilding (1995), *Welfare and Ideology* (Hemel Hempstead, Harvester Wheatsheaf) is the latest in a series of texts dating back to 1976 which puts ideology at the centre of discussions relating to perspectives within welfare. An important and rare inclusion is a discussion of green issues. V. George and R. Page (1995) (eds.), *Modern Thinkers on Welfare* (London, Harvester Wheatsheaf) can be read in conjunction with George and Wilding (1995). This collection includes chapters on the new right, the middle way, democratic socialism, Marxism, greenism, feminism, and anti-racism. P. Lee and C. Raban (1983), 'Welfare and Ideology', in M. Loney, D. Boswell, and J. Clarke (eds.), *Social Policy and Social Welfare* (Milton Keynes, Open University Press) still provides a useful discussion, particularly in relation to Marxist approaches to welfare and ideology.

CHAPTER 3

Social Policy, Social Work, and Social Problems

- Some defining characteristics
- A Fabian approach to the development of social administration
- Challenges to Fabian wisdom
- Alternative perspectives in policy analysis
- Defining social problems
- Social work, social science, and social problems

Introduction

Until the 1970s social administration and social work were concerned with the manner in which social services solved what had been defined by those designing social policy as social problems. In this chapter the emergence of social administration as a discipline will be examined. Over time the nature of what social policists have thought worthy of study has been redefined. The chapter will conclude with a discussion of some of the difficulties which emerge when attempting to define the term social problems, and the manner in which different interpretations of the social problem have influenced social work.

Some defining characteristics

Social administration and social policy have a relatively short intellectual history. Although the roots of both disciplines can be traced back to the beginning of the twentieth century (the teaching of social administration began at the London School of Economics in 1912), they have developed largely in the UK with the post-war emergence of the welfare state.

In a well-known introductory textbook Brown argues that at a 'superficial level' social administration simply means a study of social services. There are a number of 'levels' at which the social service can be defined: 'A social service is usually defined as a policy provided by the state whose object is the improvement of the welfare of the individual' (Brown 1985: 11). In this sense social services are therefore for Brown distinguishable from the public utilities. The concept of collective provision for Brown is the hallmark of social services.

A Fabian approach to the development of social administration

The development of a Fabian approach to the study of social administration owes much to the founding work of Richard Titmus, who gave social administration its academic credibility. Titmus's critical view of the market systems led him uncompromisingly towards the conclusion that industrial societies need state welfare systems (Titmus 1970). Titmus, who reflected the Fabian approach in his writings, conceptualized social services as having the following principal functions:

- to redistribute incomes usually in terms of some concept of need;
- to create social integration and harmony;
- to cope with 'diswelfares' like unemployment, the obsolescence of skills, and pollution;
- to enhance the lives of those who have particular needs;
- to be a form of investment, in that public expenditure results in healthy citizens and an educated workforce;
- to facilitate the growth of altruism, reciprocity, and social duty in the provision of social services.

The delivery of such services should be at the centre of state activities.

Challenges to Fabian wisdom

Fabianism came to dominate social administration during the 1960s. The research which resulted from this period was largely focused upon the collection of empirical data relating to the extent of poverty. Social administrators hoped that evidence would influence governments to improve welfare provision. This led to a prescriptive, remedially based approach to the solution of social problems which precluded a wider examination of the structured subordination of particular groups such as women and black, gay, and disabled people. Its empirical base took for granted certain assumptions like continued economic growth, the existence of the nuclear family, the capacity of the welfare state to solve social problems, and the recruitment of cheap labour from the colonies. It failed to provide claimants and service users with a voice in the development of services which were intended for them.

Some writers would argue that this enabled social problems and solutions to be defined in terms approved of and conceptualized by the state (Williams 1989). In the early 1970s Pinker developed a more theorized historical account of the development of sociology and social administration which amounted to a defence of the empirical tradition within social administration (Pinker 1971). Pinker argued that the tenaciousness with which writers like Titmus had defended state welfare had prevented a consideration of the potential that the market system has for enhancing welfare provision (Pinker 1979).

Until the mid-1970s social administration lacked a critical analysis of the values and political structures which underlay social policy. At this point the notion of social policy, itself a term which connoted an engagement with issues relating to underlying values and political ideologies, gained ascendancy. Social policy essentially went beyond the descriptive towards an analytical and frequently critical examination of the welfare state.

In their earlier work George and Wilding grouped thinkers into particular categories.

- Marxists who, as we have seen, conceptualize society in terms of conflict between economic classes;
- Fabians steeped in the tradition developed by Titmus, Tawney, and Crossland;
- anti-collectivists like Friedman and Hayek who reject the idea of state welfare;
- reluctant collectivists such as Beveridge who accept the welfare state as a necessary corrective to the vicissitudes of a competitive market (George and Wilding 1976).

George and Wilding (1995) have refined their typologies of welfare ideologies. The new right, as exemplified by the work of Hayek and Friedman, regard the welfare state in advanced capitalist societies as unacceptable, in that it is inefficient, produces high levels of taxation, weakens incentives to work, and stifles investment. The welfare state, it is argued by the new right, has a tendency towards monopolistic services which are antithetical to competition, and the creation of large numbers of people who are dependent on the state for benefits brings about a culture of dependency which stifles individual efforts and entrepreneurial initiative. State bureaucracies develop to the point where the freedom of the individual is undermined, which leads to a form of state-imposed serfdom. The new right advocate a return to residual welfare benefit, where market principles reign supreme and the family, informal community networks, and the voluntary sector play a far more active role in delivering state welfare.

Writers characterized as representing the 'middle way' include Beveridge and Keynes. Those of the middle way support capitalism, whilst acknowledging its limitations in that some issues cannot be left to the market alone. Further, they believe that some of the unacceptable consequences of capitalism can be remedied by government action. Although Keynes has been described as advocating as much liberalism and as little collectivism as possible, he believed that positive government intervention in the economy was necessary in order to avoid unemployment, which was 'wasteful' and inefficient. Although more concerned with the concept of unemployment than with the unemployed his ideas were of crucial importance to the development of the post-war provision of social welfare in Britain. The middle way represents a balance between economic and social policy rejecting the notion that a thriving economy can be trusted to cater for social needs. Supporters of this view come from a wide variety of political perspectives, including liberalism, as in the case of Keynes and the left of the Conservative Party. From this perspective provision of welfare is in complete accordance with Conservative principles. Whilst democratic socialists disagree on many issues, they agree that democratic socialism is a far more desirable economic system than *laissez-faire* capitalism. They argue for the continuation of state welfare through the pursuit of a variety of corrective measures. This step-by-step approach will lead, they believe, to universalist social services and a more altruistic society. Three versions of democratic socialism have been identified by George and Page (George and Page 1995).

- Private ownership of the means of production would continue whilst the abolition of poverty would be a vitally important part of social policy. This would not include any major redistribution of wealth or income.

- Means of production and reduction of income inequalities would be controlled by the state. This view tended to predominate in the 1960s and 1970s.

- A mixture of co-operative state and private forms of ownership, sometimes called market socialism, would emphasize the substantial involvement of the labour force.

Alternative perspectives in policy analysis

Until fairly recently green issues have been virtually ignored within policy analysis. 'Light greenism', now acceptable to many governments, industry, and business, accepts that economic growth must continue, but only in environmentally friendly ways. 'Dark greenism' rejects this view, arguing that increased consumerism is not compatible with the development of a clean environment and will ultimately destroy the planet. A green form of social policy would be ecocentric in that the interdependence of all the world's species would be emphasized. Greens would also claim according to George and Wilding that social problems stem from the nature of social organization in industrial societies. The reductions in economic growth advocated by the greens would require a concomitant reduction in public spending. The greens would also reject full-time, state-paid helpers such as social workers who disable their clients through forms of authoritarian provision (George and Wilding 1995).

With the disappearance of the post-war consensus about social welfare, a number of developments have made a reformulation important. In his analysis Cahill roots social policy in the context of changes in information technology, economic globalization, the internationalization of production, and flexible specialization, sometimes known as post-fordism. Communicating, viewing, travelling, shopping, working, playing, and globalization are all issues which the social policy should analyse (Cahill 1994).

Midgeley has recently put forward a 'social development' approach to social policy. Unlike social work, social development does not assist individuals by providing them with services but focuses on change within wider structures. It is, in Midgeley's words, 'A process of planned social change designed to promote the well being of the population as a whole in conjunction with the dynamic processes of economic development' (Midgeley 1995: 25). This requires the creation of formal organizations that can assume responsibility for harmonizing and managing the implementation of differing approaches to social policy. Midgeley seeks to demonstrate that both collectivism and individualism have failed. It is necessary to create a centrist position which combines the insights of individualist and collectivist ideologies within a pluralist democracy. This will ultimately create a more corporatist form of welfare state. 'Social work's most distinctive feature is its reliance on professionally educated personnel to treat social problems and enhance the well being of individuals, families, groups and communities' (Midgeley 1995: 19).

This is similar to a social partnership model described by Mishra in which employers, workers, and the state control wages, prices, and social benefits rather than market forces (Mishra 1990). The model also reflects the position adopted by 'New Labour', which separates itself from socialism by seeking to bring about structural change within capitalism through a partnership between the private and public sectors. Within social policy Williams (1989) has defined three positions:

- a non-socialist approach which argues for the development of a mixed economy of welfare (Pinker 1971, 1979; Hadley and Hatch 1981);
- a more self-critical form of Fabianism as exemplified in the work of Deakin (1987) and Glennerster (1983);
- a radical strand which combines the structural analysis of social problems with Fabian concerns. Such an approach requires a radical redistribution of resources and wealth through social planning (Townsend 1983, 1984; Walker 1984).

Defining social problems

It will have become apparent from the above discussion that one of the major problems in defining social policy and social administration in terms of offering institutionalized solutions to social problems lies in defining what is socially problematic.

In the twentieth century a number of different models have evolved in the study of social problems which have been mainly developed in the USA. The 'social pathology model' according to Manning (1985) grew out of the 'progressive era' in the United States during the early twentieth century. Particular politicians and liberal thinkers of the time argued that the individual opportunities created by capitalism in the early twentieth century were being eroded by the individual greed of politicians, trade union leaders, and powerful business interests. The perceived solution to this problem was education of those with power to become more egalitarian and less pathological.

The obvious failure of this approach to remedy social problems led to a more sophisticated analysis based on the premiss that social problems are brought about by tensions created in a society which is undergoing major institutional changes. These changes were not soluble at the level of the individual. As Manning argues, the development of an extraordinarily heterogeneous society in the United States led to a debate as to what constituted the 'good society'. Such a debate still continues in the American social problems literature. It has recently been argued that

U.S. political culture has abundant resources for talking about public good. But the cultural and political heritage of liberalism and contemporary developments in interest group politics makes definite claims to common good rhetoric difficult. (Williams 1995: 140)

Such debates led to what is often referred to as the 'value conflict' approach to social problems. Mills has argued that American society is riven by conflicts between major class groupings and professionals, some groups having the power to define what constitutes a social problem. A hierarchy of credibility enjoyed by lawyers, doctors, and journalists, and one could add to that social workers, have the power not only to define social problems, but also to make decisions as to what constitutes the 'good society' (Mills 1956). Thus as Fuller and Myers have argued:

Social Problems are what people think they are and if conditions are not defined as social problems by the people involved in them, they are not social problems to those people, although they may be problems to outsiders or to scientists. (Fuller and Myers 1941: 320)

American work on social problem theory has focused more on the way in which social phenomena come to be defined as social problems than on empirical accounts of social conditions (Jennes 1995). Social work intervention both reflects and determines the extent to which social phenomena are defined as social problems.

Social work, social science, and social problems

The relationship between social work theory and social work is a complex one. Davies (1985) notes that there have been few occasions on which social theory had a significant impact on social work practice. When Wooton published her book *Social Science and Social Pathology* (1959) she aimed at developing a critique of social casework. She argued that

Happily it can be presumed that the lamentable arrogance of the language in which social workers describe their activities is not generally matched by the work they do. Otherwise they would constantly get their faces slapped. (Quoted in Davies 1991: 3)

Wooton's intervention, according to Davies, made social workers more aware of the possible impact of structural factors on the people they described as their clients.

Early attempts to formulate comprehensive sociological overviews of social work were undertaken by Leonard (1966) and Heraud (1970). There was something of an evangelical call in this early work when Leonard concluded that 'Social work cannot long continue to depend for its knowledge predominantly upon research undertaken and theory developed in other disciplines' (Leonard 1966: 102). Subsequent writing on social work has been criticized for being reductionist and does not appear to have benefited from forms of analysis offered by social science. Social work writing, including the anti-discriminatory literature, tends to be detached from recent major debates in sociology (Howe 1988). Social workers themselves have a tendency to rely on intuition and practical wisdom rather than social science knowledge (Carew 1979, Sullivan 1987, Sibeon 1991).

The need for an understanding of social science in social work can be justified on a number of grounds. Social workers are not simply making assessments of the individual's situation in relation to available resources, but reflecting dominant social problem definitions. Some of the contradictions which result from the social worker's role in defining social problems can be seen in all aspects of social work practice. It is for instance possible for a probation officer to write a pre-sentence report on a service user charged with being in possession of an illegal drug such as cannabis, whilst enjoying a cigarette and a beer with lunch. In the afternoon the same officer may even offer a cigarette to a service user held on remand in prison or serving a sentence.

Another way of expressing this situation is that in the morning a probation officer writes a report on an individual who is charged with being in possession of a drug, the effects of which are possibly harmless, yet some hours later she or he can use two drugs (alcohol and nicotine) which are known to be dangerous to health, whilst also supplying a prisoner on remand with a dangerous drug. In Becker's words, 'moral entrepreneurs' have the power to define marijuana as a dangerous drug, yet other drugs known to be dangerous such as alcohol and nicotine are defined by policy-makers as recreational and used by the population at large. Marijuana, however, is illegal, outside the legal code, and constitutes part of the social problem of drug abuse that the probation officer is statutorily charged to address professionally, whilst nicotine and alcohol are not. Both the policy and social work response are conceptualized in terms of a complex interplay of ideas.

- The 'good' society is conceptualized as being one which is free of particular 'harmful' drugs.
- The use of particular drugs which may be harmful if not checked by the law will lead to an attack on values which are central to the functioning of that society.
- The helping professional can perform a therapeutic although increasingly controlling function by explaining to the court why a particular individual has deviated from socially acceptable behaviour whilst providing a solution, i.e. supervision in the community.

These three ideas suggest that a consensus exists about what constitutes the good society and that the social worker plays a crucial role in maintaining and promoting a questionable consensus.

Discussion relating to the role of social workers in defining what constitutes the socially problematic have formed the basis for a vigorous debate over the last twenty years. Hindness has warned against analysing social policy solely in terms of the realization of some general principle. Such an approach ignores the role of particular 'interests and objectives' (Hindness 1987).

Marxists see dominant constructions of social problems as ideas which ultimately work in the interests of the powerful who control the capitalist mode of production. Social work is an activity therefore which should enable the powerless to have a voice in order to bring about radical change (Corrigan and Leonard 1978, Bailey and Brake 1975). Social work has a distinctive role to play in addressing oppressive social policies and directly tackling social problems through political pressure.

Pluralist writers conceptualize social work in terms of maintaining the existing social structure whilst attempting to tackle social phenomena constructed as social problems. Davies was able to write when Thatcherism was at its height that 'The social worker is concerned with maintaining each individual and society as a whole, and with negotiating the interdependent relationship between each individual and society: it is a policy of reconciliation' (Davies 1985: 32). There is for Davies a clear difference between the real world of social work practice and what he refers to as the 'social administration view of inequality'. The achievement of equality and the tackling of social policy issues, he argues, lie in the domain of politics, whilst most social workers are involved with carrying out the legislative requirements of the job. The social sciences have made a contribution to social work which is 'primarily negative' (Davies 1985). It would appear that over the last decade this view of social work has gained ascendancy and is now clearly reflected in national training requirements (CCETSW 1995).

Conclusion

Social work and social policy can be regarded as providing institutionalized responses to social problems. Social problems arise from individual human needs which are common and obvious, like the need for food, clothing, housing; some are less tangible, such as the need for dignity. At a simplistic level it can be argued that when needs are not met they give rise to social problems. Much of the social worker's task directly relates to assessing individuals who are lacking basic needs. However, the relationships between need, social work practice, and conceptions of social problems are far more complex.

Social workers are centrally involved with the well-being of service users and address social problems in their daily work. How social problems are defined is linked to ideas about what constitutes the good society. Whether social workers should be involved in trying to bring about structural and policy change as part of their job is open to fierce debate although increasingly it would appear that social work is being defined in terms of discrete professional competencies rather than a political consciousness-raising activity.

Social administration is rooted in a moderately socialist, Fabian model of change and collectivity which has since the Second World War come to be challenged from the left and right. This model has also been challenged by economic circumstances from the early 1970s which have put pressure on supporting state welfare (Gladstone 1995*b*). Some writers within the field of social policy argue that the idea of promoting equality through public expenditure is an enterprise which has self-evidently failed, whilst others seek to defend the achievements of the welfare state since the war and call for a re-emphasis on intervention within welfare. Others straddle the two positions.

Exercise

George and Wilding have argued that social policies have stated and unstated aims/consequences. Consequences can be anticipated or unanticipated. The government's view of the consequences of a policy may be endorsed or challenged by other groups.

Table 3.1. **The impact of social policy**

Aims	Consequences
Stated	Intended
Unstated	Unintended

Source: Adapted from George and Wilding (1984).

Take an example of social policy and work through stated and unstated aims, anticipated and unanticipated consequences, and the way in which the consequences are viewed by the government and other interested groups (Table 3.1).

Exercise

1. Examine the following areas of government policy-making. Discuss which areas you would regard as social policy.

   (a) taxation policy;

   (b) regional policy;

   (c) overseas development;

   (d) transport policy;

   (e) capital punishment;

   (f) policy towards Northern Ireland;

   (g) defence policy;

   (h) policy with regard to the arts;

   (i) welfare benefits;

   (j) education policy;

   (k) trade policy;

   (l) the criminal justice system;

   (m) race relations policy.

2. Consider the following ways in which social policy and administration have been conceptualized:

Social Administration is concerned with social problems and secondly it is concerned with the ways society responds to these problems. (Brown 1985: 11)

Social Administration: The study of the development structure and practices of the social services. (Spicker 1995: 271)

Social policy involves an understanding of the legislation which makes it explicit, of the government machinery, and administrative procedures concerned with social provision, of the role of voluntary action, the recruitment and professionalisation of staff and the problems of financing the social services. (Brown 1985: 13)

The establishment of the discipline of social policy (or 'social administration' as it was usually known until recently) emerged from the politics of collectivism and the practice of state intervention to deal with social problems in the beginnings of the twentieth century. (Williams 1989: 4)

What do these explanations of social policy and administration mean?

How are they relevant to social work practice?

In what ways are these views of social administration and social policy similar and different?

FURTHER READING

British social policy writing which specifically addresses the problem of defining the concept of social problem is rare. Much of the work is American. G. Miller and J. Holstein (1993) (eds.), *Issues in Social Problems Theory* (New York, Aldine de Gruyter) provides a sound theoretical background to the study of social problems. N. Manning (1985) (ed.), *Social Problems and Welfare Ideology* (Aldershot, Gower) is one of the few British attempts to provide an issue-based theoretical account of social problems within social policy. Chapters on domestic violence, 'race' madness and epilepsy, delinquency, unemployment, and inflation. The American journal *Social Problems* provides a wealth of material on this area of study. P. Spicker (1995), *Social Policy: Themes and Perspectives* (London, Harvester Wheatsheaf) is a well-written and clear introductory text, which examines the nature of social policy. The book also contains a useful chapter on research in social policy. P. Taylor-Gooby (1991), *Social Change, Social Welfare and Social Science* (Hemel Hempstead, Harvester) provides a critical assessment of the position that the state can no longer provide welfare from the collectivist left, individualist right, and some feminist perspectives. An invaluable assessment of the theoretical, empirical, and philosophical arguments about the role of the state in welfare provision. M. Cahill (1994), *The New Social Policy* (Oxford, Blackwell) is a new approach to defining the nature of social policy with chapters on such topics as shopping. This book takes an importantly global account of social policy developments. J. Midgeley (1995), *Social Development: The Developmental Perspective in Social Welfare* (London, Sage) is an important book which seeks to integrate social and economic policies within a development process which will ultimately achieve social policy objectives.

CHAPTER 4

Services, Poverty, and the
Social Construction of Human Need

- What is human need?
- Who has the power to define needs?
- What needs are social policy and social work trying to meet?
- Poverty, social work, and social policy
- How do needs arise?
- Individualized explanations of need
- Structural explanations of need
- How effective are policies in tackling need?
- Social work effectiveness and need

Introduction

Empirical description of need was favoured by a generation of social administrators after the Second World War and came to characterize the subject area. Here the imperative to identify, measure, and classify need which was evident in the early work of Charles Booth and Seebohm Rowntree and continued by Abel-Smith and Townsend (1965) and Townsend (1976) is emphasized. The concept of need has a long history within the social policy literature, although latterly it has been placed at the centre of debates about welfare provision (see discussion in Chapter 16). This is reflected in the legislation which dominates the delivery of health and personal social services, the National Health Service and Community Care Act of 1990, where management is defined as the process of tailoring services to individual needs.

To some extent social workers have notions of need defined for them in terms laid down by those who formulate social policy, yet the concept and the manner in which need is operationalized in practice is contentious. By the 1990s according to Taylor-Gooby (1991) a high level of need coexisted with a growing unease about state interventionism in the field of welfare. This occurred for three principal reasons.

- British social policy had never been imbued with the same egalitarian assumption which had dominated the development of welfare states in Scandinavia.
- The response of Britain over a number of decades to the crisis on welfare had been to cut services, whilst retaining the concept of mass welfare.
- The incidence of need to welfare provision measured by poverty and unemployment had become increasingly acute by the mid-1980s.

What is human need?

Although Spicker defines needs as 'Those things which are necessary to avoid deprivation' (Spicker 1993: 15), all human needs can be considered under the two headings of physical survival and personal autonomy. These are the preconditions to individual actions in any culture and constitute basic needs. Unless these basic requirements are fulfilled it becomes impossible for individuals to participate in society in order to achieve goals (Doyal and Gough 1991). The welfare of an individual from this perspective depends not only on such basic physical needs as food, shelter, and clothing, but also on holidays, an individual's feeling of security from attack, and belonging to a community (George and Page 1995: 1).

In an often quoted taxonomy of need, Bradshaw defines the way in which different conceptions of need relate to types of service offered.

- 'Normative' needs are defined by the professional or expert.
- 'Felt' need corresponds with what the service user wants.
- 'Expressed' need is need combined with action as in the case of a service user making an application for some form of help.
- 'Comparative' need is assumption of need based on the service user being in the same circumstances as others who receive services (Bradshaw 1972).

The social worker is not in a position to fulfil expressed need since the means of satisfying needs, resources, are severely rationed. Decisions as to who is in need then come to be modified and constructed in response to the particular administrative requirements of the department (Clayton 1983).

Who has the power to define needs?

Social problems are defined by a wide variety of individuals and welfare agencies. Social work is intimately connected with making assessments and care managers have the power primarily to define the extent and nature of need in relation to available services.

Handler's view, now twenty years old, still has a remarkably clear resonance in the 1990s.

The social worker has command over goods and services that people need and want. Thus there is no problem in recruiting clients to an agency. The creation of power arises out of this command over scarce resources. It is a power relationship because the clients need their resources and the agency has discretion as to how the resources are to be distributed. (Davies 1985: 95)

One of the main difficulties faced by social workers in implementing social policy is that frequently those who have the most power to define social problems and policy measures—politicians, civil servants, academics, journalists—are least able to understand need since they have little contact with deprivation. In a study of the geography of poverty, Mc Cormack and Philo argue that it is a failure on the part of politicians to look and listen which has led 'To the present situation where a powerful minority is able to deny the existence of poverty or to claim as ideological those who insist on the existence of poor places' (Mc Cormack and Philo 1995: 3).

The study of mass communications is based on the premiss that the media can affect the manner in which people perceive policies. Experimental psychology has ascribed enormous power to the media in shaping public opinion. McQuail (1987) argues that it is difficult to make this case, given that comparatively little is known about the psychology of perception and cognition.

The media by selecting particular events have not simply reflected but shaped public consciousness. Moral panics are symbolic expressions of profound social change awaiting some episode to throw them into focus (Galtung and Rudge 1965). Moral panics relating to social work have been most evident in the coverage of child abuse tragedies where social workers are portrayed as being at best incompetent, but at worst responsible for the deaths of young children in the care of local authorities. It will be argued in Chapter 5 that the treatment of anti-discriminatory practice by the media influenced policy-makers (see Chapter 5). Aldridge (1994) in her analysis of social work in the media has described the occupational ideology of the journalists who have the power to define human need as being far removed from and antithetical to social work.

Schlesinger, Tumber, and Murdock (1991) have described a struggle for media attention between professional associations, campaigning pressure groups, and government departments (see Fig. 4.1). It is not the case that some agencies have the absolute power to define issues like need. Although the apparatuses of state, e.g. the Home Office, occupy the most powerful defining role other groups can achieve change and define need by threatening publicity. Although professional workers including social workers

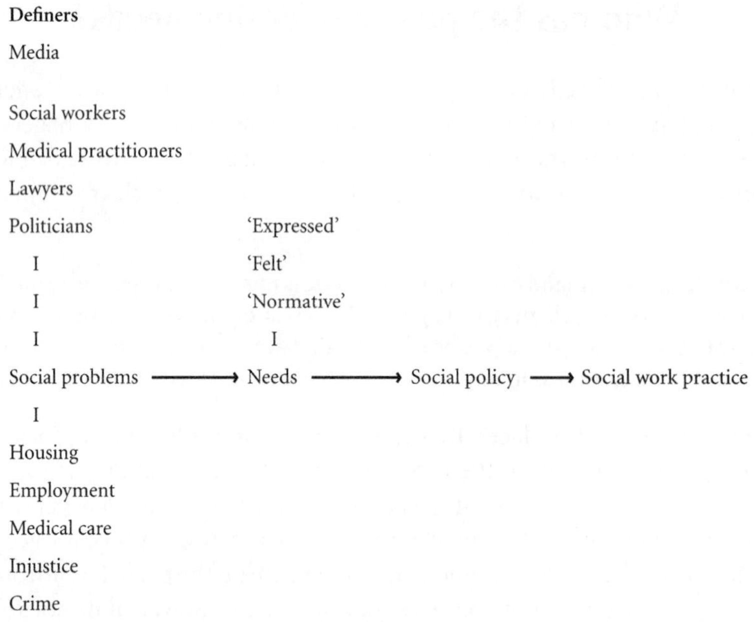

```
Definers
Media

Social workers
Medical practitioners
Lawyers
Politicians              'Expressed'
    I                   'Felt'
    I                   'Normative'
    I                       I
Social problems ———→ Needs ———→ Social policy ———→ Social work practice
    I
Housing
Employment
Medical care
Injustice
Crime
```

Fig. 4.1. Defining need: policy and practice

may object to the direction of a particular policy development, they rarely have the power to change the direction, or even modify policy. Thus those who have gained power are able to frame social policy around ideas rather than felt need.

What needs are social policy and social work trying to meet?

Concentration on need has enabled policy-makers to delineate the focus of social work particularly in relation to community care. The NHS and Community Care Act 1990 emphasized the notion of 'needs-led' assessment which is described in official documents as the requirements of individuals 'To enable them to achieve, maintain or restore an acceptable level of social independence or quality of life as defined by the particular care agency or authority' (Braye and Preston-Shoot 1995: 14). Need here is expressed in terms of nine broad categories:

- personal/social care;
- health care;

- accommodation;
- finance;
- education;
- employment;
- leisure;
- transport;
- access (Braye and Preston-Shoot 1995: 15).

What is unclear from this is the nature of an acceptable level of social independence and quality of life. It will be argued in Part III of this book that what policy-makers define as acceptable is becoming increasingly unacceptable to service users.

Poverty, social work, and social policy

Throughout its history social work has been concerned with the morality and condition of the poor. Poverty has also been the concern of social administrators with much effort being expended on researching the impact of poverty on vulnerable groups and defining the meaning of the term itself. Two principal forms of poverty have been described in the social policy literature. Absolute poverty is the minimum level necessary for subsistence and is often associated with an individualist, residual model of welfare. Here welfare is regarded as a safety net designed to meet the basic needs of those who are unable to rely upon their own or families' resources. Relative poverty on the other hand is more likely to be associated with the principle that all individuals at some point in their lives require welfare, the responsibility for which is a collective one (Spicker 1993).

Far from diminishing, a position of social polarization in the UK has continued to develop throughout the 1980s and 1990s. Between 1979 and the 1990s, according to Townsend, there was a loss of purchasing power which particularly affected the poorest 20 per cent of the population. As the poor become poorer, according to Townsend, the rich are becoming richer at a rapid rate. On 14 April 1996 the richest 500 people were worth £71 billion, 28 per cent more than twelve months earlier. Privately invested, the wealth of the 500 richest people could educate 5 million children aged from 5 to 7 (Townsend 1996). By the 1980s inland revenue statistics indicate that the wealthiest tenth of the population still own 49 per cent of total wealth (Hills 1995: ii).

Jones argues that poverty is overwhelmingly the most common problem which faces service users. Social work is dominantly concerned with those sections of the population who are in a state of poverty. Nine out of ten social work clients were dependent on state benefits in the mid-1980s, whilst one in ten children between the ages of 5 and 9 years in families on state benefits were admitted to care. This compares with 1 in 7,000 for children living in families not on income support (Jones 1997).

How do needs arise?

Living in a particular place where some of these factors are more prevalent creates a cascading and interrelated set of needs. In areas where need is high there are often fewer services within both the private and state sectors. The busiest commercial organizations in areas of high deprivation are bookmakers and bingo halls, which siphon money out of poor places into national entrepreneurial organizations with few local loyalties (Mc Cormack and Philo 1995).

Need should not simply be viewed as a localized problem. Midgeley has pointed to the problems of persistent poverty in the midst of economic affluence. In many parts of Africa and Latin America poverty actually increased during the 1980s. In industrial countries like Britain and the United States poverty increased significantly during the same period (Midgeley 1995). The debates relating to the causation of need are grounded within the differing ideological positions which can be broadly summarized into explanations based upon individuals and social structure.

Individualized explanations of need

Individualized explanations of poverty attribute it to the personality and abilities of people who are in need. In a society rooted in competitive values some people, it is argued by the new right, have simply not made it for a variety of reasons. Some are incompetent, others may have made the wrong decisions, or have suffered bad luck, whilst others are simply feckless. The distinction leads to a further individualized explanation based on the division between the undeserving and deserving poor which, as was noted in Chapter 1, is still a potent argument in explaining how state welfare resources should be allocated. Those arguing from the new right would advocate minimalist welfare being given to the deserving who have fallen on hard times through no fault of their own, whilst the undeserving must face the consequences of their own decisions (Spicker 1993).

Social work, even if it be called 'needs led', to a large extent reflects individualized assessments. Other explanations emphasize the importance of cultural factors which perpetuate need (Lewis 1966). Such a culture creates a paralysing dependency on welfare which bolsters the existence of an underclass which will ultimately lead to a form of totalitarianism (Hayek 1949). Although these arguments, based in the case of Lewis on studies of Latin America, lost credibility in the 1970s, they have found a resurgence in the dominance of new right ideas. Sir Keith Joseph, one of the intellectual architects of the early Thatcher years, argued: 'The only hope we can give to the poor is helping them to help themselves; to do the opposite, to create more dependence is to destroy their morality whilst throwing an unfair burden on society' (quoted in George and Wilding 1995: 33).

Joseph also believed that deprivation was cyclical and transmitted across generations. The only way of finding out what people wanted from services, and consequently how best to organize welfare provision and lift them out of need, was through the market. Social work to some extent reflects this view. The emergence of the task-centred form of casework in the 1970s required the setting of clearly defined time-limited goals through contracts, and in some cases the use of positive reinforcement for socially acceptable behaviour. Recently 'needs-led' community care legislation provides inducements for service users to help themselves towards independence.

Structural explanations of need

In the early 1980s one justification amongst many utilized by the Conservative Party for reducing taxes and public expenditure was that the economy needed to be more competitive within international markets. One benefit of this was so-called 'trickle-down'. In a buoyant economy wealth created by entrepreneurs would 'trickle down' to those in most need. However, the Conservative government's own figures suggested that between 1979 and 1991 the poorest tenth of the population experienced a 14 per cent fall in their real incomes. The total number of people living in poverty has risen from 5 million in 1979 to 13.5 million in 1990/1. This was despite a 36 per cent increase in overall incomes (Hills 1993). The households below-average income statistics indicate that between 1979 and 1992/3 the poorest half of the income distribution has seen its share of income drop from 32 per cent to 25 per cent. During the same period the richest half increased its share of income from 68 to 75 (Oppenheim and Harker 1996).

The accumulated evidence suggests that being older, unemployed, on low earnings, chronically sick and disabled, a single parent, a woman, or a black person increases the likelihood of need. Others would argue that social work techniques which encourage service users to be more independent ignore the contradictions which have created the need in the first place. Those on the left usually cite the importance of structural factors in creating need. Marx believed that the immiseration of poor people would be endured as the crisis in capitalism developed. Unemployment increases, driving down what Marx called the exchange value of labour, thus increasing the levels of exploitation.

Class is still a crucial factor in determining one's position within society and vulnerability to need. People's poverty for the most part is reflected by their income, which is again determined by their position within the marketplace. This has led some Weberian sociologists to describe the poor as an underclass or possibly more accurately a group of underclasses (Spicker 1993).

How effective are policies in tackling need?

After 1979 expenditure on social security increased to the point at which each working person was paying £13.00 per day towards financing the system (Deacon 1995). Extra revenue needs to be raised in order to cope with the demand of a population with an ever increasing number of older people of pensionable age, a growth in the number of one-parent families, and the rise in unemployment (Alcock 1996). It was assumed until the 1970s that the NHS had dealt with major inequalities in health (Allsop 1995). The publication of the Court Report in 1976 (D.o.H. 1976) and the Black Report in 1980 (DHSS 1980) indicated that poverty was directly related to ill health.

Expenditure on community care services is the subject of intense competition at local government level where departments battle for funds from the general rate support which is distributed by the Department of Environment to each local authority. Standard Spending Assessments (SSAs) are calculations built into the block grant. The Department of Environment determines the amount of money each authority should have to spend. SSAs are not built on need but are a device for distributing funds from the Treasury (Harding 1992). Allocation of funds within this mechanism is divided into three blocks—children under 18, elderly people, and other adults. The expenditure on particular blocks is decided upon with reference to population and deprivation factors. The formulae used to calculate SSAs tend to create different results for populations with similar problems and population profiles. The effect of this is that most local authorities overspend and are forced to take money from budgets intended for other purposes, or cut services.

Social work effectiveness and need

Effectiveness in the delivery of social work to those in need is a relatively new area of research, and has been neglected (Sheldon 1982). In an overarching study of the personal social services in the late 1980s Webb and Wistow called for more systematic and rational forms of assessment, review, and allocation. This they argued would produce a more effective targeting of resources and services which would in turn lead to an enhanced level of service user welfare. Too much care, it is argued, can be as damaging to individuals as too little, if it undermines autonomy and establishes or reinforces dependency on others (Webb and Wistow 1987). It is possible to be over-pessimistic about the effects of social work, since there is some evidence to indicate that social work can be successful in meeting need, and also bring about increased levels of independence. Some service users feel that they benefit from social work intervention (Cheetham, Fuller, McIvor, and Petch 1992). The bad news about social work's ineffectiveness and incompetence appears to gain more attention particularly in delicate areas such as child care. One of the most detailed studies of research using controlled experimentation has been carried out by Sheldon (1986). He claims that studies dating back to the early 1970s indicate that, with more focused forms of social work assessment, outcomes become more favourable.

Conclusion

Questions relating to the effectiveness of social work in meeting need are to some extent determined by the manner in which these terms are defined. Effectiveness defined in terms of enabling individuals to function more effectively can be characterized by those holding an opposing ideological position as failure to address underlying exploitative social relations which create need in the first place. From this perspective social workers who are effective in enabling service users to function more effectively within existing social arrangements are failing to address the source of the need and are effective only in allowing the social structure which creates need to continue unchallenged.

Exercise

1. Attempt to prioritize the needs which exist in Britain in the 1990s.

2. Josie and Michael have four children aged 12, 10, 6, and 3 years. Michael was made redundant from his job as an industrial cleaner and has been unable to find employment that would provide a salary which after tax exceeded his benefit level. Josie used to work as a cleaner but is afraid that if she continues it will affect the family's benefit. As the months have progressed the family have found themselves in arrears with their rent, and have accumulated debt. Josie and Michael say that they simply cannot manage on their present level of assistance. In desperation Josie recently stole some food from a supermarket and faces criminal proceedings as a result.

Describe the needs of this family from an individualist and structuralist perspective.

How best could a social worker assist in this case?

Can it be argued that this family is caught in a poverty trap in that they cannot hope to earn a sufficient amount to match their inadequate income benefit level?

How would the social worker ensure that the family were claiming and receiving all their welfare benefits? (This would include child benefit, income support, weekly premium payments designed to provide for some associated costs of child care, entitlement to social fund payments.)

3. Is there any evidence to suggest that poor people are becoming poorer in the 1990s?

FURTHER READING

There are problems in discussing need as a concept without locating the notion within the daily experiences of service users. Need is a concept which runs through this book and will be considered in more detail in relation to particular groups, e.g. older and disabled people. R. Cohen (1992) in *Hardship Britain* (London, Child Poverty Action Group) gives an excellent account of the experience of being in poverty. J. Bradshaw (1972) provides a now dated but still highly relevant classification of forms of social need in 'A Taxonomy of Social Need', *New Society*, 496: 640–3; see also G. MacLachlan (ed.), *Problems and Progress in Medical Care* (Oxford, Oxford University Press). L. Doyal and I. Gough (1991), *A Theory of Human Need* (Basingstoke, Macmillan) is much quoted. A. B. Atkinson (1989), *Poverty and Social Security* (London, Routledge) will assist in being more precise about the meaning of the term 'poverty'; a broad discussion of needs which will be particularly helpful in discussing how social workers allocate care resources and access need. Joseph Rowntree Foundation (1995), *Inquiring into Income and Wealth*, vols. i (York), and J. Hills (1995), *Income and Wealth*, vol. ii (York, Joseph Rowntree Foundation) provide extremely well-presented materials illustrating the gaps between rich and poor and possible future policy developments. J. Mc Cormack and C. Philo (1995) (eds.), *Off the Road: The Social Geography of Poverty in the UK* (London, Child Poverty Action Group): a useful text which systematically documents the geography of poverty in the UK including useful chapters on rural poverty and the Celtic divide. With regard to welfare rights, annual editions of the Child Poverty Action Group's *Rights Guide to Means Tested Benefits* and *National Welfare Benefits Handbook* are useful sources for practitioners and social work students. Janie Percy-Smith (1996) provides a useful edited collection which relates needs to public policy with particular reference to community care policies in *Needs Assessments in Public Policy* (Buckingham, Open University Press).

CHAPTER 5

Discrimination and Oppression: Policy and Practice

- Anti-discriminatory practice
- Equal opportunity: social work orthodoxy
- Criticisms of equal opportunities policies; anti-oppressive practice
- Development of and challenges to anti-discriminatory and anti-oppressive social work

Introduction

There is evidence of overt and covert forms of discrimination within social work which have been given insufficient attention by policy-makers. This realization has created complex areas of debate. A full examination of these issues needs to encompass a discussion of disability, age, gender, 'race', and discrimination directed towards gay and lesbian people. The issues raised by specific user groups will be considered in Part II. This chapter will consider some of the broader issues which have emerged, including problems of definition, developments of and challenges to anti-discriminatory practices, and the importance of listening to service users.

Anti-discriminatory practice

Taylor and Baldwin (1991) have conceptualized discrimination in terms of the systematic use of power by some groups which devalue other less powerful groups on the basis of perceived difference. Such differences can be conceptualized in terms of 'race', ethnic or national origin, religion, age, gender, class, sexuality, or disability. The term anti-discriminatory practice is fraught with conceptual difficulties and raises fundamental and, as yet, unanswered questions. This is not surprising given that intra-group divisions ensure that terms used to describe the relations between men and women, white people and black people, heterosexuals and homosexuals, disabled and able-bodied people will depend on the perspectives from which the form of discrimination is conceptualized (Ramazanoglu 1989).

The distinction between direct and indirect discrimination is reflected particularly in the legislation relating to race (1976 Race Relations Act). Direct discrimination, which was reflected in race relations legislation of the 1960s, occurs 'When someone, or a whole group, is treated differently (either positively or negatively) from another solely or mainly because they belong to a particular social category' (Blakemore and Drake 1996: 9). Indirect discrimination was not recognized in the legislation until the mid-1970s. Indirect discrimination is more difficult to define since it invokes the significance of 'Inbuilt patterns of inequality rather than the particular actions of individuals' (Blakemore and Drake 1996: 9). A pattern of inequality can persist even when an institutional policy of treating people equally exists. Thus if for instance there is a tendency to draw employees from a particular geographical area in which black people are less likely to live, then this makes it more difficult for minorities to meet employees' requirements.

In 1991, CCETSW set out the *Rules and Requirements for the Diploma in Social Work*, which appeared to herald a new emphasis on ADP issues. This was at odds with the anti-collectivist thrust of social policies which had dominated political discourse since 1979. All qualifying social workers were therefore required to show the ability to 'Understand and counteract the impact of stigma and discrimination on grounds of poverty, age, disability, and sectarianism' (CCETSW 1991*a*: 16). Social workers were also expected to demonstrate an awareness of both individual and institutional racism. All these issues were to be addressed in all aspects of qualifying training.

Equal opportunity: social work orthodoxy

Except for a short period in the 1990s equal opportunities policies have been seen by social work managers and trainers as the most appropriate way of challenging discrimination. The origin of the concept of equal opportunity is often ascribed to Tawney, who believed that there should be equal access to basic necessities. Whilst individuals differed profoundly, a 'civilized society' would aim at eliminating inequalities. Tawney believed that the source of inequality was not located within individual differences but constructed by society (Deakin and Wright 1995). Equal opportunities policies should then be aimed at the elimination of discrimination. Edwards (1990) has argued that there are two distinct ways of seeing equality of opportunity. First, there is the idea that everyone irrespective of their morally arbitrary characteristics should have the same opportunities to develop their lives as they wish, or to pursue their chosen life plans.

The second formulation, Edwards argues, is quite distinct in that every individual should have an equal opportunity unfettered by arbitrary boundaries like race or ethnicity to compete for a given goal or a scarce resource. The glittering prizes constitute what Edwards refers to as the rewards system and are allocated on the basis of merit (Edwards 1990). A spectrum of equal opportunities policies have been identified ranging from the first-generation equal opportunities policies to the development of affirmative action and more latterly the 'managing diversity' approach. Affirmative action sought to introduce preference for particular individuals from disadvantaged and previously unrepresented groups. The managing diversity approach has emerged in the light of the perceived failure of both affirmative action and equal opportunities policy. The managing diversity approach seeks to maximize the potential of all employees whereas equal opportunities policies and affirmative action target particular groups. The managing diversity approach concentrates on the culture of the institution and not on discrimination (Blakemore and Drake 1996). One of the major problems with this approach is that it is couched in generalist terms, although its aims are to turn diversity into a resource and not a problem for the organization. Its effects remain to be seen.

Criticisms of equal opportunities policies; anti-oppressive practice

Equal opportunities policies can appear attractive since they can be associated with quality and 'good management'. In reality equal opportunities can be used as a tool for impression management, incorporating minimal equal opportunities policies, which are frequently defined so widely as to be devoid of meaning (Wilding 1994). Equal opportunities statements can give the appearance that policies are in place to counter discrimination, yet in practice the policies themselves become a smokescreen for inactivity. Equal opportunities can thus be seen as failing to address social exclusion and inequitable power relationships between people. The stated aim of many equal opportunities policies is to create respect and understanding of diversity in an attempt to counter unfairness. Anti-oppressive policies aim more directly at locating power within dominant ideological discourse which legitimizes negative beliefs about particular user groups. In relation to the position of women, Ramazanoglu has argued that oppression can be seen in terms of 'The various ways in which men have been seen to dominate women, and in which structural arrangements have been seen to favour men over women' (Ramazanoglu 1989: 21). Oppression focuses directly on the power relations which give some individuals the power to discriminate against particular social groups.

Dominelli has described anti-oppressive practice as

A form of social work practice which addresses social divisions and structural inequalities in the work that is done with people, whether they be users (clients) or workers. AOP aims to provide more appropriate and sensitive services by responding to people's needs regardless of their social status. AOP embodies a person concerned philosophy; an egalitarian value system concerned with reducing the deleterious effects of structural inequality upon people's lives; a methodology focusing on both process and outcome; a way of structuring relationships between individuals that aims to empower users by reducing the negative effects of social hierarchies on their interaction and the work they do together. (Dominelli 1996: 170)

Whereas anti-discriminatory practice emphasizes the importance of consulting user groups with regard to types of provision and individual needs, anti-oppressive practice emphasizes the urgent need for the elimination of structural oppression. The objective of such practice is a wider variety of user-led and -controlled choice in service provision (Braye and Preston-Shoot 1995). Anti-oppressive practice thus seeks to penetrate dominant ideological discourse which legitimizes negative beliefs about particular user groups, and differential practices.

Development of and challenges to anti-discriminatory and anti-oppressive social work

During the 1980s the need to challenge structural discrimination in the personal social services was to some extent recognized by social work employing authorities and CCETSW. In its Paper 30 CCETSW required that all qualifying social workers should demonstrate 'An awareness of the interrelationship of the processes of structural oppression, race, class and gender' (CCETSW 1991a: 16). Although this statement referred to 'awareness' rather than any particular form of action, it acknowledged the structural and oppressive base of discrimination. Subsequently this initiative has been used as a weapon to attack social work and justify a shift towards its deprofessionalization and further privatization. John Major in his speech to the Tory Party Conference in 1996 referred to the 'absurdities' of political correctness in his pledge to increase the role of the private and voluntary sector in the provision of social care. Although it is always easy to be wise with hindsight, there were a number of factors which contributed to the use of this issue to change the nature of social work.

Over-generalization and evangelism

The generality combined with absolute certainty of some anti-discriminatory writing allowed for crude caricatures of political correctness to be developed. Anti-oppressive forms of social work were presented in ways which reduced all social work issues to oppression and were consequently oversimplistic (Macey and Moxon 1996). This allowed unlikely coalitions to develop against the development of ADP. Liberals on the one hand saw ADP as an authoritarian threat to free speech. The right of British politics presented ADP as a metaphor for a supposed neo-Marxist conspiracy—yet another manifestation of the enemy within.

It can be argued that the use of a single term like 'oppression' to describe the experiences of women and black, disabled, and gay people is too general since there are important differences in the way in which particular groups experience the social world.

Although the need to tackle racism in social work was critical, other forms of discrimination existed which also affected people's life chances, but appeared to receive less attention in the early 1990s by social work trainers and writers. Specific issues relating to gay and lesbian service users and social work staff still have not received equal coverage. It is possible to present initiatives designed to address anti-discrimination in ways which make race and gender appear more important than other issues.

The media: political correctness as moral panic

A concerted media campaign directed at attempts being made to implement anti-discriminatory and anti-oppressive policies followed in the wake of the decision of a Norfolk County Council adoption panel to refuse Jim and Roma Lawrence permission to adopt a 'mixed-race' child in July 1993. Melanie Phillips argued that the activities of politically correct social work lecturers were not benefiting black people. The drive to eradicate all 'politically incorrect' attitudes was an abuse of power and a corruption of traditional liberal values of open-minded education and honest inquiry (Phillips 1993). Other articles followed in the same vein (e.g. Appleyard 1993). Virginia Bottomley, the then Secretary of State with overall responsibility for social services, herself briefly targeted by the media as being one of the politically correct, separated herself from political correctness by attempting to neutralize the approach to these issues.

The impact of the critique

Many of CCETSW's activities in this area centred around publications, conferences, and professional presentations. Dissemination of ideas in this form was required in order that the ramifications of oppressive practice could be made clear to as many as possible. As the political correctness panic developed, and became increasingly directed at CCETSW, a gap appeared to develop between service users (social work students, social work academics, social work clients) and trainers. The media presentation of

CCETSW's approach to anti-oppressive practice appeared to legitimize the scepticism of many within social work who sought to discredit the anti-oppressive position taken by CCETSW in Paper 30.

The immediate impact of the critique was to steer national training policy in the direction of equal opportunities, which was seen by CCETSW as a position more acceptable to the government. The new competency-based requirements for the Diploma in Social Work training programme required providers to:

Ensure that candidates have the knowledge and skills to counter unfair discrimination, racism, disadvantage and injustice in ways appropriate to their work with children, adults, families and communities, applied to the roles and context in which they are working. (CCETSW 1995: 9)

It is important to note that this statement does not mark a retreat from a concern with anti-discriminatory issues but puts less emphasis on the need for students to understand and incorporate into their work explanations of discrimination and structural accounts of oppression.

The political significance of attacks on ADP, particularly those launched through various forms of media, is now manifest. The removal of probation students from the Diploma in Social Work programme (Dip. SW) to an employment-based form of training makes the future of all full-time professional social work courses look less than secure (Targett 1995). In an atmosphere in which the very continued existence of professionalized full-time social work education could be in doubt, CCETSW has opted for an apparent rapid decentring of anti-discriminatory and anti-oppressive practices evident in the reworked Paper 30 (CCETSW 1995). The adoption of an 'equal opportunities' statement acceptable to central government appears to be less vulnerable to attack and more politically acceptable. During the 1990s anti-discriminatory social work appeared to offer a new future yet came to be parodied and derided as an uncoordinated set of simplistic authoritarian notions. Although the initiative taken by CCETSW and some employing authorities in the 1980s was imaginative, timely, and essential it did not touch many of the forms of discrimination it sought to tackle.

Conclusion

Social work has been utilized in the production of a social category, political correctness, which for a period created a moral panic. Political correctness has been presented by the mass media and some politicians as ridiculous and dangerously situated on the far left of British politics. Dominant ideas fundamentally affecting social work practice emanating from the right (e.g. market testing of services, curfews in relation to probation) are not described in terms of 'political correctness' by the media. The widespread acceptance into the vocabulary of 'PC' as a derogatory term can deflect attention from the relationship between social policy and social work practice. It is at the interface of ideas and practices that attention should be focused if we are to understand the origin, transmission, and impact of oppression. The form in which oppression and discrimination are conceptualized by social workers will have a crucial bearing on the services offered.

Exercises

1. What do you consider to be the central elements of an anti-discriminatory strategy?

Examine the problems and benefits of creating an anti-discriminatory policy in the following areas:

- the National Health Service;
- the personal social services;
- education.

2. Questions on 'political correctness':

Summarize any theme which is common to the articles on pp. 59–61.

How are the arguments developed and sequenced to give most persuasive impact?

How is political correctness being defined in these articles?

In what ways are these articles similar and different?

Select two differing theoretical perspectives in providing an explanation for the selection of this topic as being newsworthy.

Do you recognize any form of code emerging from these articles?

FURTHER READING

The area of race relations now contains vast amounts of literature. E. Cashmore and B. Troyna (1990), *Introduction to Race Relations* (2nd edn., Basingstoke, Falmer Press) provides an invaluable guide to those unfamiliar with the issues surrounding race relations, and a clear and readable introduction. J. Solomos (1993), *Race and Racism* (2nd edn., London, Macmillan) and J. Solomos and L. Back (1996), *Racism and Society* (London, Routledge) both provide scholarly accounts of the central issues and debates in this area. P. Ely and D. Denney (1987), *Social Work in a Multi Racial Society* (Aldershot, Gower) provides an introduction to the way in which racism operates within the social services, whilst L. Dominelli (1988, 2nd edn. 1997), *Antiracist Social Work* (Basingstoke, Macmillan) develops anti-racist concepts in relation to social work practice. Similarly the literature on gender and welfare has become extensive. C. Glendinning and J. Millar (1992), *Women and Poverty in Britain* (2nd edn., Brighton, Wheatsheaf) and M. Maclean and D. Groves (1991) (eds.), *Women's Issues and Social Policy* (London, Routledge) provide good introductions to some of the central issues in the area. Particularly the chapter by Joshi on sex and motherhood and the labour market in M. Langan and L. Day (1992) (eds.),

Concepts, Context, and Ideas

Women, Oppression and Social Work (London, Routledge) and L. Dominelli and E. McCleod (1989), *Feminist Social Work* (Basingstoke, Macmillan) provide important contributions to some of the debates relating to feminist social work practice. Research and writing which examines issues of sexuality as they impact on social work practice and policies is urgently needed. J. Hart and D. Richardson (1981) (eds.), *The Theory and Practice of Homosexuality* (London, Routledge) still contains some excellent accounts of the debates. The theoretical chapters are excellent and the chapters on presenting problems in part iii are extremely helpful to practitioners. C. McCaughey and K. Buckley (1993), *Sexuality, Youth Work and Probation Practice* (Sheffield, Pavic) have produced a collection on sexuality which is relevant to practice and policy and which includes a discussion by M. Powell of the impact of the HIV epidemic on probation practice. On disability see M. Oliver (1990), *The Politics of Disablement* (London, Macmillan), also M. Oliver (1996), *Understanding Disability: From Theory to Practice* (London, Macmillan), and C. Barnes (1991), *Disabled People in Britain and Discrimination* (London, Hurst). K. Blakemore and R. Drake (1996) provide a clear and lucid account of the debates relating to equal opportunities policies in *Understanding Equal Opportunities Policies* (London, Harvester Wheatsheaf). See also 'Further reading' for Chapters 7, 8, and 9.

'POLITICALLY CORRECT'

Anti-racist zealots 'drive away recruits'

Melanie Phillips

University teachers are abandoning social work teaching because they say they are being forced to teach 'politically correct' attitudes on race and gender in a climate of intimidation and fear.

Anti-racist zealots, they say, have captured the social workers' training body, the Central Council for Education and Training in Social Work, which has built into the new social work diploma, the DipSW, the assumption that society is fundamentally racist and oppressive.

Some social work professors have been engaged in running battles with the central council over the requirement to teach social workers anti-racist practice. It can refuse to validate courses that do not meet its criteria.

Robert Pinker, professor of social work studies at the London School of Economics, said these criteria implied that every British institution was racist. 'It's the given pre-sumption that racism is an institutionalised phenomenon. We may or may not conclude that from an inquiry into the evidence; but it seems we're no longer supposed to do that.'

The tutors claim that some students and staff are being intimidated. *The Observer* has spoken to several tutors who asked not to be identified for fear of reprisals. One said: 'I've had students come to me crying. Tutors have said to them, you're white, so you must be racist: confess. And if they're going to get through the course they confess.'

Students' marks, say these tutors, depend on whether their work displays the 'correct' attitudes on race. Some, when sent on practice placements, do not qualify until they have satisfactorily challenged 'racist' attitudes even where none exist. Another tutor said: 'If they're placed among old white people in a home, it becomes absurd because they still have to show they've questioned the home's management about their anti-racist policy to get a good mark.' The tutors say students spend so much time on ideology they end up ill-prepared to deal with people's real problems.

Some directors of social services say the anti-racist preoccupation is depriving vulnerable clients of adequate standards of service.

'At its worst, white social workers are frightened to deal properly with black families for fear they will be labelled racist. So I hear workers telling me it's quite normal for black families to beat their children. Well, I don't think it's right for anyone to beat their children,' one said.

Tony Hall, the council's director, denied the organisation assumed all white society was racist. Its criteria were designed, he said, to help social workers understand, recognise and deal with racism wherever they found it.

'Some people may adopt a more extreme view than others, but that's not done with my endorsement,' he said. It would not be 'desirable or effective' if students were being browbeaten. He also denied that his council gave anti-racism dis[pro]portionate emphasis.

One tutor said the prospect of a place on her university's social work course improved with the number of references made to racism or structural oppression on the entrance form.

'Students and tutors who question some of CCETSW's assumptions run the risk of being labelled racist,' she said. 'That's not education but indoctrination.'

Source: Observer 1 August 1993.

A social work directive elevates racism to a national epidemic. It is a national disgrace

Why paint so black a picture?

Bryan Appleyard

Social workers usually earn abuse and bad publicity from cases of obvious incompetence. The highly specific nature of these cases is, however, confusing: they do not reveal whether there is something wrong with individuals or with the system. But the latest round of social worker abuse engages with the ideological basis of the whole enterprise as embodied in a document known as Paper 30.

This paper is being blamed by some social work academics for a wave of oppression and corruption in university departments of social work. It has, they claim, inspired Stalinist demands for political rectitude, and launched persecutions of students and teachers who fail to comply or who insist simply on freedom and openness of discussion.

More alarmingly, Paper 30 is said to lie behind the justifications of social workers who refused to allow a Norfolk couple to adopt a mixed-race child because they displayed a 'lack of understanding of racial issues.'

At first glance this paper, published by the Central Council for Education and Training in Social Work (CCETSW) and now in its second edition, is no more than an averagely incompetent piece of bureaucratic illiteracy. Over 48 pages it rambles with burbling imprecision in an attempt to define the 'rules and requirements' for the Diploma in Social Work. A general intention is discernible, but the terms are laughably vague. Students or teachers could more or less do what they liked and find justi-fication for it via some elementary juggling of this worthy vocabulary of skills, assessments, commitments, models and validations. It is, in short, routine garbage of the sort that clogs all of our lives some of the time, and can usually be safely binned along with everything from American Express.

Yet on the academic front there can be little doubt that the charges against the paper have substance. A significant number of social work courses have been poisoned by Paper 30-inspired political correctness, and in those courses serious teaching and free debate can be said to be impossible. Many have not succumbed, simply because there remain enough tough-minded academics prepared to resist and, if necessary, to exploit the CCETSW's own incompetence with language.

In the real world, blaming Paper 30 directly is more dubious, since the causal chains are longer and because stories of stupid social workers are so attractive to newspapers. The result is that it is difficult to assess whether there really is something uniquely stupid or wrong-headed about this profession. Lawyers or doctors could, I am sure, be equally successfully pilloried. But it is social workers who are in the dock, and Paper 30 is Exhibit One.

Having studied this document at some cost to my powers of reason and sense of style, and engaged in a shouting match/calm discussion with a representative of CCETSW lasting nearly two hours, I have reached a verdict. The bureaucratic definers of the profession of social work are desperately wrong-headed, and Paper 30 is lethal.

Amid all the unfocused wittering of the document, one clear obsession is detectable: race. Racism is, in fact, the only specific social problem that is repeatedly emphasised. And the terms in which the subject appears are quite distinct. For example, the section headed 'What CCETSW expects' begins with four paragraphs of organisational chat, and then launches into the insistence that 'students are prepared not only for ethnically sensitive practice but also to challenge and confront institutional and other forms of racism.'

Later there is an insistence that students have a knowledge or understanding of 'processes of structural oppression' and 'the notion of ethno-centricity'. These are heavily loaded and dangerously ambiguous terms bearing intellectual assumptions and values on a scale that is not to be found elsewhere in this document. Both 'structural oppression' and 'ethnocentricity' have been employed in other contexts, especially in the US, to justify black Fascism and, indeed, a form of left-wing apartheid. They allow zealots to insist that racism can be detected anywhere at any time and, in the name of anti-racism, people can justifiably be persecuted.

I was given relatively anodyne definitions of these terms by the CCETSW, but more vicious ones are current and they are emphatically not excluded by the terms of the paper.

But the real climax of the race issue in Paper 30 is Annex 5—the three-paragraph 'statement on anti-racism.' This is a horror that makes explicit the dishonest and coercive politics implicit in all the preceding references: 'CCETSW believes that racism is endemic in the values, attitudes and structures of British society, including those of social services and social work education. CCETSW recognises that the effects of racism on black people are incompatible with the values of social work and therefore seeks to combat racist practices in all areas of responsibilities.'

A cursory reading of this sentence might lead

you to think that it says simply: there is a lot of racism about and we are against it. But here, for once, the paper's language is precise; there is not simply a lot of racism, it is 'endemic' in 'values, attitudes and structures'. This might reasonably be interpreted as meaning that everybody and everything is racist and that Britain has a particularly acute problem. Furthermore, since everybody is a racist, we are racists, too, and because we hate racism so much we have a special duty to fight it.

Books could be written on the intellectual arrogance and dishonesty of these assertions, as well as on their close structural kinship to certain ideas that have justified totalitarianism and murder in the past. For the moment, however, only these points need be made: racist attitudes exist and there are many nasty incidents with a racial component that can be proved; it is meaningless and utterly unjustified to inflate this into the conviction that all British society is riddled with it; to elevate racism as the one specific enemy of social work cripples the profession's ability to think and to consider other factors; the conviction that we are all racists is an old totalitarian trap that means if you argue with any part of the case you are directly providing evidence for the case; such presuppositions, as demonstrated by the Norfolk fiasco, encourage the inhuman conviction that blackness or whiteness is the overwhelmingly dominant factor in individual identity, and that if you are not absolutely defined by your skin colour, then you are racially naïve.

In fact, Britain in world terms is a society relatively free of racist tension and, historically, it was the British rather than the equally implicated Arabs and Africans who abolished the slave trade, so we might reasonably congratulate ourselves on being the most anti-racist culture on earth.

Yet, in a sense, such arguments are beside the point. Bureaucrats have decided to formalise their extreme and—to blacks—highly offensive views about race in this and a stream of other papers; many young social workers will accept them and the damage will be done. Reasoned argument is unlikely to be effective—when, for example, I pointed out the meaning of their own words to the CCETSW, the reply was simply that they could not be responsible for misinterpretations—a frightening indicating of how remote they are from real history, functioning language and an elementary sense of responsibility.

Perhaps, in such a context, Professor Robert Pinker of the London School of Economics was right to say on Monday that this body should be abolished at once. But presumably this disabling obsession with racism will remain, and this is what really needs to be confronted. It is evident that racism is perceived by these people as a social problem of such magnitude and pervasiveness that it either dwarfs or defines all others. Indeed, the language employed—the word 'endemic' being the grossest example—indicates that racism is understood not as a series of simple incidents or nasty attitudes, but rather as a condition, a syndrome, a virus or even some metaphysical entity that silently invades all our lives and perverts all our judgements.

This elevation of racism into disease or original sin is the real clue to the obsession. Ever since the 19th century there has been a tendency for social work to manifest itself as a group of well-meaning 'experts' moving among the lower orders with the conviction that they have some clear understanding and explanation of their problems.

It is not enough merely to help, there must also be some explanatory mechanism. This, of course, changes with time, and racism happens to be the explanatory model of the moment. Furthermore, race conveniently replaces class as the point of conflict required by much left-wing political theory; it is an issue that usefully inspires the same generalised guilt and provides the same material for a pseudo-scientific explanation of social developments.

Finally, and most banally, social workers are politically tied to local government, and race is a devastatingly effective and apparently simple issue for firing up the councillors. The truth is that racism is neither a virus against which we need social workers to inoculate us, nor an abstract force of history or metaphysical entity to which we must all confess or whose blemish must be wiped from our souls. It is simply a stupid and occasionally evil distortion of the natural human impulse to treat the alien with caution and some unease.

The racist elevates uncertainty to aggression, as does the rapist or the socially inadequate domestic murderer. Racism, in short, is nothing special, it is just one element in the spectrum of human nastiness.

Paper 30 is a miserable document that can all too easily be used to justify divisive and vicious attitudes. It encourages racism by placing it so relentlessly in a category of its own and by insisting on the certainty of its ubiquity and its effects. Virginia Bottomley and Jeffrey Greenwood, the new chairman of the CCETSW, should withdraw it at once.

Source: The *Independent* 4 August 1993.

CHAPTER 6

Ideological Perspectives and Older People: A Case Study

- Ideology, social policy, social work, and need assessment: a case study: Eileen and Ann
- Application of theoretical approaches
- Criticisms of perspectives as they apply to Eileen and Ann
- New right, new left, postmodernity

Introduction

It has become fashionable to argue that there is a growing convergence between new right and new left social policy. Although there is an unquestionable closing of the ideological gap on the question of social service provision a distinction of sorts still exists. Before losing the 1997 general election the Conservative Party announced their intention to extend compulsory competitive tendering in the personal social services. The reaction of Chris Smith, Labour Party shadow Health Secretary, at that time was significant: 'To force councils to go to the private sector, no matter what is best for the individual citizen, smacks of clapped out ideology rather than sensible provision for the most vulnerable in our society' (*Sunday Times* 1997: 1). Despite such polemical statements made in opposition, the approach taken by the Labour Party following their 1997 general election victory is not markedly different.

In this chapter it will be argued that differences in ideological approaches even if not reflected in policy still exist. The case study below approaches an example of practice from three distinct perspectives—new right, new left, and postmodernism—which are of contemporary significance. It examines the way in which decisions made by social policy-makers at the macro level and social workers and care managers at the micro level impinge on the lives of two people. It demonstrates both the power that professionals have in controlling people's lives, and the severe limitations that are placed on social workers in bringing about change.

Ideology, social policy, social work, and need assessment: a case study: Eileen and Ann

Eileen, aged 78, and Ann, aged 72, both white women, had spent their working lives nursing in a general hospital on the south coast of England. Whilst Eileen had been principal nursing officer Ann had worked very closely as her deputy. Since retirement they had lived in a bungalow near to where they had previously worked and were both in receipt of modest occupational pensions. Eileen had savings exceeding £10,000 and they owned their own bungalow.

After her first stroke Eileen suffered a further stroke and was left with difficulties in her walking and talking whilst also suffering some occasional bouts of incontinence. After treatment and recovery in hospital she was assessed by the social worker as being 'frail and in need of constant care'. The medical social worker in the hospital received a call from the ward saying that the consultant on his last ward round had decided to discharge Eileen into the community. Ann insisted that she wanted to continue to look after Eileen at home, claiming that she was able to help Eileen with all her needs.

The social worker working as part of a multidisciplinary community care team explained to the two women that since Eileen's savings exceeded £10,000 she would have to make a major contribution towards the cost of her care. The occupational therapist visited the bungalow and recommended the installation of a number of aids. The social worker constructed a package of care for Eileen which consisted of a visit from a home care worker twice each day, meals on wheels for five days, and a weekly visit to a club for older people. The GP was also contacted by the social worker and promised to 'look in from time to time' in order to monitor the situation.

Two weeks after Eileen was discharged from the hospital the social worker received a call from Ann to say that neither woman could eat the food provided by meals on wheels and requesting that this service be cancelled. The visit to the day centre had proved to be an ordeal for both women, since the journey in the minibus, which was run by a voluntary group, had been in Ann's words traumatic, and Eileen did not like the people whom they had met. The social worker expressed her concern to both women as to how Ann was going to manage with cooking and the care of Eileen. Three days later the social worker visited the bungalow, finding Eileen in a very distressed condition. Eileen was upset since she had continually woken Ann during the night. Ann was clearly exhausted. The social worker left the bungalow recording that she would discuss the case with her community care team manager, but was concerned that the situation might be breaking down. Before that discussion took place the social worker had a call from the ward to say that Eileen had been readmitted to the hospital after a fall which had occurred whilst Ann was attempting to lift Eileen out of a chair.

After Eileen's recovery from the effects of the fall the social worker discussed Eileen's discharge with the medical team and community care manager and it was decided that the level of support required by Eileen was beyond that which could be supplied by the community care system. Overnight care from a private agency was not available in the area at that time due to financial restrictions, and respite care was not available at this point due to lack of resources. In any event respite care was not deemed appropriate given the extent of care that Eileen appeared to require. The only option appeared to be residential care for Eileen. Despite the reluctance of both women, the medical house officer, ward sister, occupational therapist, and social worker were able to persuade them that the best course of action was for Eileen to be placed in a private residential home. It was clear from early days that the residential home was unsatisfactory. Ann found difficulty in visiting Eileen regularly since the area in which the two women lived was badly served by public transport. Eileen was becoming increasingly distressed and worried by being away from Ann.

This case has been constructed to demonstrate some of the major problems faced by social workers and care managers. It does illustrate that social work professionals to a large extent accept particular social definitions of social problems which are grounded in ideological positions. A discussion of perspectives found in the social policy liter-ature can assist in locating social work practice within such debates. The perspectives do not reflect political positions in the sense that the new left model represents New Labour and the new right the Conservative Party. Each perspective approximates to what Weber referred to as an 'ideal type'. By this he meant

One-sided accentuation of one or more points of view and . . . the synthesis of a great many diffuse, discrete, more or less present and occasionally absent concrete individual phenomena which are arranged according to those one-sidedly emphasised viewpoints into a unified ana-lytical construct. (Weber 1949: 90)

In other words the perspectives which are examined in relation to Eileen and Ann, and the social work practices associated with them, will not exist in discrete forms. Social workers might be attempting to incorporate ideas from differing perspectives. Social workers are subject to severe ideological and practical constraints which can result in them being forced to work from ideological perspectives with which they do not agree. It is difficult to find a social worker possessing all the characteristics ascribed to any one perspective.

Application of approaches

The new right perspective

Good practice from this perspective is inextricably linked to working within an internal market which requires local authorities to allow the private sector, charities, and the voluntary sector to bid for most of the £8 billion a year budget which is spent on care by social services. This perspective also incorporates a transformation from the idea of social work as enabling the client purposefully to express feelings, empathy, and individualization towards a care management approach (Biestek 1961; see Part III below). Care management involves the social worker undertaking core tasks in costing and tailoring services to individual needs, assessing need, implementing, monitoring, and reviewing a care plan (D.o.H. 1991*a*).

Whilst taking cognizance of the needs of the two women, the cost of the level of resource required to provide assistance would form a dominant concern (see Table 6.1). The internal or quasi-market system is regarded by the new right as being the most

Table 6.1. **Perspectives in policy and practice**

Perspective	Problem location	Social policy goal	Social work goal	Implications for social work practice
New right	Individual failure. Burgeoning local state. Creation of a culture of dependency.	Reduce costs of welfare. Competitive testing in market.	Consumer independence within the community. Lowering cost of welfare through competition.	Increased managerial control.
New left	Individual failure. Imperfect economic system. High rates of unemploy- ment, homelessness. Poverty, ignorance, and associated inequalities.	Tackle social problems. Efficient, realistic provision of services for those in need. Pursuit of equality through a variety of corrective measures including the possibility of raising taxes.	Community development. Rights of citizenship.	Counselling. Groupwork. Casework. Advocacy. Welfare rights.
Postmodernity	Oppressive programmatic notions of truth which promote the idea of one authentic reality.	Policies should reflect individual consumer interest. Decentralization and fragmentation of services.	Possible disappearance of social work profession.	Inappropriate state response.

effective and cost-efficient way of providing care in the community in this case. The justification for this can be related both to the quality of service which is provided and to the wider concerns relating to the functioning of the economy. Successful providers in the market will sell services at an economical rate. This in turn will enable tax levels to be kept lower, which is instrumental in the creation of profits for providers within the state, private, and voluntary sectors. Such competition also ensures that waste and bureaucracy are minimized. This will act as a counter to increasing uncontrolled state welfare expenditure as the demands made by people of Eileen and Ann's age increases. Reduced taxation levels provide incentives, and an environment in which entrepreneurs will invest to provide increased revenue, some of which will be spent on welfare. A by-product of this will be more employment opportunities for welfare workers in the private sector, who might otherwise be unemployed, claiming benefit, and creating a further burden on the benefit budgets. A healthy economy cannot sustain unlimited welfare services for older people.

The internal market and the private sector is seen as providing cost-effective, flexible, and adaptable service provision for the women, whilst ensuring that Eileen does not become institutionalized until it is absolutely necessary. From the new right perspective a costed attempt was made to keep Eileen out of residential care, which was in keeping with the wishes of both women. Services were tailored to the needs of the women at the lowest cost to the taxpayer. Eileen and Ann were directed towards the private residential sector since, it is argued by the new right, state funds cannot supply a bottomless pit of

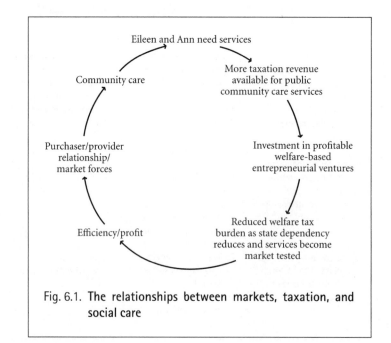

Fig. 6.1. **The relationships between markets, taxation, and social care**

demand. Scarce community resources can best be used in cases which are more likely to lead to independence. Both social workers and medical professionals acted upon the supposition that this perception constituted the way forward for the two women and indeed appeared to have little else to offer the two women apart from home care, which would eventually have proved to be a strain on the financial resources of the two women given that they were forced to make a contribution (see Fig. 6.1).

Equality is not a major priority from this perspective since unequal rewards resulting from the market are necessary inducements for providers to compete in the internal market. It is oversimplistic to suppose that all proponents of this view of Eileen and Ann's situation are driven simply by lack of consideration for those in need. Some writers who have entered the policy debate from this perspective believe that the reduction of state activity in the field of welfare and a growing dependence on the mixed economy of welfare can ultimately enhance the well-being of those in need (Friedman 1962). If the levels of state assistance are expanded taxation will become prohibitively high and discourage wealth producers from investing in any potential market. Such entrepreneurs ultimately provide the tax revenue which resources welfare services. Recipients of welfare are seen as suffering in the long run if expenditure on welfare is increased beyond the limits which revenues can support.

The new left model

Good practice from this perspective would promote a policy which met the aspirations of Eileen and Ann whilst providing an efficient, moderately priced, state welfare service. The new left wish to avoid burgeoning state activity but would recognize that state welfare is designed to serve the best interests of Eileen and Ann. Costings would also be based upon the need to provide economical services within clearly stated budgetary constraints. The need for financial constraint would be acknowledged but there would be some acknowledgement that the state has a responsibility for the care of Eileen. The 'problem' from this perspective would be couched in terms not of the need to restrict access to scarce resources but of the possible danger to both women if services were not provided. Services need to be cost effective but also responsive to need. The possible failure of the women to cope would guide the way in which assessments were made. On the surface the objectives listed in relation to the new left and new right do not appear to be remarkably different. Assessment, care-planning, monitoring, and review are also present within this perspective. A prime aim of the intervention would be to attempt to enable Eileen and Ann to live together for as long a period as possible through a partnership between Eileen, Ann, and service providers. Whilst recognizing that Ann and Eileen could experience severe difficulties in coping, a social worker might also employ a more individualized, psychodynamic form of practice which moves beyond the mechanics of designing a care package for the women. The worker for instance might think it appropriate to assist both women to prepare for the day when they would live apart

(Hollis 1964). This perspective would also place an emphasis on evaluating the results of practice on a more individualized basis. A working model has been developed by Preston-Shoot and Williams, who describe a number of steps which emphasize a more evaluative approach to intervention:

- a description of the situation as precisely as possible;
- a description of the broad aim of the intervention and desired outcome;
- the identification of feasible objectives;
- a description of the intervention designed to achieve the desired objective;
- the identification of indicators which reveal change
- a decision as to who will record what and why;
- a plan for establishing the evaluation of processes 1–6;
- review: the results of the intervention should be reviewed prior to a return to step 1 or termination and subsequent follow up (Preston-Shoot and Williams 1987).

The new left social worker would accept the need for more services to be purchased from the private sector; other services like home help could still be controlled and provided directly from local authorities if this was the most efficient, effective, and cost-effective way of providing the service. The worker could take a far more adversarial role, focusing on the need to obtain resources both from the state and from voluntary agencies which were more appropriate for Ann and Eileen. This could involve attempting to put pressure on care managers to provide more resources for Eileen and Ann, and being critical of the current mode of service delivery. Overnight care, for instance, although very costly, would have enabled Ann to gain more rest.

The worker would have concentrated more clearly on the difficulties faced by both women and the 'interactions between people and their social environment'. Following Pincus and Minahan (1973), a more integrated approach could have been taken within this perspective which focuses attention on the systems through which people experience welfare, and the possible change agent systems which can be utilized by workers in order to improve the situations faced by service users. This would also involve utilization of systems within the community, in this case volunteers, who might have been willing to help with transporting Ann to the private residential home, or local support groups for older people, the services of neighbours, or local church groups.

The worker would be concerned with ensuring that Eileen and Ann secured their rights under the present legislation, and for the development of machinery for complaints procedures if services were lacking.

From this perspective it would have been possible to tailor opportunities for participation to take account of the physical limitations of the women. This could have been achieved through Ann and Eileen taking part from home. Although they require careful planning and facilitation, telephone meetings can involve older people collectively without the need for them to leave the home. Social workers need to develop skills in listening to older people like Ann and Eileen in order to establish how best to involve them in the process of participation, which it is argued can have a significant impact on community care practices. In two years one of the organizations studied by Thornton and Tozer became part of the local health authority and trust planning process. The planning forum was consulted before policy was made and a functioning consultation process on health issues was created. National representation on the Department of Health's National Users and Carers Group was also developed (Thornton and Tozer 1995). We will return to the theme of rights participation in Part III of this book.

In order to secure change and extra resource the worker would be seeking to negotiate collaboratively with other agencies and professionals with a view to creating changes which would ultimately work to the benefit of Eileen and Ann. One example of this might be to work with non-fund-holding GPs who might also feel that the level of care offered to their patients was inferior to GP fund-holders.

The new left would place less emphasis on the responsibility of the women to care for themselves and a greater onus on the state and community to develop appropriate services. This would be achieved within budgetary constraints. The social worker as a state employee would understand the position faced by the women in terms not of their own 'inability to cope', but of the inability of the state to care for people who are in genuine need.

Modernity and postmodernity

Reference has previously been made to the importance of postmodernity in understanding the manner in which social work could develop in the future (Howe 1994). Modernity emerged out of the seventeenth-century Enlightenment and represented a way of understanding the physical and social world which went beyond divine intervention. Rationality and science could ultimately provide the means whereby human beings could control their destinies. Modernity was based upon the notion that history had a definite progression, and tended to develop universal categories of experience. Modernity has had a profound affect upon the development of economic and social systems like welfare, since reason can be seen as constituting the basis of social work (Parton 1996). Social work as a profession was thus built upon such a view of reality and provides a means whereby qualified professionals like social workers with reference to a corpus of professional knowledge can distinguish between what is normal and pathological, risky and safe. In some respects Eileen and Ann experienced a modernist approach to social care. Both medical and social work expertise based upon learned and examined theoretical and practical knowledge appeared to impose a form of professional truth upon the two women which ultimately worked to their detriment. The dominance of supposed professionally agreed insights based upon scientific or quasi-scientific concepts formed a professional reality which was contrary to the wishes of the two women. Modernity in this sense is disempowering since it removes the right of Eileen and Ann to make decisions about their own lives.

Parton has argued that the ambiguities which surround current social work practices are related to the development of new forms of social regulation which move beyond modernism. Recent interest has focused upon the manner in which the development of social work is connected with the postmodern condition. The emergence of the post-modern is represented in Parton's words by 'Increasing uncertainty, fragmentation, ambiguity, and change' (Parton 1996: 12). No professional group such as social workers has any particular access to truth, since truth itself is a problematic and contested concept. Although there is no agreement as to how postmodern conditions have impacted upon the development of social work a number of possibilities occur.

- Competency-based training, as seen in the development of professional social work training in the late 1990s, is composed of categories which are arbitrary and fragmented (Dominelli 1996).

- The purchaser/provider split provides a further example of fragmentation. The local authority increasingly becomes a purchasing authority for services provided by a disparate group of service suppliers drawn mainly from the voluntary and in-dependent commercial sectors.

- The overall tendency is towards heterogeneous service provision. Packages of care and varying types of contractual arrangements will create more differentiated services.

- Social work will become increasingly deprofessionalized and integrated within the work of other professionals. Much of the work previously carried out by social workers is now and will increasingly be allocated to care managers from a wide variety of ancillary medical professions.

- The notion of a discrete theoretically based social work will be incorporated into the notion of social care. As social work disappears, social care workers drawn from numerous disciplines will identify with corporate structures dominated by man-agement, rather than any quasi-body or contested body of professional social work.

Postmodern theories also focus attention on the way in which meanings are created through discourse. Discourse can be defined as that which mediates between meaning and the sentence. Forms of powerful discourse are often associated with professional techno-language. In this case neither Eileen nor Ann was able to construct a discourse which could compete or even be heard against the dominant expert-based discourse of the welfare and medical professionals. The formulation of technical concepts which were used between social workers and medical staff created the impression that shared meanings existed as to what was the best course of action, which led both women towards an unquestioning compliance. For the postmodernist such assertions of abso-lute professional truth are untenable and remove power from vulnerable people. Social workers and medical staff persuaded Eileen and Ann that they were using professional power on their behalf. They had effectively assumed the right to make decisions on the basis that their professional technical knowledge was ultimately best for both women. Postmodernism renders Eileen and Ann as being unique, allowing the possibility for care to be developed in less formal and possibly more imaginative ways. The views of the experts would be less likely to be imposed upon service users, as professional authority and reliance upon a corpus of powerful professional forms of knowledge lose their legitimacy. Although some writers are increasingly sceptical about the use of terms like postmodern or indeed post-anything one could argue that social work is in a state of transition or may possibly disappear in its present form from the UK (Clarke 1996). Social work in a postmodern world becomes an increasingly ambiguous, uncertain, and dissipated activity.

Criticisms of perspectives as they apply to Eileen and Ann

The new right perspective has constituted a dominant orthodoxy for the last decade and the mixed economy will structure the future of welfare provision for the foreseeable future. There is no reason to believe that any other major political party would change the basic principles of the purchaser/provider relationship, including competitive tendering and a greater involvement of the voluntary and private sector in respect to the provisions of welfare services (Le Grand and Bartlett 1993). What has emerged on the left is a form of rhetoric advocating market socialism which seeks to forge an accommodation between individualism and collectivism (see Chapter 2).

Criticisms of the new right

The inadequacy of the level of resources offered to Eileen and Ann had a crucial bearing on the breakdown of the situation. Whilst it is true that the post-war welfare state has failed to provide anything other than minimal services, the level of support envisaged by the new right falls below that which is necessary for basic need to be met. Although service provision will vary from area to area, Eileen's package of community care would probably have amounted to nine home help hours and between two and five home care attendances per week with additional meals on wheels help for five days. Such a package provides care at an extremely basic level. Thus Eileen's assessment was technically needs led, whilst decisions were made in the context of fixed budgets. A criticism frequently made of the developments of quasi-markets is that of 'cream-skimming', which might well have affected the level of resource allocated to Eileen and Ann. Le Grand and Bartlett (1993) have pointed out that in order to achieve some equity within quasi-markets, there must be discrimination in favour of the relatively healthy in order to maximize the effect of rationed resources. Put another way, given that resources levels are capped, community care resources must be used in such a way as to ensure that those who have a chance of living within the community receive a fair share of the assistance available. This leaves the most difficult situations unresourced. There is evidence to suggest that welfare services are vulnerable to cream-skimming (Means and Smith 1994). Eileen and Ann faced a situation which required intensive welfare support, yet the care manager would view them as requiring considerable sums of money over a long period of time if the situation in the community was not to break down. They were not part of the 'cream', which was reflected in the levels of service supplied. Although the notion of need has occupied a central position since the passing of the National Health Service and Community Care Act, little attention appears to be given to the way in which service users express their needs. The result has been oversimplified assumptions which appear to have been driven by a political ideology. When service users attempt to articulate their own perceptions of need or at least gain the right to express their needs, their views appear to become dissipated. Neither Ann nor Eileen appears to have had much influence over the determination of their needs or the services supplied. The women also do not appear to have had any access to published grievance procedures.

A number of consumer studies have indicated that recipients of such assessments are unhappy with the apparent disparity between assessment, community care management, and the way in which service users perceive their own needs (Borsay 1986, Baldock and Ungerson 1994). Thus the change in policy towards a system which is market driven and needs led does not appear to have addressed this power imbalance.

One of the criticisms frequently made of social work during the 1980s by those advocating a new right position (Brewer and Lait 1980) was that it paid too much attention to process and too little to outcome. This de-emphasized both the importance of evaluating the measurable effects of practice, and the active participation of the service user in the process of change. In this case the broad aims of the work were unclearly defined and the objectives, i.e. independent living and living in a residential home, appear to have been confused. No indicators were identified to reveal change. This would have involved taking into account the views of the 'consumers' who in some respects in this case were right.

The quality of the service being offered to the women appears to have been in question. Quality in a complex quasi-market is extremely difficult to monitor. In an atmosphere in which keeping overheads low in order to maximize profits is regarded as being a high priority, it is not surprising that the quality of services provided in relation to the service users' need may be an early casualty.

Criticisms of the new left position

Whilst social workers witness the shortcomings of social welfare systems on a daily basis, they are usually employed by voluntary agencies or local government bodies which are part of existing institutional arrangements. The central contradiction lies in the fact that social workers critical of services are part of the system which reproduces the oppression in the first place, whilst the results of inequality and need constitute the basis of their daily work. The solution to this dissonance for new left social workers enables them to locate themselves within existing social relations whilst justifying their interventions on the basis that they will bring about relief of immediate need and change the worst effects of institutional structures. The new left social worker accepts that welfare services are cash limited, and resources determined by democratically elected government. It is not the role of social workers fundamentally to challenge this authority. Martin Davies, writing in the mid-1980s, denounces social workers who attempt to incorporate political perspectives of a left-wing 'radical' variety into their work.

There is nothing logically impossible about social workers, along with other groups, pursuing radical ends with a view to overthrowing the present balance of power. They might even choose to do so as a result of what they have seen and experienced in the course of their social work duties. But for them to claim that what they are doing is social work seems of doubtful validity. Social work as it has emerged in the twentieth century, undoubtedly depends for its existence on its acceptability to the political regime within which it practices and significantly social work exists as an occupational activity in nations of many varied political hues. (Davies 1985: 11)

Social work according to Davies should not be located within debates about structural change, since the social work task is professional with definable and assessable skills.

The critique of the new left approach to social work from the new right is now familiar and has been enunciated by successive Conservative governments since 1979. State social workers have yet to prove that they offer anything more than wasteful and ineffective services which create welfare dependency (Brewer and Lait 1981, Marsland 1996a).

Criticisms of postmodernism

The postmodern perspective has been criticized from both a policy and a social work perspective. One of the major criticisms of the postmodernist position is that it leads to a form of relativism which fails to give social policy or social work any real purpose or direction. Destructuring and decentring knowledge could have a number of negative effects as Taylor-Gooby (1994) has pointed out. The development of a rational and systematized approach to human betterment through public-funded and -organized agencies became the *raison d'être* for social work. The cultural transition from the monolithic to the diverse, or put another way from the absolutism of modernity to the relativism of postmodernity, presupposes a homogeneous past. Postmodernists are to some extent suffering from what Clarke refers to as a form of historical amnesia.

Social work's past is marked by challenges, resistances and refusals in both collective and individual forms. From its nineteenth century origins, social work has been viewed ambiguously and sceptically by both its beneficiaries and commentators. (Clarke 1996: 43)

Postmodernist interpretations of social work fail to recognize the complexities inherent in debates and struggles relating to class, culture, ethnicity, race, and gender.

Conclusion

This chapter has sought to demonstrate that social work practices are subject to changes which are guided by political values and beliefs, and by changes which are occurring in the structure of society. Even though the stated aim of current community care policies is the creation of a responsive needs-led service, the demand for service constantly outstrips supply. The relationship between social work methods, quality, choice, and ultimately the service experienced by the user should be understood in these stark terms. Part III will examine these issues in greater detail.

Exercise

Thornton and Tozer (1995) in an examination of older people in the community studied three initiatives which sought to reflect the perspective of older people on welfare services. The first project studied was of a service users' action forum which as well as being reactive in the consultation process took up a number of issues like co-ordination of hospital discharge, and environmental planning. The second organization studied was 'healthlink', a postal network developed by a Community Health Council which aimed to bring services to people who had difficulty in living in their own homes. Older people were asked to identify their health-related concerns, environmental issues such as pollution, house repairs, adaptations, help at home, and transport. The third project was a telephone discussion group which also was designed to enable isolated older and disabled people to gain friendship and support. Social services managers entered into dialogue with discussants. A number of important 'practice points' emerged from this study which are relevant to Eileen and Ann, who needed to know about the community care changes. Comment on the way in which these models of participation might be applied to Eileen and Ann.

FURTHER READING

V. George and P. Wilding (1995), *Welfare and Ideology* (Hemel Hempstead, Harvester Wheatsheaf), and V. George and R. Page (1995) (eds.) in their collection *Modern Thinkers in Welfare* (London, Harvester Wheatsheaf), offer accounts of the positions discussed in relation to Eileen and Ann. Particularly useful accounts of Friedman are given by Jim Tomlinson, and Hayek by Norman Barry. P. Sharkey (1995), *Introducing Community Care* (London, Collins Educational) is a clear introduction to practice and community care policy. R. Davidson and S. Hunter (1994),

Community Care in Practice (London, Batsford) contains seventeen short chapters on all aspects of community care practice and care management which also constitute good introductory material. Two books by Malcolm Payne (1991), *Modern Social Work Theory: A Critical Introduction* (London, Macmillan) and (1995), *Social Work and Community Care* (London, Macmillan) provide accounts which attempt to utilize theory and policy to inform constantly changing practice situations. J. Clarke (1993) (ed.), *A Crisis in Care* (London, Sage) provides critical accounts of some of the issues raised in the case example.

PART II

User Groups

CHAPTER 7

Disablement:
Social Work and Social Policy

- Legislation
- An agenda for rights
- The struggle for anti-discriminatory, anti-oppressive legislation
- Social policy and the creation of dependency
- Learning disabilities
- Normalization
- Social work and disabled people: policy and practice
- The social model and empowerment
- Independent living
- Issues of language
- Monitoring
- The impact of policy and practice
- Some fundamental requirements

Introduction

In this chapter it will be argued that although the oppressive position occupied by disabled service users and employees has been partially recognized through equal opportunities statements, stated intentions have not been coherently reflected in practice. A reactive rather than proactive managerial approach has led to particular groups being temporarily targeted for attention at particular points, whilst the needs of others are consistently neglected. Disabled people fall into the latter category.

Legislation

The history of provision of post-war personal social services for disabled and impaired people can according to Sainsbury be divided into three broad periods—Promotional welfare 1948–63, which established services for disabled people; the 'rights to services' phase between 1963 and 1975 which increased control and choice over the daily lives of disabled people; and the burden of care approach from 1976 to the present (Sainsbury 1995). There are problems with the way in which each historical period has been described here. Welfare for disabled people has never been actively promoted, rights to basic services have never been achieved, and governments of all political parties have tended to regard disabled people as a burden on public expenditure. It is more accurate to say that arguments about rights for disabled people emerged in the late 1970s. Policy and practice with regard to disabled people has to some extent been subject to ebbs and flows of underlying political ideologies although some gains have been made in particular areas. Overall progress has been painfully slow and brought about in the main by the efforts of disabled people themselves. State provision in many areas has been non-existent and has tended to create dependency on dominant able-bodied professionals, which has had a disempowering effect on disabled people themselves.

In briefly describing the legislation it is more helpful to describe:

- philanthropy, less eligibility, and the Poor Law 1834–1945;
- the post-Beveridge 'welfare' consensus, 1945–75;
- the development of an agenda for rights by disabled people within the disability movement, 1975 to the present day.

Philanthropy, less eligibility, and the Poor Law

Although it is possible to trace legislation relating to disabled people to the Elizabethan Poor Law of 1601 which created a parochial system of welfare, brevity makes it necessary to move forward to the mid-nineteenth century. The emerging pattern of social policy at this point bears remarkable similarities to the situation which emerged after the publication of the Beveridge Report. Throughout the nineteenth century individual philanthropists set up organizations to assist the 'deserving' poor, which is how the disabled population were designated. The charitable organizations were in decline and experiencing difficulties in finding funds by the turn of the century. Despite this the report of the 1905 Royal Commission on the Poor Laws and the Relief of Distress recommended that the relief of all forms of poverty should remain primarily in the hands of the voluntary organizations (Thane 1982).

The Blind Persons Act of 1920 was intended to remove most visually impaired people from pauperism by providing rehabilitation, training, and employment. Under the Poor Law which it replaced, minimum services had to be provided on a means-tested basis.

The emergence of a welfare consensus

The 1948 Act was premissed upon services being supplied on the basis of need although the concept had been introduced in the regulations concerning the 1944 Education Act. The Education Act of 1944 effectively created a complex system of segregated schools for disabled children. Such provision was based upon a number of medical categories of disability (Tomlinson 1982). Section 29 of the 1948 Act required local authorities to promote the welfare of disabled people. The emphasis appears to have been on the supply of employment, training, and rehabilitation. Local authorities were given the power to establish sheltered workshops, hostel-based accommodation, and home working schemes. They were required to provide residential care for older people and the disabled, although the Act made no distinction between these two groups. The 1944 Disabled Persons Employment Act established a registration system. Disablement resettlement officers (DROs) were intended to assist disabled people in finding employment. The 1944 Act also required larger organizations to employ 3 per cent of disabled people. In 1951 the Ministry of Health issued a circular (32/51) encouraging local authorities to provide escorts for disabled people to places of worship and entertainment. This, according to Sainsbury, began to shift the balance away from the provision of employment-based services towards the need for the development of recreational and social facilities, whilst also allowing local authorities to use voluntary organizations as their paid agents. As a result of the ever increasing cost of the National Health Service in 1961 circular 15/60 initiated the replacement of beds in long-stay hospitals with community care.

Growing pressure from disabled people for a disability income and access to public buildings and transport drew attention to the deficiencies of the provisions under the 1948 National Assistance Act and single-issue disabled groups generated the pressure to create new legislation. This came in the form of the Chronically Sick and Disabled Persons Act of 1970 which ostensibly brought disabled people under the control of the newly genericized post-Seebohm social service departments. The stated intention of the Act was to strengthen the provisions for disabled people under the National Assistance Act to ensure access to buildings, adapt homes, and register disabled people, and provide home help and service-planning based upon estimates of the numbers of disabled people in a particular area. Attendance allowance was introduced in 1970 and a new benefit, mobility allowance, in 1976.

An agenda for rights

By the mid-1970s disabled people had begun to agitate for participation in the management of their own services in order to create greater control over their lives. Oliver has described the chronological development of five types of organization:

- Charitable organizations like RADAR (Royal Association for Disability and Rehabilitation), RNIB (Royal National Institute for the Blind), and the Spastics Society were organizations for disabled people which sought to develop a consultative and advisory role with professional organizations.
- Economic Parliamentary groups such as DIG (Disablement Income Group) and the Disability Alliance were primarily single-issue groups for disabled people.
- Consumerist self-help groups like the Spinal Injuries Association were organizations *of* disabled people as distinct from those that were *for* disabled people. Organizations of disabled people aim at problem-solving, providing services, and working in collaboration with local and national voluntary and statutory agencies.
- Populist activist organizations like the British Deaf Association and UPIAS (Union of the Physically Impaired Against Segregation) developed as organizations of disabled people and focused on issues of empowerment.
- Umbrella groups are organizations of disabled people who reject divisions within the disabled population based upon clinical classification, and may function at international, national, or local level. These are primarily political organizations which aim to facilitate the empowerment of disabled people.

Only populist, activist, and consumerist self-help groups can be regarded as constituting a new disability movement, since they are organizations of disabled people (Oliver 1990).

In the late 1970s local authorities began to respond to the increasing anger of deaf people by introducing specialist workers who were signers. This development was erratic, and deaf people were highly critical of social work training which has tended to pathologize the experience of deafness. The struggle relating to the use of sign language to some extent diverted attention from hearing-impaired people who were reliant upon speech for communication (Sainsbury 1995).

The struggle for anti-discriminatory, anti-oppressive legislation

Some commentators have argued that the goal of providing appropriate state services based upon need was supplanted by a general atmosphere of state crisis management brought about by the oil crisis, and public expenditure cuts imposed by the International Monetary Fund. Other writers have argued that, far from being in a state of crisis, the welfare state of the late 1970s and early 1980s bore a steady continuity. The crisis was in terms of perceptions of welfare (Manning 1985). The election of the first Thatcher government in 1979 occurred in an ideological climate favouring minimalist provision which was cost centred.

The Barclay inquiry into the personal social services, new right critics of social work (Brewer and Lait 1980), and liberal academic research sought to demonstrate that services for disabled people could be provided more effectively by informal and formal networks (Hadley and Hatch 1981). By the end of the 1970s there was a growing realization amongst disabled people that disability was created not by tragedy but by social oppression. Despite the growing confidence of the disabled people's movement the beginnings of the attempted restructuring of the welfare state began directly to affect disabled people.

In 1981 the Education Act which followed the report of Lady Warnock of 1978 supported the principle of integration in schools. The Act also increased the rights of parents to some degree in having access to records which related to their children. The 1988 Education Act marked the introduction of the discipline of the market into education but allowed for the disapplication of the national curriculum to disabled children in particular situations at the discretion of the head teacher (Barton 1993).

In 1983, in an attempt to encourage participation of the private sector in care, the government relaxed its social security rules, enabling people in receipt of social security payments to enter private residential establishments, the state paying the difference between a resident's income less the guaranteed personal allowance and the price of accommodation. The Conservative government responded to the resulting increased cost by placing an upper limit on the level of fees that it was prepared to meet, whilst stepping up its regulatory function by introducing the 1984 Registration of Homes Act.

The 1986 Disabled Persons Act gave disabled people the right to an independent assessment of need by the local authority, and some limited rights to be involved in their own assessment, if necessary through a representative, although as we will see later this legislation was never fully implemented. In 1988 the Conservative government failed to include social security payments in its social security reforms and in the same year it commissioned a survey of disability.

The stated aim of the NHS and Community Care Act (1990) was to provide more value for money through the working of an internal market and the development of an independent sector (for a full discussion of the community care legislation in relation to disabled people see Part III). Packages of 'needs-led' care would, it was argued, provide a more sensitive and responsive service whilst also providing more support for carers. The 1990 NHS and Community Care Act, with the 1970 Chronically Sick and Disabled Persons Act as amended by the Disabled Persons (Services, Consultation and Representation) Act 1986, also requires local authorities to gather and disseminate information relating to services available to disabled people. The disability working allowance introduced in 1992 encouraged disabled people to top up low earnings. This was intended to be an incentive for those on invalidity benefit and severe disability allowances to take up low-paid employment. The means-tested nature of the benefits and the potential for disabled people to find themselves in the poverty trap has not made this policy initiative a popular option. It was estimated that some 50,000 disabled people would claim, whereas two years after its introduction there were only 5,000 claimants. Of those claiming 805 were already in work, so it cannot be argued that the new measure acted as an incentive to find employment (Thornton and Lunt 1995).

The 1995 Disability Discrimination Act makes it illegal for large employers (including social services and probation departments) to discriminate on the grounds of disability in the areas of recruitment, training, promotion, and dismissal. It also requires employers to take reasonable steps to adjust disabled workers' working conditions and working arrangements in order to assist them in performing their job. Complaints can be made to an industrial tribunal and compensation is not subject to any upper limit.

Social policy and the creation of dependency

The dependency of disabled people on services provided and organized by the state can be traced back to the development of legislation and practices which emerged during the nineteenth century.

Since at least the nineteenth century, Britain in common with most western societies has witnessed the gradual and sustained growth of a multi billion pound 'disability industry' dependent on the disabled people's continued dependence for its survival. (Campbell and Oliver 1996: p. ix).

Four themes can be identified with the 1834 Poor Law Amendment Act which have resonated through the years.

1. The less eligibility principle devised by Chadwick as a guiding principle for the administration of relief made paupers less eligible for relief. This principle was reinforced by tougher regimes within the workhouses which forced poor people to rely on friends, relatives, and informal networks of care. The state was the very last resort, and fear of the workhouse grew throughout the nineteenth century. We will see in Part III of this book that the less eligibility principle is now applied to disabled people following the new community care legislation in that local authorities are failing to comply with community care requirements laid down by the legislation on cost grounds (Travis 1996). The 1834 Poor Law Amendment Act, based as it was upon the strict

control of public spending and the less eligibility principle, transformed impairment into a problem which created a burden upon the taxpayer.

2. The patronizing and disempowering distinction between the deserving and the undeserving poor has also been a constant theme. Chadwick made this categorization clear in 1834 in that the deserving poor should be eligible for some form of relief since their position had not been brought about by fecklessness, or lack of industry, but misfortune. Disabled people clearly fell into the deserving category and were to be offered pity and charity given that they had no hope of ever becoming productive. During the 1980s this image was powerfully reinforced by media images of voluntary events like telethons, Children in Need, and red nose days, which portray disabled people as pitiful, dependent, and entitled to charity. This theme is also clearly echoed in approaches to disabled people in the 1990s. The deserving poor are the passive recipients of the proceeds of red nose days and other charitable extravaganzas.

3. The link between needs-led assessment and dependency is another important theme. The local state would offer limited help based upon needs as assessed by the local boards of guardians. One of the central planks upon which policy and practice has been based is that of needs-led assessment. Assessment is currently conceptualized on social work training courses as 'Working in partnership to assess and review people's needs, rights, risks, strengths, responsibilities and resources' (CCETSW 1995: 27). In practice we can substitute here social workers and more latterly care managers for the function of the boards of guardians. Both groups have the power to establish what constitutes need and who is deserving of resources ostensibly designed to meet the needs of the deserving.

4. The oppressive practice of warehousing disabled people in institutions can also be traced to nineteenth-century roots. The 1834 Poor Law Amendment Act was intended to make workhouses more strict and discourage the able-bodied from being dependent on the local state. Yet the Poor Law Commission of 1905 found that 30 per cent of the populations of the workhouses were either sick or disabled. Despite charity, pity, and being deserving, disabled people through a needs-led form of assessment ended up in total institutions which were designed for the feckless able-bodied. Like the workhouses the Cheshire Homes after the Second World War rescued the destitute disabled but effectively segregated young disabled people, denying them the basic right to live where and how they chose (Oliver, 1996).

The Chronically Sick and Disabled Persons Act of 1970 extended the needs-based approach which had been enshrined in the 1948 National Assistance Act (Keeble 1979). The only additional duties imposed upon local authorities by the Act were to compile a register of disabled persons and publicize services. Neither of these measures appears to have been effective in providing new rights to disabled people; they simply reinforced the notion of needs-based services.

The 1981 Education Act supported the principle of integration, although no additional funding was made available. The Act has done little if anything to extend the rights and entitlements of disabled children whilst the government's own inspectorate have shown that the level of provision in most remaining special schools is inadequate (Oliver 1996).

The 1986 Disabled Persons Act, although conferring certain rights of procedural fairness on disabled people, has not been properly implemented (Doyle and Harding 1992). Local authorities have simply been able to claim that they are underfunded to the point where they are unable to implement the legislation. Even though the NHS and Community Care Act offers the potential for disabled people to purchase their own packages of care through direct payments, it is unlikely that this will happen in a situation in which community care budgets are severely capped and in some cases community care denied illegally (Travis 1996). It is more likely that the concept of needs-led assessment will replay the nineteenth-century themes.

One of the major problems with the 1995 Disability Discrimination Act is that organizations employing less than twenty persons would not be affected by these new arrangements, which would leave some 96 per cent of firms exempt. This measure follows the rejection of the Civil Rights (Disabled Persons) Bill in 1994 which if passed would have offered more comprehensive rights to disabled people. The 1996 Direct Payments (Disabled Persons) Act which enables payments to be made to disabled people in order for them to purchase their own services marks an important break with the 1948 National Assistance Act which gave local authorities the responsibility for supplying services for disabled people. Some influential writers in social policy place need at the centre of the policy agenda (e.g. Doyal and Gough 1991). It must be acknowledged that, since the Second World War, needs-based legislation and practices have provided more access to more services, thus reducing the likelihood of disabled people being segregated within institutional settings.

What may appear to able-bodied social work professionals to be a reasonable set of propositions based upon needs-led assessments made by social workers and care managers has, according to a number of disabled commentators, become the basis upon which policy and practice has structurally subordinated disabled people into dependency. Relatively small gains have been achieved at the price of invasion of privacy and the acceptance of service prescribed by the state, rather than the services that disabled people themselves say they need. The emphasis on need offers the state more opportunities to gain access to the private lives of disabled people, thus removing independence and control over personal life (Borsay 1986, Hugman 1991).

The new reforms fail to challenge the balance of power which is now held by the care manager, who will essentially be performing the same task as the pre-1990 caseworker and the Poor Law guardian. The only thing that has changed as far as many disabled people are concerned is the job title.

The impact of direct purchasing on the lives of disabled people is a major breakthrough. It remains to be seen whether resource levels make it possible for disabled people to purchase the services they need. If history repeats itself disabled people will still find themselves in situations dominated by material poverty.

Learning disabilities[1]

It is estimated that between 2 per cent and 3 per cent of the population have a learning difficulty ranging from mild to profound. There are approximately 30,000 children in the UK under 16 who have severe or profound learning difficulties. Children with learning difficulties tend to live with their parents or other carers. One-fifth of adults with learning difficulties live in hospital and NHS community units and just over one-quarter live in residential accommodation provided by local authorities or the independent sector. Few people with learning difficulties have jobs, since the benefit system effectively provides a disincentive to work, forcing individuals into a life of 'training'. Adult Training Centres and Social Education Centres are the main source of daytime occupation for adults (Booth 1997).

People with learning difficulties have suffered similar forms of social exclusion to disabled people, having failed to gain access to basic rights of citizenship (Walmsley 1991). Chappel has used a number of case examples to draw attention to the way in which people with learning difficulties are treated within the criminal justice system.

Case examples

Stekan Kiszko, described in court as having a mental age of 12, was convicted of murder in 1976. During the court proceedings it emerged that he had confessed to the crime during his sixth interview. Much of his sentence at Ashworth Special Hospital was spent in solitary confinement, and Kiszko suffered major bouts of depression. In 1992 he was freed by the Court of Appeal and in May 1994 a senior police officer and forensic scientist who had been instrumental in the case were charged with attempting to pervert the course of justice. Vital forensic evidence which could have freed Kiszko at his original trial had been withheld. Stekan Kiszko died in 1993.

Colin Lattimore, an 18-year-old with learning difficulties, was convicted of murder in the late 1970s and later freed by the Court of Appeal after serving a two-year period in Rampton Hospital. It was clear as a result of this case that not all senior police officers were aware of the Judges' Rules and their relevance to the Lattimore Case. The gate-keeping procedures to protect people with learning difficulties during police investigations appear to be highly problematic. The function of the 'appropriate adult' who according to Judges' Rules must be present during police questioning can constitute a 'let-out clause'.

[1] There has been considerable controversy concerning this particular term (see D. Race in Malin (1994)). Most organizations providing services in the UK use either 'learning difficulties' or 'learning disability'.

Although Chappel acknowledges that as a result of PACE (Police and Criminal Evidence Act 1984) the safeguards in this area have been clarified, it still remains the responsibility of the police to identify whether a suspect has learning difficulties before invoking the codes of practice. Research carried out for the Runciman Commission found that police officers only decided that a suspect required an appropriate adult in 'exceptional circumstances'. Appropriate adults do not have to be present when a probation officer interviews an offender, and it is at this point that vital decisions are taken which may have a long-term impact on the individual. Chappel argues that groups who are economically, politically, and socially weak are particularly easy targets when demands exist to secure a conviction at any cost (Chappel 1994).

Normalization

In relation to people with learning difficulties the concept of normalization has been influential in the development of services. Although normalization has its origins in Scandinavia it developed as a practice in America and was transported to Britain. Normalization emphasizes the importance of reproducing the lifestyle of able-bodied people by creating routines during the day, the development of sexual relationships, and self-determination. Normalization has developed into a theory which suggests that people with learning disabilities should have roles which are socially valued (Wolfensberger and Thomas 1983). However, such a theory when applied could enable social workers to retain a professional role and concomitantly the power to control people's lives. More radical attention needs to be given if the main source of difficulty faced by people with learning disabilities, i.e. poverty, is to be tackled (Chappel 1992). Although some commentators (Means and Smith 1994) regard this as a somewhat harsh judgement given the role that normalization has played in deinstitutionalization, user groups have generally followed the line taken by Chappel.

Social work and disabled people: policy and practice

Despite the presence of numerous 'equal opportunity posters' and other forms of stated good intention, disabled people see institutional discrimination as a major obstacle in their daily lives. They challenge the right of able-bodied social workers to distribute services which affect their lives. As Davis comments: 'At this juncture our lives are substantially still in their hands. They still determine most decisions and the practical outcomes' (Davis 1993: 199).

Table 7.1. Discrimination: policy and practice

Perspective	Causes of discrimination	Social policy perspective	Social work perspective
Personal tragedy	Misunderstandings of individuals. Prejudice, handicap.	Needs led.	Working with grief—adapting to a new situation.
Liberal pluralism	Established systems malfunctioning.	Rights to needs-led services, equal opportunities.	Assess need. Utilize professional expertise.
Social model	Medicalization, professionalism structured in dominance of able-bodied. Oppression, capitalism.	Anti-discrimination. Rights to appropriate services as defined by disabled people.	Enabling disabled people to purchase their own choice of services. Assisting disabled people to live independently. Centrality of user empowerment.

Ideas have formed the basis for policy and practice in work with disabled people. 'Personal tragedy theory' enables disabled people to be conceptualized as essentially passive pitiful individuals, in need of insightful assessment and intervention by able-bodied social workers. This position substantiates the view that formal training and experience in social work bestows particular skills upon social workers which gives them a professional form of insight into the 'trauma' and 'grief' felt by the disabled person.

Like the assimilationist ideology which frequently pervades social work and probation practice in relation to black people (Ely and Denney 1987), personal tragedy theory is essentially a deficit theory which has had a powerful impact on the assessment and 'treatment' of disabled people. Disability becomes a form of bereavement, the social worker's job being to counsel the bereaved person through the loss and make the best of a tragic situation. Such an approach serves to disempower, aiming at the creation of passivity and dependency. Here the emphasis is placed on the disabled person's diminished ability and responsibility to adapt to the demands of an environment experienced by disabled people in a less than perfect society (Wood and Badley 1978) (see Table 7.1).

From this perspective disabled people are conceived of as being legitimately dependent on an essentially imperfect but benignly beneficent state. Within the legislative framework created by the state social workers can represent disabled persons' rights since disabled people themselves are seen as being unable to fight for their own rights. A text based upon the 'needs-led' approach delineates the professional skills which are required for developing 'excellence in community care'. These include self-insight to make objective judgements on another's needs, costing and resource targeting (see Chapter 6), and pursuing equal rights in employment. Whilst noting that the user's progress towards independence should be encouraged, and recognizing the clients rights to self-determination, the workers stress the importance of 'Understanding, empathy, compassion, patience, and the ability to be positive in handling clients' difficulties in learning or coping' (Seed and Kaye 1994: 21).

The notion of compassion connotes the familiar theme of personal tragedy, whilst one is left wondering why it appears to be self-evident that the disabled person is dependent on the professional to cope. The important point about gaining rights from within the liberal pluralist perspective is that the rights are rarely defined or conceptualized by disabled people themselves but through the practices of able-bodied social workers/care managers. Directors of social services and the Association of Chief Probation Officers are publicly committed to 'equalizing' services and providing an environment which caters for the needs of everyone in order to avoid 'reinforcing negative stereotypes which causes offence to disabled people'. The equal opportunities approach, however, still places able-bodied professionals at the centre of the decision-making and budget-holding processes whilst failing to grasp the fundamental link between the creation of dependency and the kind of services which are being offered at present in most areas.

Equal opportunities policies effectively create parameters for organizations to define lists of services which able-bodied professionals consider appropriate for disabled people, which further limits their opportunities to gain the right to control their own lives. Such equal opportunities discourse gives the impression that disabled people have in some way been empowered by actions taken by the able-bodied managers who control resources. It is also a means by which the same managers and professionals can retain control of budgets. Wilding (1994) has drawn attention to the requirement of complex and expensive organizational back-up for rights enforcement, the difficulty of defining precisely the quality of service to which the user is entitled, and the ultimate use of charters of rights to protect the service provider. The result can be the legitimization of elaborate forms of 'tinkering' with a system which is fundamentally flawed.

The social model and empowerment

The idea of empowerment has been constructed around what has become an increasingly influential alternative social model of disability (Finkelstein 1980, Shakespeare 1993, Oliver 1990, 1996). Disability from this perspective must be defined in terms of restriction caused by a social structure which not only fails to take account of people who have physical impairments but excludes them from basic rights such as employment, decent housing, and education. Such a perspective on disability represents a shift in focus from the individual person's limitations towards a consideration of how disability is ideologically produced.

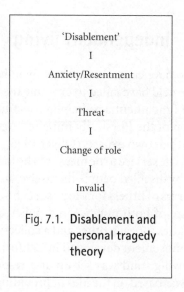

'Disablement'

I

Anxiety/Resentment

I

Threat

I

Change of role

I

Invalid

Fig. 7.1. **Disablement and personal tragedy theory**

Despite a number of criticisms of this position from within the disability movement it has enabled a new vocabulary to emerge. Here tragedy becomes an oppression, a personal problem a social problem, individual treatment becomes social action, and medicalization self-help. The expertise of professionals is transformed to become personal experience of disability, care becomes rights, and individual adaptation is transformed to social change.

The term 'empowerment' has also come to be used by policy-makers who seek to reduce services to disabled people. An essential blurring between purchasing power and empowerment lies at the heart of the difficulty (Ramon 1991). To some degree the concept of empowerment has been objectified and appropriated by social care managers within the discourse of equal opportunities which redesignated disabled people as consumers. Crucial to the development of this model in practice is the development of a vociferous and autonomous disability movement which bases its critique on the proposition that disability becomes possible in a society which is hierarchically ordered, where social exclusion and discrimination are tolerated. The politics of disablement is therefore not restricted to disabled people but refers to all forms of social oppression within a hierarchically ordered society.

A number of writers provide accounts of the disability movement, evolving as it did from the traditional voluntary organizations, the failure of single-issue pressure groups such as the Disablement Income Group, and the emergence of groups set up by and for disabled people. Morris (1993) sees the formation of the Disabled People International, following the rejection of Rehabilitation International that 50 per cent of the members of each national delegation should be disabled, as a defining moment in the history of the movement.

Independent living

Disabled people in order to have control over their own lives wish for independence. Able-bodied 'experts' in the field have failed to examine the cause of disability but only its effects. The statement of fundamental principles constitutes a clear statement of the position taken by the Union of the Physically Impaired Against Segregation, that disabled people must become their own experts (Oliver 1996). It is self-evidently essential for a professionally appropriate service to be measured by the extent to which it provides services which are defined by disabled people themselves as being needed. If quality of service is to be defined in terms of fitness for purpose such an arrangement provides the essential basis for the future of both practice and policy. Independent living should entail collective responsibilities for each other and a collective organization.

The independent living movement developed in California during the late 1960s. In the UK the independent living fund was set up as a response to the social security changes of 1988. The fund was based on the idea of providing weekly payments in order that disabled people could provide services for themselves. Disabled people were able to use the allocation to create packages of care which were appropriate for them. However, the government phased out this development on cost grounds in 1993 (Means and Smith 1994). The popularity of the scheme amongst disabled people far exceeded any expectation (Craig 1992). This is not surprising given the fact that, as Kestenbaum (1992) has argued, such schemes can increase the quality of disabled people's lives. The ILF was replaced by two other funds designed to curb costs. One fund from local authorities provides up to £210 worth of vouchers, whilst application can be made for cash up to a total of £300 from the independent living fund. This is despite other research evidence to suggest that independent living schemes offer the possibility of providing a more cost-effective service through the transfer from the over-production of welfare services to a situation in which services are purchased (Oliver and Zarb 1992).

Issues of language

Questions of language are vitally important when considering how professional dominance and control are exerted over disabled people. Barnes has argued:

The first and most important thing to remember about discussion of language and disability is that they arise because disabled people experience discrimination daily and are denied the same rights and opportunities as the rest of the population. (Barnes 1993: 8)

Both social policy and practice texts are infused with language which both subordinates and supports a personal tragedy, individualized view of disability. In the sixth edition of his basic text on social policy Brown was able to write in 1985: 'Disablement arouses severe anxieties and strong resentment in people. Not surprisingly, a disabled person, suddenly threatened by a role change from head of the family to dependent invalid, can become bitter and frustrated' (Brown 1985: 231).

Personal tragedy theory as exemplified in the above quotation provides a conceptual link between individualized casework and a form of state intervention which compensates deserving victims for the tragedies which have befallen them. There is a familiar sequence within this quotation which broken down can be characterized as follows. From this perspective disability is seen as arising from the functional or psychological limitations of impaired individuals.

Report writers should ensure that sign language interpreters are available whenever necessary. It should also be remembered that deaf people whose first language is British Sign Language should be seen as a linguistic minority. (Campbell and Oliver 1996)

The use of language by the social worker will have a crucial bearing on the way in which individual circumstances are considered by care managers, adoption panels, courts, and other official collectivities. Although many social workers may be aware of the important relationship between language and discrimination within the personal social services, a combination of legal and professional conventions and expectations leads them to speculate in an individualized, subjective, and quasi-scientific manner on the causal factors which lead to offending behaviour.

Care managers assemble materials from a number of sources including other social workers' reports, the medical profession, and in some cases the police. From this variety of sources, an official explanation of the individual's problems is created and an Individual Programme Plan produced. The collation and translation process is fundamentally important to the understanding of the way in which disability is officially conceptualized by social workers and frequently results in the construction of disability in terms of the disabled person's problem and not the manner in which disability is produced by society. Terms like 'subnormal', 'limited intelligence', 'X has a low IQ', 'X's prospects for employment are severely limited by his disability' are used. Disabled people can frequently become 'wheelchair bound'. If accessible community services are unavailable does this effectively mean that a disabled person is denied access to a particular service?

Monitoring

Put crudely the argument for monitoring services for disabled people is that without such a process the needs of disabled people cannot meaningfully be assessed, which results in the unthinking discrimination which now prevails. The number of disabled people who come into contact with the social service in any context as employees or service users is to some extent shrouded in mystery.

The impact of policy and practice

Current legislation has barely touched the surface of the complex interaction of oppression, discrimination, poverty, and structured subordination which pervades the lives of most disabled people. Limited rights to basic services under current legislation are frequently ignored by service providers (e.g. provisions of the 1986 Disabled Persons Act, 1990 NHS and Community Care Act). Some critics argue that if anything the measures further consolidate and institutionalize discrimination against disabled people on a daily basis in social services, housing, employment, transport, the media, and education (Barnes 1993). The incomes of most people with disabilities are below those of the rest of the population. Despite the requirements of the 1944 Act only 0.7 per cent of county council employees are disabled people and only 0.9 per cent of London boroughs' employees. Educational institutions are also likely to be below the 3 per cent quota (Barnes 1991). Craig reports that 78 per cent of people with disabilities live in households without earners whilst disabled people in work earn less than the able-bodied, and incomes drop with the severity of the disablement (Craig 1992).

Parker and Lawton found that the impact of caring can be seen in the depressive effect on income, in that carers are less likely to be in paid employment and, when they are, will probably earn less than non-carers (Parker and Lawton 1994).

Some fundamental requirements

The social model of disability demands that fundamental changes must be made to the way in which society is organized. The degree to which social work or any form of social care can bring about this change is debatable. Gillespie and Campbell recommend a disability action plan based upon specific targets. Underlying their approach is the idea that integration should be based upon difference and not 'normality'. The following are required:

- A full analysis should be made of problems which might be encountered in attempting to improve services for disabled people.
- Social workers should be proactive in attempting to bring about independent living for disabled people. It is fundamental that in doing this social workers ensure that disabled people are central in the running of such independent living schemes.
- Social workers should be working with local organizations run for and by disabled people and be proactive in the setting up of joint working groups possibly with representatives from other agencies, local disabled people, and local government representatives.
- Social workers should research national and local organizations which provide

services to disabled people. This may well provide information relating to grants or funds available to disabled people in relation to particular projects or work opportunities.

- Disabled people must be placed in a position to decide the purpose of social work intervention.
- It should no longer be possible for social workers to decide unilaterally on the duration, location, frequency, content of contact, and outcome.
- Social workers must enable disabled people to decide about the appropriateness of their own services. Most crucially this must involve understanding how disability is viewed and understood by disabled people themselves. Core skills need to be extended in ways which support empowerment of disabled people who have the right and ability to define their own needs (Gillespie-Sells and Campbell 1991).

Attention must also be given to the removal of barriers to employment of staff with disabilities. Although basic grade social workers may feel remote from the managerial decision regarding recruitment, they can collectively bring pressure to bear upon management whenever possible.

Consideration could also be given to the need to interview people with learning impairments in the presence of an appropriate adult. This may be a relative, guardian, or a person professionally qualified in the field. The role of the person would be to advise the service user and ease communication, whilst also ensuring that the interview is conducted in a fair manner.

Gillespie-Sells and Campbell suggest that in dealing with such problems workers can reprioritize, and seek discussions with senior managers and other groups of colleagues in order to research options for funding.

Is the service user claiming the benefits to which she or he is entitled (disability working allowance, disability living allowance, attendance allowance)? Assessments for local authority services are available under section 4 (Duty to Assess) of the Disabled Persons (Services, Consultation and Representation Act) 1986. Legislation providing the right to services exists under section 2 (Provision of Services) of the Chronically Sick and Disabled Persons Act 1970. Are mobility allowances being fully claimed?

Conclusion

This chapter has merely scratched the surface and in many ways failed to do justice to this group of users. Social workers are more likely to leave problems connected with disabled people unresolved even when levels of risk are comparable with other areas of practice such as child care, where action would be taken. Intervention is dominated by forms of casework which individualize and can trap disabled people into dependency. The most important principle which should guide practice is the importance of approaching tasks on terms defined by disabled people. What emerges in relation to disabled people is a weak and apparently contradictory set of intentions which create the impression that 'something is being done'. The ineffectiveness of policies to be translated into action is dependent on a number of factors including specificity as to what constitutes discriminatory practice, the meaning of 'quality service', and more developed user rights. Without an engagement with these issues and a firmly directed desire for change, there is a danger that equal opportunities statements will simply become a smokescreen for inaction; thus disabled people will not only continue to be neglected, but their basic civil rights will be flagrantly ignored. Most important is the recognition by social workers that disability is created by social oppression, and that social work practices hitherto have contributed to and indeed constituted a central plank within forms of oppression which have been professionally created and reproduced. Despite the achievements of disabled people's movements it is clear that all change is painfully slow and is reflected in Oliver's description of a journey which could take another 'hundred years' (Oliver 1994: 2).

Exercise

Table 7.2. Applications to Dip. SW programmes (1994 entry)

	Total no. of applicants	Successful no. of applicants	% successful
No disability	10,342	2,752	27
Dyslexic	114	26	23
Blind/sight impaired	36	10	28
Deaf/hearing impaired	76	22	29
Wheelchair/mobility difficulties	44	11	25
In need of personal care and support	1	—	—
Mental health difficulties	17	2	12
Unseen difficulties	363	80	22
Multiple disabilities	26	4	15
A disability not listed above	126	16	13

Source: CCETSW (1994*b*).

1. In Table 7.2 comment on the way in which the disabilities have been classified by CCETSW in the left-hand column.

2. Are any assumptions being made about the nature of disabilities?

Monitoring is necessary if the needs of disabled people are to be understood. This has to be balanced against a fear of intrusive questions and fears as to how information will be used. Social work personnel must be aware of the fear and anger created by unnecessary intrusion. What information may be fed back to a government department? What are the implications for information affecting benefit? Who has access to this information?

Exercise

Alan, a social work lecturer, invited Garry, a disabled speaker, to give an introductory overview on a sequence in the programme entitled 'disability awareness'. Alan booked a room in an adjacent building since the social work programme was situated in an inaccessible part of a seven-storey building. The room selected for the presentation was on the ground floor although there were a number of steep steps to be negotiated from the car park to the building in which the room was situated. Alan phoned the domestic bursar who agreed to arrange for a ramp to be constructed.

On the day of the presentation, Garry arrived and was met by Alan in the car park. When they reached the specially erected ramp from the car park to the building, Garry refused to use it since he feared that it would not withstand his weight. In addition there was rain, which made the ramp quite slippery. Garry had noticed from his car that the height difference between the building and the car park lessened at the back of the building. With the help of Alan and two other members of staff Garry was pulled up to the level of the building. On reaching the interior of the building Garry asked if he could use the lavatory only to be told that no 'disabled facilities' existed in that building.

Questions

1. Comment on the use of the term 'disability awareness'.
2. What actions should have been taken to avoid the situation that developed?
3. What are the long-term implications of the incident on
   (a) the institution;
   (b) the social work programme;
   (c) the academic staff;
   (d) the students;
   (e) disabled people.

Exercise

The probation service: discrimination in a 'helping' agency

The probation service, which is itself a government-financed and -organized helping agency, appears to pay somewhat haphazard regard to the rights of disabled people in its own employment policies. The National Association of Probation Officers is committed to dismantling 'The barriers which are constructed by lack of thoughtfulness and lack of resources, and which transform disability into handicap' (NAPO 1993*b*: 2). However, the number of disabled people who come into contact with the probation service in any context as employees or service users is shrouded in mystery.

In April 1991 a NAPO sub-group on disabled people wrote to all probation areas seeking information about policies on disability. Only one met the conditions laid down under the 1944 Employment of Disabled Persons Act which requires 3 per cent of disabled staff to be employed. The 1944 Act also requires exemption certificates from the above requirement. Only fifteen areas were applying for exemption certificates. Very few probation areas indicated that they were taking into account issues relating to service delivery. Further, little if any attention appears to be given by probation services to the need for ramp access. Although a number of areas expressed good intentions in affirming that they are committed to non-discriminatory services, policies appeared to hinge on terms like 'whenever possible'. Some areas admitted that they were doing nothing in connection with issues raised by disability, whilst others made reference to general statements about equal opportunities. Specific measures which were thought to be necessary by the majority of probation areas which responded to the questionnaire included circulating job advertisements to a disablement resettlement officer, and ensuring that all new buildings are adapted to the need of those who have mobility problems. Probation areas in this study appeared to equate disability with motor disability, making few references to hearing loss or visual impairment (Bodlovic 1992).

Questions

What practical steps could be taken to counter the level of discrimination described above? How can good intentions be translated into action?

Exercise

'Quality' is a term now deeply infused within the discourse of all public services, including personal social services. There is a debate as to the reasons underlying the proliferation of quality-based policies. In a book entitled *Quality Assurance for Social Care Agencies: A Practical Guide*, it is possible for the following statement to be made in relation to desirable goals for the future direction of policy and practice.

To improve society's awareness of its responsibilities to provide for and accept the handicaps of disabled people. (Cassam and Gupta 1992: 124)

1. Comment on the use of the word 'handicaps' in this quotation.
2. In what way is the word 'disabled' being used in this context?
3. Construct an alternative aim utilizing the social model of disability.

FURTHER READING

Michael Oliver's *The Politics of Disablement* (1990) and *Understanding Disability: From Theory to Practice* (1996) (both London, Macmillan) are important basic texts in this area, placing social work practice with disabled people in an ideological and policy context. C. Barnes (1991), *Disabled People in Britain and Discrimination* (London, Hurst) gives an extremely useful account of the ramifications of discrimination against disabled people whilst making some useful comments about policy-related issues. For an account of the impact of caring on the lives of people see J. Twigg and K. Atkin (1994), *Carers Perceived: Policy and Practice in Informal Care* (Buckingham, Open University Press). J. Campbell and M. Oliver (1996), *Disability Politics* (London, Routledge) powerfully describes the shape and development of the disability movement. Christopher Williams (1995) describes crimes and abuse against people with learning difficulties in *Invisible Victims* (London, Jessica Kingsley).

CHAPTER 8

Black People:
Social Work and Policy

- Legislative developments
- Discrimination and black people
- Black people and the criminal justice system
- Black people and the social work literature
- The development of black perspectives
- The development of anti-racism in social work
- Criticisms of anti-racism

Introduction

This chapter will examine some of the wider issues which affect black[1] people in the delivery of personal social services and community care. More detailed discussion relating to black people, child care, mental health, and the criminal justice system will follow in chapters which examine specific user groups.

---

[1] The word 'black' is frequently used to refer to people of African/Asian/Caribbean descent irrespective of the country of their birth. Fevre points out that the word has a deeper meaning: 'Some readers may complain that Asians are not black. Certainly research in this area is plagued by confusing language. "Asians" for example do not look like people born in Saigon or Tokyo. Nor are whites the colour of this page nor blacks the colour of print, but these terms have some use. They emphasise the need recognised as non white is to be treated differently to these with white skin' (Fevre 1984: 9).

Legislative developments

The wider canvas of national post-war race relations legislation provides a context for understanding the nature of discrimination within social policy and social work practice. The 1948 Nationality Act ensured the right of colonial passport holders as well as those holding passports issued by independent Commonwealth countries to enter the UK freely to settle and find work. Such a policy reflected not only a post-war need for labour but also the American melting-pot ideology, whereby 'immigrants' would be assimilated into a flexible and tolerant society. The goal of assimilation was reflected in social policy throughout the 1960s. The 1962 Commonwealth Immigrants Act restricted the automatic right of Commonwealth citizens to entry into Britain, creating a voucher system which was related to occupational status.

In 1966 Roy Jenkins, the then Labour Home Secretary, changed the policy agenda from assimilation to integration, calling for a policy which reflected equal opportunity, cultural diversity, and an atmosphere of mutual tolerance. The legislation with regard to 'race' does not appear to have followed this pattern since 1968. The 1968 Commonwealth Immigrants Act withdrew the right of settlement of those who had a 'close connection'; an individual had to be born in the UK or descended from a parent or guardian resident in the UK. Controls on immigration became tighter with the creation of the 'patrial' status in 1971 and the introduction of the 1971 immigration legislation. Non-patrials were granted permission to work initially for a period of one year.

The 1981 British Nationality Act was ostensibly introduced to clarify the concept of British citizenship but in practice created even greater restrictions to entry. A child born in the UK can only acquire British citizenship if either parent is a British citizen or ordinarily resident in the UK. The concept of 'ordinarily resident' is difficult to define and in any event is subject to the interpretation of an immigration officer and not a court of law.

Legislation designed to curb racism was introduced in 1965 and 1968. The current legislation contained in the 1976 Race Relations Act made it unlawful to publish or distribute written material or use language in any public place which is threatening or abusive to black people or likely to incite racial hatred. The Act has jurisdiction over employment, education, and the provision of goods and services, defining both direct and indirect discrimination as unlawful (Denney 1985). It is widely accepted that the Act has been largely ineffective in combating racial discrimination. New legislation should be introduced which clarifies the definition of indirect discrimination, whilst improving the procedures and remedies available to those who have suffered discrimination (Hepple 1987, Luthra 1997).

A new offence of intentional harassment was introduced under section 154 of the Criminal Justice and Public Order Act which amended the 1986 Public Order Act. The new offence was meant to deal with more serious cases of harassment. In the case of *R. v. Ribbans, Dugley, Ridley* the Court of Appeal ruled that it was appropriate for a court to deal with any offence containing a proven racial element in such a way as to make the offence even more grave.

Many parts of the 1996 Asylum and Immigration Act (1996) have been found to violate basic human rights. Under section 1 of this legislation the UK government can refuse asylum to people from certain countries where it deems there is no danger of persecution. Several of these countries have been designated by Amnesty International and other human rights organizations as infringing human rights. Sections 9 to 11 of the Act have also been challenged by human rights campaigners, since they remove entitlements of welfare and housing from asylum seekers. In June 1996 the Social Security (Person from Abroad) Miscellaneous Amendments regulations were ruled *ultra vires* by the Court of Appeal. Section 10 of the legislation removes the right of asylum seekers to claim child benefit and section 11 the rights to other benefits. These are clearly in breach of the 1951 UN Convention on the Rights of the Child regarding the right of children to humanitarian assistance. Section 9 of the Asylum and Immigration Act and the Housing Act of 1996 restricts the access of asylum seekers to local authority housing. At present the only way in which asylum seekers can gain some of their rights is through the implementation of other legislation (e.g. the 1948 National Assistance Act).

The race relations legislation forms a bewildering set of contradictions, since on the one hand the state imposes ever more stringent immigration controls whilst on the other it has a history of introducing measures with the stated aim of challenging racism.

Discrimination and black people

As Williams has noted, the Fabian tradition which was at the forefront of the establishment of the discipline of social administration largely ignored the issue of racism in the welfare state. Williams suggests that Fabian empiricism allowed imperialist immigration policies and institutionalized racism to be taken for granted. Williams has described how Titmus in his writing on the problems of population regarded western society as slowly evolving a higher form of social organization compared with the 'teeming millions of India and Africa'. Titmus combined his observations with a concern to help and guide less 'civilized' peoples (Williams 1989).

During the period of labour shortage which followed the Second World War black people from the Commonwealth were encouraged to enter the UK to take up employment. Evidence in relation to the employment of black people indicates that, whilst black people are involved in a wider range of employment than used to be the case, disadvantage continues to operate. The labour force survey indicates that 80 per cent of white men aged between 16 and 24 are in employment whilst only 69 per cent of all 'ethnic minority' men are in employment. Figures for women between the ages of 16 and 59 indicate that 66 per cent of all white women are in employment. This should be compared with 48 per cent of all 'ethnic minority' women and only 16 per cent of Pakistani women in employment. The figure of 59 per cent unemployed for Pakistani men is particularly high. By 1990 the rate of unemployment for Afro-Caribbeans, Pakistanis, and Bangladeshis was double the rate for white people. This pattern is confirmed by the 1991 census which reveals highly differentiated labour markets in different geographical areas. Some 38 per cent of the Afro-Caribbean labour force in Liverpool, and 45 per cent of south Asians in Tower Hamlets, are unemployed. Although in more recent years, according to Blakemore and Drake, no employment ghettos have existed in the UK, the position regarding the influence of race on employment has become more complicated (Blakemore and Drake 1996).

The emphasis on parental choice in education is unlikely to benefit black people, many of whom are locked into an underclass. Black people also experience discrimination in housing (Karn 1984, Luthra 1997). In the area of housing during the 1970s black people gained access to better-quality local authority housing, whilst south Asians have tended to move into the owner occupier housing sector. However, this has not led to any overall decline of residential segregation.

Residential segregation remains one of the most potent symbols of the disadvantages faced by ethnic minorities in the UK society. It is also an indicator of the continued inequalities between ethnic groups. This is important because segregation mediates the distribution of society's material resources. (Hudson and Williams 1995: 209)

Recent developments follow a similar discriminatory pattern. Discrimination against black people in the personal social services has now been well documented over a considerable period of time. Studies dating from the late 1970s show a broadly consistent pattern of white people being resistant to the supply of services for black people, believing that 'they look after their own' (Barker 1984). Relatively little is known about informal care networks in the black community. Take-up of services is low amongst black people and over the last decade has been lower than for white people. Services for black people, as will be argued in the later chapters on children, mental health, and crime, are often provided in an insensitive and inappropriate manner.

In 1985 the National Council for Voluntary Organisations suggested a more active role for the voluntary organizations in working with black people. Some voluntary organizations show little recognition of the multi-racial nature of British society (Connelly 1990). If voluntary organizations are to play a more active role in the service-providing aspect of the mixed economy of welfare through such mechanisms as compulsory competitive tendering, they will need to be more cognizant of anti-discriminatory issues.

Sickle cell anaemia and thalassaemia, two disabling conditions, occur disproportionately in the black community. Community care for people with mental health problems has left black people marginalized, with legitimate demands for change in mental health services being frequently ignored (Watters 1996). Mizra has shown how the government's flagging of complaints procedures in 'ethnic minority languages' gives the impression that institutionalized procedures exist for black people who are dissatisfied with service delivery. Such measures as multi-lingual complaints procedures can divert attention from the need to provide resources which enable black people to make choices about the kinds of services which have meaning for them. Only fifty-seven lines of the White Paper 'Caring for People: Community Care in the Next Decade and Beyond' were devoted to the needs of black people (Mizra 1991: 123).

One could be forgiven for thinking that the government also believe that their policies should be based upon the premiss that black people are generally able to cope, by utilizing their inner strengths derived from ethnicity, when the cursory nature of the attention given to the needs of black people in the community care measures is considered. Mizra powerfully argues that a 'package' which gives local authorities duties, without providing any rights to the consumer, disadvantages people who already face discrimination in the delivery of services. Many who are in need of services will not approach social services departments until problems have reached a crisis, if at all (Jadeja and Singh 1993).

Black people and the criminal justice system

The evidence relating to the sentencing of black people is complex and at times contradictory (see also Chapter 14). Whilst some studies describe differences in sentences which work to the detriment of black people (Stevens and Willis 1979, Walker 1988), other studies show no significant differences in the use of custodial sentences (McConville and Baldwin 1982, Moxon 1988). The use of differing statistical techniques and other factors adds to the complexity of analysing sentencing processes in relation to black people (Mair 1989). It would appear to be the case that where offences are similar black people are receiving custody and harsher alternatives to custodial sentences (Hudson 1989). Reiner in the late 1980s reached the conclusion that it was difficult if not impossible to apportion with certainty the relative contributions of either racism or offending patterns to the growing involvement of black people in the criminal justice system, arguing that both factors play a part (Reiner 1989). A similar conclusion was reached by Smith, who argues that race is less important that either age, sex, or class in determining the nature of an individual's interaction with the criminal justice system (Smith 1994).

The Home Office has a stated goal of tackling discrimination in the probation service. In its three-year plan published for the years 1993–6 the stated goal of the probation service nationally is to 'Achieve equality of opportunity throughout the service' (Home Office, 1992b). The existence of section 95 of the 1991 Criminal Justice Act has the specific aim of 'Facilitating the performance by such persons of their duty to avoid discriminating against any persons on the ground of race or sex or any other improper ground' (Home Office 1992c: 3). In practice, however, of the proposed seventeen performance indicators any requirement relating to anti-discrimination is absent. Thus the right of a woman or black person to be treated equally is not regarded as a factor worthy of performance indication despite government stated policy. It also seems possible for a probation user to be subjected to a discriminatory form of practice without any form of regularized institutional redress. The combination of frustrations could result in service users, particularly black offenders, subsequently being breached by probation officers (Denney 1992). As far as the probation service is concerned the evidence points to three general conclusions:

- that there is some evidence of probation officers perceiving women and black offenders in ways which incorporate varying degrees of prejudice and racism;
- that probation officers, although aware of discriminatory issues and possibly anti-racist and anti-sexist, are constrained by court procedures, the criminal justice system, and professional conventions, leading them to include some irrelevant information in reports and exclude other relevant information;
- that differences in styles of report writing are indicative of an attempt to present the reality of offending as perceived by the service user. What is unclear is the nature of the relationship between such attempts and practice.

The 1984 Police and Criminal Evidence Act, which followed the Scarman Report, established statutory police–community liaison committees. These measures were ostensibly aimed at improving relations between the police and black people. The allegations frequently made by black people that the police failed to investigate racially motivated crimes were countered by what some would argue were tokenistic measures which included the setting up of help lines, and the monitoring of racial incidents. Recruitment campaigns were also specifically targeted at black police recruits.

Although Scarman emphasized that the roots of community disturbances lay partly in police practices, some critics argue that he failed to grasp the fact that oppressive policing is not simply a set of fortuitous isolated events, but a 'structural condition'. In other words he failed to link civil disturbances with the structural bases of racist practices, which marks a clear limit to his recommendations. During the 1980s policing practices were riven with complex contradictions veering from coercive over-policing in the 'swamp' operation in 1981, to the development of more consensual forms of community-based police practices. The 1984 Act extended powers of arrest, detention, and stop and search, but was ostensibly accompanied by clear codes of conduct which governed powers to stop and search, the search of premises, seizure of property, detention, treatment, and questioning of persons, and identification procedures. Subsequently a code of conduct relating to the tape-recording of interviews was also introduced. The Act also set up a full-time Police Complaints Authority which was meant to supervise investigations into serious complaints. Despite this the principle still remains that the police investigate themselves.

The beginning of the 1990s was marked by major disturbances at Strangeways and a number of other prisons including Bristol and Cardiff, and at a number of young offender institutions. An independent inquiry was set up under the chairmanship of Lord Justice Woolf. The report was published in 1991 and made twelve major recommendations which included closer co-operation between different parts of the criminal justice system, more visible leadership from the Director-General of the Prison Services, increased delegation to governors of prisons, a contract for each prisoner, a national system of accredited standards, and a new rule that no prison should hold more prisoners than is provided for in the certified normal level of inmates (Davies, Croall, and Tyrer 1995).

In prisons black people are likely to encounter discrimination and often find themselves at the bottom of numerous complex pecking orders (Genders and Player 1989). In one study, 53 per cent of black inmates and 14.5 per cent of white inmates felt that they had been badly treated in prison (NACRO 1991).

Black people and the social work literature

Until the mid-1980s social work literature did not reflect the presence of black people either as service users or as social work practitioners. The isolated pieces of literature which did emerge (e.g. Fitzherbert 1967) appeared to condone assimilation whilst to some extent blaming black people for the inappropriate use of services. Within this framework white perceptions of reality appeared to be inherently superior to those of black people.

Following the integrationist stance developed by policy-makers in the mid- to late 1960s, social work and the literature appeared to be dominated by a form of liberal pluralism (Denney 1983). Here society was conceptualized in terms of competing groups deriving their power from a variety of sources, military, religious, and economic. Discrimination in these terms was seen as emanating from practices which excluded black people from gaining resources. Corrective action is seen in terms of education and altering the mechanisms of the welfare and other social institutions in order to challenge discrimination (Cheetham 1972).

Another strong theoretical current which emerged during the 1970s was cultural pluralism. Here emphasis was placed on the way in which several ethnicities could ameliorate the worst injustices of a society in which positions of power were occupied by white people (Ballard 1979). During the 1970s, those advocating a culturalist analysis appeared to be suggesting, according to some critics, that black people needed to pull themselves up by their 'ethnic bootstraps' (Bourne and Sivanandan 1981).

A structuralist perspective which emerged in the 1980s was firmly rooted in a variety of Marxist perspectives. Here institutionalized racism is located within a dominant ideology which excludes black people from provision, whilst ensuring that they are over-represented within the criminal justice system. Welfare services, it is argued, should be designed to remove racially structured subordination. Personal problem-solving capabilities and cultural factors are seen as being less important than structurally based discrimination (Denney 1983).

The development of black perspectives

Black writers who have emerged during the 1980s, according to Williams,

Have a common intellectual concern which may be summarised as an attempt to give full recognition to the material and ideological ways in which 'race' and racism are experienced and struggled over by people both black and white and as members of a particular class and gender. (Williams 1989: 100)

These writers do not fall into a reductionist trap, in which all inequalities are based upon the ramifications of capitalism, which ultimately leads to the conflating of race with class. A number of black writers have warned against the dangers of anti-racism becoming such a monolithic concept (Singh 1992). Black identities are dynamic and constantly changing. 'Solutions' to the problem of racism in social work have been criticized from a black perspective. One example of this is the prescriptive suggestion that the employment of more black social workers could at least ameliorate some of the worst manifestations of racism. Gilroy has warned that the result of this might be that black social workers could be drawn into a form of managerialism which distances them from the daily realities of racism (Gilroy 1987).

The development of anti–racism in social work

As has been suggested in Chapter 5, anti-racism rests upon a critique of the liberal pluralist assumption that developed in the 1960s and 1970s, which located racism and not misunderstanding as the underlying cause of discrimination. Anti-racism has its roots partly in urban disturbances of the 1980s and the resulting post-Scarman era which emphasized the importance of tackling racism in the police force and the participation of the local community in policing policy. Racism from this perspective is defined as an ideology created and reproduced principally by the capitalist mode of production. Although the term anti-racism covers a diverse group of writers, there is a challenge being made to analyses which focus primarily upon cultural and ethnic differences. Some anti-racist writers have argued that an overemphasis on the cultural created a diversion from practices which perpetuated and legitimized racism. This critique of cultural pluralism developed in the early 1980s, although some writers continued to make such a criticism of the culturalist position for a decade (e.g. Dominelli 1979,

1988). From the mid-1970s black writers were drawing attention to the lack of power that black people had over their own lives (Hall, Clarke, Critcher, Jefferson, and Roberts 1978, Gilroy 1987). Anti-racism invoked a form of social work practice which marked a break from the liberal notion of equal opportunities, and developed an agenda for change which challenges dominant power relations. Whereas advocates of equal opportunities approaches, of which there are many, define the causes of discrimination in individualized terms, those who advocate an anti-racist position emphasize black persons' lack of access to powerful white-dominated institutions. The inhuman nature of the institutions which exclude black people is reflected in Naik's call for a form of social work which concentrates on the needs of black people collectively defending their own interests.

Local community-based institutions must be specifically conceived, designed and managed by members of the black community. They must exert their energies to humanise the larger society by developing strong black alternatives to existing policies and institutions which will serve the needs of black people as a whole. (Naik 1991: 164)

Criticisms of anti-racism

Combined with polemical allegations of 'political correctness' made in the media, numerous more seriously considered critiques of anti-discriminatory practice have been formulated from a number of differing perspectives. Some of these critiques were more sophisticated and elaborate versions of journalistic criticisms described earlier.

In the area of race relations a culturalist critique of anti-discriminatory practice developed, claiming that a form of conventional wisdom, 'deprivationism', had emerged. This had its conceptual foundations rooted not within an authoritarian form of neo-Marxism, as was suggested by the more journalistic critics, but within Fabian socialism. Such accounts, which sought to expose the extent of racism which exists in society, were limited since they presented the 'victims' of exclusionism as lacking the capacity to change their own destiny. Ballard calls for a more relativistic position, in order that the nature of racial and ethnic diversity can be best understood.

People are not pawns, unable to negotiate the terms of their own existence, according to Ballard. Differing cultures can be effective in the resistance of oppression. Thus hegemonic ideologies which oppress can be challenged through the establishing of alternative conceptualizations of reality based on what Ballard refers to as 'mental', 'spiritual', and 'cultural' resistance (Ballard 1992).

Anti-racism, based as it is in the notion of structural oppressions, presents the 'victims' of exclusionism as lacking the capacity to change their own destiny. Behaviour, according to Ballard, is not wholly determined by the forces that constrain it. The anti-racist preoccupation with urban proletarianization does not take sufficient cognizance of the part that differing cultures have played in the 'extraordinary effectiveness' of the resistance to hegemony demonstrated by the 'migrant minorities'. Creative human energy can be effectively utilized to circumvent or resist oppression.

This position has been challenged by Sivanandan, who when addressing a group of black social workers argued that:

You do not have time, you do not have energy, your morale is being undermined, there are so many political decisions which restrain you, you have so many cuts in the services that you cannot extend yourselves in terms of individuals and thus the interpreting of an individual in terms of his/her personal culture becomes the be all and end all. This is a cul de sac, a false track into which you must not go because culture is not static, culture is not stable, culture is moving and changing with the political impact you as black people have put into it. Culture cannot be voided of its economic and political content. (Sivanandan 1991: 31)

Other writers mirror the concern that anti-racism has become an absolutist form of discourse, describing a change within CCETSW's stance on these issues from self-doubt and hesitancy to a position of certainty albeit based on a commitment to social justice (Macey and Moxon 1996).

Webb notes that a similar sense of certainty is presented by neo-conservatives in their desire to change the status quo in another, more individualist direction (Webb, 1991). Gilroy in a withering attack on anti-racism has argued that it fails to locate racism as being at the core of British politics. The 'coat of paint approach' to anti-racism essentially sees racism as being outside social and political life and has dominated local government policies. Here racism constitutes an unfortunate

Excrescence on a democratic policy which is essentially sound, and it follows from this that with the right ideological tools and political elbow grease, racism can be dealt with once and for all leaving the basic structures and relations of British economy and society essentially unchanged. (Gilroy 1990: 74)

Gilroy acknowledges that anti-racism to some extent is intrinsic to the equal opportunity approach but comments that the anti-racist 'coat of paint approach' is doubly mistaken in that it fails to recognize, as equal opportunities policies do, that issues relating to social justice and democracy are important weapons in the battle against racism. Anti-racism as currently expressed also reduces and trivializes the rich experience of black life to 'nothing more than a response to racism'. This then leads towards a reductionist conception of black people as victims. Like Ballard, Gilroy argues that anti-racism mistakenly conflates racial divisions with class divisions. Anti-racism is not redundant but needs to be reconstituted in order to take account of both the criticisms and the complexities of defining racism itself. Table 8.1 indicates some of the differences between an unreconstituted and reconstituted form of anti-racism.

Following Gilroy (1990) it can be seen that racism cannot simply be defined in terms of prejudice combined with power but must incorporate the idea of the nation as a unified and cultural community. The sources of racism must also be extended to encompass historical development and not focus solely upon identity and culture. Recent

Table 8.1. Varieties of anti-racism

	Reconstituted	Unreconstituted
Racism defined	Nation is a unified and cultural community.	Prejudice + power. Biological inferiority and superiority.
Sources of racism	Politics/history.	Identity/culture.
Manifestations of racism	Cultural nationalism.	Thatcherism; anti-collectivism.
Site of struggle	Voluntary organizations; community groups.	Local authority bureaucracies.

developments in social policy which emphasize the mixed economy of welfare and the involvement of the voluntary and private sector in care management create the need to extend the site of struggle away from the local authority.

Perhaps most worrying is the possibility that anti-racism fails to take into account the voice of service users who have experienced discrimination and becomes an academic industry benefiting trainers and consultants rather than the recipients of services. This is reflected in the patterns of practice familiar to members of other oppressed groups (Oliver 1990).

Conclusion

The notion of anti-racism has been subjected to vociferous attacks from a number of quarters. To some extent anti-racism, being at the forefront in the conceptual development of anti-oppressive social work practice, has been most vulnerable to attack. The overarching certainty which is now so often derided must be placed in its historical context. Until the early 1980s racism within the personal social services had barely been addressed. Although there is now a need to be more precise about anti-racist ideas and their applicability to changing systems of personal social services delivery, it is easy to be critical with hindsight. Racism is an enduring feature of social life about which anger is justifiably felt. Current policy-makers have misrepresented the aims of anti-racism in terms of a closed-mindedness which has been structured into public consciousness. The moral panic created around the concept of anti-racism has been used by the government as a justification for removing most providing functions out of local authority control, into the safer hands of the voluntary and private sector. Until policy-makers recognize the existence of racism and the part that black people can play in nurturing new ideas about the delivery of social services, they will be denying the existence of an enriching challenge, falling back on the use of moral panics to further their own political agendas.

Exercise

Prioritize measures which could be taken by policy-makers at national and local levels to combat racism in the areas shown in Table 8.2.

In what respects are the identified policy proposals similar and different at national and local level?

Are issues for social work practitioners different from or similar to those for professionals working in education or housing or health?

Table 8.2. Exercise

	National	Local
Housing		
Education		
Personal social services		
Health		

Case study

Helen is a recently qualified white social worker located in an all-white multidisciplinary purchasing community care team. Other colleagues come from a variety of professional backgrounds including occupational therapy, physiotherapy, and nursing. She is currently working with Mrs G, an older Asian woman who has recently suffered a stroke. Mrs G has a history of mental illness and, apart from occasional visits from her son who lives some distance away, appears to be quite isolated. In her efforts to construct a package of care which is sensitive to Mrs G's requirements particularly with regard to diet, she has been told by her colleagues not to bother too much 'because they always look after their own'. Helen has also been told by her senior care manager that 'any attempt to accommodate any ethnic requirements must be balanced with the need to distribute resources fairly'.

What is an appropriate course of action in this case?

How can Helen ensure that Mrs G has appropriate care management?

FURTHER READING

W. I. U. Ahmad and K. Atkin (1996) provide a recent and useful account of anti-racist issues in the development of community care in *'Race' and Community Care* (Buckingham, Open University Press). L. Dominelli's (1988) *Antiracist Social Work* (London, Macmillan; 2nd edn.

1997) provides a clear and influential account of the issues raised by racism in practice. D. Denney (1992) examines some of the issues concerning anti-racism and probation in *Racism and Antiracism in Probation* (London, Routledge). J. Solomos and L. Back (1996), *Racism and Society* (London, Routledge) provides a well-written theoretical account of racism and social relations in contemporary societies. Luthra's (1997) *Britain's Black Population* (Aldershot, Arena) provides extensive empirical evidence of the conflicts and problems facing black people. This book also contains a welcome European dimension.

CHAPTER 9

Women:
Policy and Practice

- Women and the development of the welfare state
- The development of industrialized exploitation
- The early struggles for civil rights
- Welfare rights and early feminism
- Equal opportunities and 'second-wave' feminism
- Forms of feminist analysis
- Feminism and social work
- Community care
- Social work education and training
- Criticisms of feminist perspectives in policy and practice
- Women and the criminal justice system
- Work with male perpetrators

Introduction

One of the constant themes which runs throughout this book in relation to all user groups is the position of structured subordination occupied by women in relation to men. There is insufficient space in this chapter to chart the struggles of women against discrimination. Attention will be focused upon the position occupied by women within the welfare state.

Women and the development of the welfare state

It is possible to identify four discernible periods when examining the welfare state and women:

- the development of industrialized exploitation;
- nineteenth-century civil rights struggles;
- early twentieth-century welfare rights phase;
- equal opportunities and second-wave feminism from the 1970s onwards.

The development of industrialized exploitation

In the eighteenth century Mary Wollstonecraft argued that since women had equal reasoning powers to men they should be granted equal rights. She also emphasized the waste of talent that male dominance created. Throughout the eighteenth century women and young children were used as cheap slave labour in an unregulated factory system, working sometimes up to sixteen hours each day.

There is considerable evidence to suggest that legally sanctioned domestic violence has always existed in Britain and throughout the world since historical records were first kept. In 1782 Judge Buller declared that legally a husband could beat his wife as long as he did not use a stick thicker than his thumb. Until the late nineteenth century British law gave men the right to beat their wives, this practice being referred to as 'lawful correction'. A wife had no legal status beyond that of her husband. She was effectively the chattel of her husband, to whom her body belonged. Effectively in law man and wife were one person.

The early struggles for civil rights

Throughout the first half of the nineteenth century women and children worked long hours in mines and factories. In 1842 the Mines Act regulated these practices. In 1847, with the victory of the 'ten hours' movement, women were restricted to twelve hours per day, allowing two hours for meals, although shifts could still be twelve hours long.

Smart has focused upon the period between 1860 and 1890 as being a period of particular significance within the development of policies which were related to women. The 1861 Offences against the Person Act contained clauses which dealt with rape, procuring abortion, concealment of birth, and exposing children to dangerous acts. Contagious Diseases Acts passed in 1866 and 1869 imposed what Smart refers to as a form of 'sanitary incarceration' on working-class women who became registered as prostitutes in the vicinity of garrison towns. The Criminal Law Amendment Act of 1885 was concerned with the encouragement of English girls to work in foreign brothels, the regulation of brothels at home, exploitation of underage girls, and the age of consent, which was raised to 16. All this legislation constructed sexuality and mothering as both physiological, i.e. the product of a woman's nature, and a danger to the social order. The mother who farmed out her baby was not, as Smart puts it, the 'idealised mother' presented in Victorian literature. The fallen woman was constructed in terms of the frailty of femininity, prey always to immoral influences (Smart 1989).

A series of Property Acts between 1860 and 1880 gave married women rights to their own property and earnings. Effectively during this period there was no system of civil divorce beyond Act of Parliament, which was expensive and rarely used. Ill-treated and neglected women could apply to a church court for a form of separation order— divorce a mensa et thoro—but in principle it was not easy for wives to separate because the husband maintained the right to take away all the woman's earnings and property whilst retaining custody of her children. In 1857 civil divorce was introduced with the Matrimonial Causes Act. In 1878 the Matrimonial Causes Act granted women the right to live separately from their husbands, to retain custody of children, and to receive maintenance from that husband. This was only the case where the husband had been found guilty of an aggravated assault upon the wife. The insistence that this law only applied to men convicted of such a crime made the Act less effective than it otherwise might have been. The main problem was that the woman was forced to live with her husband whilst the action was going through the courts. In 1895 it became easier for women to qualify for separation orders.

The Women's Co-operative Guild, formed in 1883, had a membership the bulk of whom were women married to working men. Margaret Llewellyn Davies advocated the creation of co-operative shops in poverty-stricken districts. The Guild were also active in local government, where they were critical of the workings of the Poor Law, education, housing, and public health despite the opposition of men (Thane 1982).

Welfare rights and early feminism

The liberal health insurance policies dating from 1911 were deemed to apply only to men, which enshrined the belief that families depended upon the male wage, despite the fact that many women worked in male occupations (Williams 1989). Despite the extension of elementary education for women in the mid-nineteenth century they did not gain entry into Oxford University until 1879 or gain degrees at that and other similar institutions until 1919. Women's struggles were dominated by the fight for the right to vote until the outbreak of the First World War. Mrs Pankhurst with her daughters Sylvia and Christabel and the women that constituted the suffragette movement gained success after the First World War. In 1918 all women over the age of 30 were granted the vote and in 1928 this was extended to all women over the age of 21. In 1919 Lady Astor became the first woman to take her Parliamentary Seat and in 1924 Margaret Bondfield became the first woman member of the government. It was not for another fifty years that the first woman prime minister was elected.

After the First World War women's struggles shifted towards gaining state welfare benefits for maternity and child health. The campaign for infant health centres which culminated in the passing of the Maternity and Child Welfare Act in 1918 gained tremendous support amongst women.

Following the defeat of the 1926 general strike, the feminist movement became more gradualist than it had been during the suffragette period. The goals of feminism tended to be restricted to welfare reforms and, less prominently, equal pay. Welfare feminism, as it came to be called, became a dominant theme in feminist struggles against the Beveridge reforms (Williams 1989). The Midwives Act of 1936 created a full-time salaried service in place of the previous uncoordinated combination of public and voluntary effort in this field. At the same time the number of maternity beds increased, although most births took place at home.

The incidence of abortion as a cause of maternal mortality is not known, but certainly constituted a powerful incentive for women to disseminate information relating to birth control in the 1930s (Thane 1982).[1]

The Beveridge settlement has been shown to have discriminated against women in a number of important respects. Beveridge approached issues concerning women and the family from the position that women should be placed in the home caring for the family. The woman should serve her husband and care for her children. For the purposes of national insurance a married woman was treated as if she were dependent on her husband. If she worked she was eligible for a lower rate of benefit. Effectively women were pushed back into the home by low pay and poor status within the workplace, to make way for demobilized men (Gladstone 1995a).

Feminists have argued that this was a major weakness in the post-war Beveridge plan. Collectivists justified the welfare state after the Second World War by presenting women primarily as mothers and secondarily as wage earners. The assumption appears to have been made that men's wages were sufficient to support an entire family, which possibly provides a commentary on the privileged class background of the architects of the welfare state. Carol Pateman argues that the welfare state is 'patriarchal' in that it created notions of citizenship which were based upon the assumption that women would, if

---

[1] Abortion remained illegal until the Abortion Act of 1967; after this it became possible for women to have an abortion up to twenty-eight weeks after conception if two doctors agreed that the child would be disabled.

employed, perform two full-time jobs, having an additional full-time job in domestic care work (Pateman 1988). The solution within the British welfare state is for women to become honorary men or to celebrate maternity.

This was part of a dominant ideology of 'familism', that is to say, a set of ideas which characterised the normal or 'ideal' family form as one where the man was the main breadwinner and his wife's contribution to the family was through her role as mother, carer and housewife, rather than as wage earner, and who was therefore, along with the children, financially dependent upon her husband. (Williams 1989: 6)

Equal opportunities and 'second-wave' feminism

Women faced discrimination even in the organizations which had grown up ostensibly to serve the interests of oppressed people. It was not until women themselves brought pressure to bear on trade unions that any action became effective in relation to equal pay. Following the direct action of women at the Ford works in 1968 legislation relating to equal pay reached the statute book in 1970 but was not in force until 1975. The Equal Pay Act required women to be granted equal pay if they could prove that their work was comparable in all practical respects to that of men. It was possible for firms to call for a job evaluation, although firms were not obliged to undertake such comparative reviews (Bruegal 1983). Responsibility for redress lay with the individual or with the often male-dominated unions. The requirements of the Act were easy to avoid.

In 1975 two other pieces of legislation, the Sex Discrimination Act and the Employment Protection Act, ostensibly provided more equitable treatment for women. The former piece of legislation was meant to create equal opportunities in the workplace, whilst the latter introduced statutory maternity provision on a sliding scale of benefit which was dependent upon length of service.

Although the legislation represents some, albeit limited progress, most feminists have been critical of the equal opportunities approach. Employment law has made little impact on the position of women within the labour market (Braye and Preston-Shoot 1995).

The Domestic Violence and Matrimonial Proceedings Act (1976) has the stated aim of protecting women in their homes, but as we will see later does not impact sufficiently to afford appropriate protection from violent men behind closed doors.

Forms of feminist analysis

Feminist analyses of welfare gained momentum within social policy during the 1980s (Gladstone 1995a). Although there are a number of ways in which feminist thought can be conceptualized, Williams in her writings on welfare has helpfully described the major strands of thought (Williams 1996b):

- Libertarian feminism identifies the state as the cause of women's oppression. Libertarians emphasize the importance of individualism and minimalist state intervention in all aspects of welfare (see Chapter 6).
- Socialist feminism emphasizes the importance of conceptualizing discrimination in structural terms of patriarchy and capitalism.
- Black feminism encompasses various critiques of the welfare state, whilst arguing for the creation of black provision which challenges current social and racial divisions.
- Postmodernist theories emphasize particularism, difference, relativism, and fragmentation in contrast to the modernist concerns with universalism, truth, structures, essentialism, and determinism (Williams 1996b).

Feminism and social work

Social workers operate in a professional ethos where the failure to make professional judgements based on intuition and subjectivity can be seen as failure. In such a professional arena the understanding of feminist forms of analysis becomes more important in helping the social worker to understand the nature of inequality, and integrate perspectives at both the structural and individual levels.

Commentators have argued that social welfare organizations reproduce a gendered society whilst devaluing the skill of women. The manner in which social work both creates and reproduces discriminatory practices is well documented (Braye and Preston-Shoot 1995, Dominelli and McCleod 1989, Dale and Foster 1986). Women during the 1980s have been differentially affected by poverty when compared with men, and constitute the majority in almost identical proportions to the number of women in poverty at the turn of the century. This would indicate that the welfare state has had little impact on the position of women as recipients of benefits (Lewis and Piachaud 1987).

Particular aspects of service delivery appear to have discriminatory elements. These include community care, child care, social work training and education, social work and the family, psychiatric work, work with women offenders, and the failure of social workers to understand the nature of domestic violence. Feminist analysis of statutory social work sets out to penetrate the predominance of women as clients, carers, and workers who suffer from the sexist nature of the organization and practice of statutory social work.

Community care

Developments in the field of community care place an even greater burden on women as carers whilst social workers are increasingly required to police the maternal role of women in the home. According to some commentators the growing reliance on informal caring increased inequalities experienced by women (Land 1991). Publication of the 1985 General Household Survey revealed that in the United Kingdom 15 per cent of all adult women were carers compared with a figure of 12 per cent for all adult men. Thus the number of carers who were men had to some extent been underestimated. Such figures fail to take account of the complex qualitative dimensions involved in caring. Caring frequently involves loss of income and restricted employment possibilities, loss of personal freedom, a low likelihood of receiving caring services for oneself (a factor which differentially affects women), and gender differences in the response of agencies to calls for care (Braye and Preston-Shoot 1995). In the UK care work has been narrowly conceptualized as caring for adults, whereas in Scandinavia the notion extends to child care. Although some researchers acknowledge that men can be more involved in caring than is often supposed, research would indicate that women are more likely to be involved in non-spousal caring (Baldwin and Twigg 1991).

In Chapter 6 of this book it was argued that discrimination against older women manifests itself in many ways, most obviously in the provision of specific services like home help and social care (Hughes 1995). Similar patterns of discrimination work against the admission of older women into local authority residential establishments (Wilkin and Hughes 1987). Older women are often assessed by social workers as requiring fewer social work skills and less complex forms of social work intervention when compared with other groups such as the mentally ill or children. Women are further discriminated against in favour of older men.

According to Dominelli and McCleod, by its very definition the construction of respite and auxiliary care reinforces the notion that women should have the prime responsibility for providing care for the very young or infirm. Statutory social services fail to lift such a burden from women or to be the means of its being discharged collectively through comprehensive day care and night watch provision (Dominelli and McCleod 1989).

Lonsdale in her study of women and disability found that there was an assumption amongst health and welfare professionals that disabled women are asexual and unable to cope with motherhood. Although this spared women sexual harassment, women with disabilities were discouraged from having children (Lonsdale 1990).

Psychiatric discourse, closely allied to and frequently utilized within social work discourse, is dominated by the ideology of forensic medicine, which authorizes psychiatrists to make medical, moral, and judicial judgements of women which renders them understandable within psychiatric discourse. These ideologies create a narrow range of gender-stereotyped classifications.

Social work education and training

Despite the heterogeneity of perspectives within feminism a dominant line of argument emerged within the social work and social policy literature which to some extent was publicly accepted by social work bodies such as CCETSW. Social policy and social work practice have reflected structured patriarchal power relations which need to be fundamentally challenged (Dominelli and McCleod 1989, Langan and Day 1992). Such a proposition appeared on the surface to have gained acceptance at CCETSW during the 1990s with the development of anti-discriminatory policies. Subsequent developments, as we have already seen, appeared to represent a shift in emphasis on this and other anti-discriminatory issues. Just as Pascall (1986) has argued that women are marginalized within most aspects of social policy, in practice gender issues are marginalized within social work training and practice. This is despite the fact that most social workers and service users are women. Women tend to be concentrated at the lower end of social services structures whilst men dominate in positions of power, so women are concentrated in domestic care and home help jobs (Howe 1986).

Women are more likely to apply for social work training and are more likely to be accepted. Seventy-three per cent of successful applications for social training in 1994 were made by women (CCETSW 1994a). Within social work practice and social work education feminist perspectives are largely hidden or given a grudging marginal place (Carter, Everitt, and Hudson 1992). Feminist social work, as is the case with anti-racism, is frequently incorrectly perceived as being 'work with women'. The assumptions made about the role of women in relation to care perpetuate a pattern whereby women are discriminated against as recipients and as carers (Taylor-Gooby 1991).

Such assumptions, as we will see, are reflected in the theories which have formed a basis for generic social work, and more latterly the assumptions made about the role of women in the implementation of community care policies. Following the creation of the welfare state it was some time before any action was taken to address glaring contradictions which testified to the position of structured subordination occupied by women.

Criticisms of feminist perspectives in policy and practice

Feminists' writings within social work are according to some critics crudely reductionist, in that complex problems are monolithically conceptualized. Moreover, it is argued, feminist critics have little to say which can assist social workers in countering the structural subordination of women. Criticism of feminist approaches to policy and practice have come from a wide variety of sources. Popular media figures, as we have seen in Chapter 6, have been able to caricature the link between feminism, social work practice, and education. Feminism and feminist critique have been the subject of vociferous criticism from a number of sources.

Some of the most vociferous critics have predictably come from the new right where the link between common sense, morality, lone parents, and the evils of collectivism seem so self-evident as not to require qualification. Marsland cannot contain his anger on this theme which constantly recurs in his work:

Britain by contrast, has become so much a haven of fraudulent welfare speak that even allegedly right wing Ministers respond to the shameless, bitchy demands of Lone Parents Incorporated in the fawning, honeyed tones of ideological surrender. In yielding thus cravenly to the campaigning bluster of collectivist ideologues, we are denying commonsense, betraying rational political principles, and subverting the family. (Marsland 1996a: 126)

Marsland relies upon what is for him the unproblematic idea of 'commonsense' a concept which has an obvious and unproblematic meaning in an absolutist world. The family and family values will somehow transform social relations over time if only the state will leave everybody alone. If we all uphold specific and prescribed forms of behaviour lone parents and crime will simply disappear. Such a direction within policy is at best naive and at worst dangerous for those who are least able to defend themselves against abuse and violence. Other men writing about social policy who do not share Marsland's position on many aspects of social policy can also become vehement in their criticism of some feminist work. Spicker in refuting Dominelli's claim that the Beveridge Report was sexist (and racist) argues:

One might as well argue that pensions are racist because the ethnic minority population is relatively young, that child benefit is sexist because it favours better off families over older women, and that public transport is both racist and sexist because it is mainly used by better off people in employment. (Spicker 1993: 107)

Other writings have sought to deny a clear link between dominant feminist critiques within social work and the reality of day-to-day life for social workers and service users. In his criticism of feminist critiques of male social work managers Sibeon argues:

To the client waiting for his giro cheque, or the young black unemployed person or the teenage mother struggling in the face of having to make ends meet, it does not matter very much whether the prestige and material rewards of their status are enjoyed by affluent male managers or affluent female managers substituted in their place: clients of the social services have more pressing concerns, none of which involve much sympathy for the plight of affluent managers of either sex. (Sibeon 1991: 124)

Sibeon goes on to argue that most social service users are predominantly working class and poor, and would wish for a democratization and decentralization of services and not replacement of one social work bureaucratic hierarchy dominated by men by one which is dominated by women or any other oppressed group (Sibeon 1991). Sibeon raises the important question as to whose interests are best being served: the substituted managers or the service users who desperately need resources.

Although Sibeon and Spicker point to a basic problem relating to the vague manner in which both Marxist and anti-discriminatory texts have directly addressed practice, Sibeon and Marsland appear to characterize feminist thought in a somewhat monolithic and undifferentiated manner. Dominelli has vociferously challenged the critics of anti-discriminatory policy, arguing that anti-discrimination was not simply a response to perceived discrimination driven by CCETSW, but resulted from the efforts of black people and feminists who have compelled CCETSW to take their position. She also takes issue with Webb, denying that certainty is a feature of anti-discriminatory ideas since many controversies exist between those who advocate anti-discriminatory practice (Dominelli 1988, 1991a, 1991b).

Pascall writes:

Egalitarian changes are superficial. At the foundation of social security policy and practice is a model of family life in which women are wageless and dependent, and a model of work as paid employment mainly carried out by men. (Pascall 1986: 231)

Others have argued that an overemphasis on women's oppression and women's need for autonomy has resulted in a lack of emphasis on children's needs. Traditional family ideology has the pernicious effect of localizing responsibility for children to the safe haven of the family whilst disregarding any communal responsibility for children (Havas 1995).

Women and the criminal justice system

The greatest gender differences within the criminal justice system relate to recorded crime. Women commit fewer offences than men and constitute a small but increasing percentage of the prison population (Heidensohn 1994). Courts appear to use the full range of the tariff less for women than men (Moxon 1988). The use of fines is declining and women are less likely to be the subject of community service orders (Heidensohn 1994). Although there is a general assumption that women are treated more leniently than men due to a chivalrous attitude of the male-dominated bench, some would argue that some women are dealt with more harshly. For indictable offences in 1990 18 per cent of women received probation compared with 9 per cent of men. The number of women on community service orders has increased from 1,600 in 1981 to 2,300 in 1991 (Worral 1993). According to Home Office research women are less likely to receive a custodial sentence for all indictable offences which are not drugs related. When women do receive custodial sentences they tend to be shorter than those imposed on men. Women are less likely to receive prison sentences irrespective of the number of previous offences.

Some women are punished for deviating from conventional views of femininity, and the criminal justice system reacts in a manner which is permeated by forms of overt and covert sexism (Eaton 1986, Worrall 1990).

Work with male perpetrators

Dominelli (1991*a*) in a study of sex offenders identified masculinist ideology as providing the main legitimizing force in a sex offender's behaviour which enables him to transcend acceptable behaviour. Men who are unable to exercise power in a public domain will exercise power in private over less powerful women and children, so it is argued. Thus work with male perpetrators should be a fundamentally important element in probation work, but as yet does not appear to be regarded as a high-priority issue for probation officers working with sex offenders (Dominelli 1991*b*).

Conclusion

Gender issues are marginalized within social work and social policy, obscuring the location of issues within social work practice. Although the 'mainstream project' of policy analysis has been cast in gender-neutral terms, its analytical concepts frequently have men as the point of departure. This has resulted in mainstream comparative policy analysis telling us little about how women fare in welfare systems since larger social categories like class, occupational group, or household have been utilized (Sainsbury 1994).

Non-abusive forms of social work practice must seek to change the context in which the abuse happens, or the consequences which follow the abuse (O'Hagan and Dillenburger 1995).

Exercise

Jane is a recently qualified black social worker in a local authority juvenile justice team. The team consists of four white men and one other woman. After only eight weeks problems have arisen. On arriving at work Jane overheard three of her male colleagues discussing the possibility of supplying pornographic videos and magazines to service users to keep them off the streets, one man going on to suggest that he could supply them. The suggestion was followed by muffled giggling and laughter. The conversation was taking place in the office adjoining the reception area. Jane immediately left the room. Later that morning Jane had finished making a phone call in a small interview room when one of the three men involved in the previous incident knocked and entered. He suggested that she could not take a joke and that a sense of humour is a basic requirement for social work. Jane asked her colleague to leave the room since she was busy but he continued asking her if she 'had a problem'. Jane then left the room.

1. Comment on the manner in which Jane dealt with this situation.

---

2. What possible course of action is open to Jane in this situation both in the team and in the wider organization?
3. What would be an appropriate managerial response to such a situation?

FURTHER READING

The length and breadth of feminist scholarship is huge and for those unfamiliar with the area a useful text to start with is B. Madoc-Jones and J. Coates (1996) (eds.), *An Introduction to Women's Studies* (Oxford, Blackwell). This is clearly written, containing materials and exercises which are accessible and readable. D. Sainsbury (1994) (ed.), *Gendering Welfare States* (London, Sage) provides a well-written collection giving a comparative perspective on the way in which mainstream typologies and models of the welfare state can be used to understand gender relations in modern welfare states. F. Williams (1996*b*), 'Post Modernism, Feminism and the Question of Difference', in N. Parton (ed.), *Social Theory, Social Change and Social Work* (London, Routledge) is a useful introduction to the contribution of postmodernism to feminist theory. These theoretical developments are then related to the delivery of welfare services. G. Pascall (1997), *Social Policy: A New Feminist Analysis* (London, Routledge) provides an excellent account of the impact of Thatcherism upon the position of women.

CHAPTER 10

Working with Families

- The family as a changing structure
- Families, women, and poverty
- The impact of poverty
- The Child Support Act
- Violence and the family
- Working with families

Introduction

The family has been identified by both major political parties as the mainstay and basic building block of a healthy society. Yet it would appear that policy-makers are seeking to re-create an idealized form of family life. There have, as we will see in this chapter, been major changes in patterns of family life which social policy has failed to accommodate. Such a view of the world encompasses the central role of the woman as carer for men, children, and the sick. This model of social organization assumes a male breadwinner, and a female homemaker who has central responsibility for the rearing of two or three children (Langan and Day 1992). The nuclear family is also supported by the system of taxation, welfare, and social security. Women and particularly lone parents tend to be targeted for investigations of all kinds, whether it be for means-tested benefits or related to child care. This chapter focuses on some of the major issues which are relevant to social work practice in families. These include the break-up of the nuclear family, family poverty, and the relationship between lone parenting and domestic violence.

The family as a changing structure

Throughout the 1980s social policy was increasingly predicated on the primacy of the family. The family was defined in terms of a heterosexual married couple and their own children, conceived naturally, with the man being responsible for the financial support of his family whilst the wife was responsible for the care of the house and children. A belief in the naturalness of this structure was reflected in Mrs Thatcher's frequent reference to the 'problem' of young single girls who deliberately become pregnant in order to jump the housing queue and get welfare payments (Carabine 1992).

In the early 1970s comparatively few heterosexual couples cohabited outside of marriage. By the 1980s cohabitation had become a dominant form of engagement. In 1971 there were 570,000 lone-parent families, but by the time the Children Act was passed in 1989 this figure had doubled. During the 1970s lone-parent families were most likely to be created by divorce, whereas in the 1990s they are more likely to be single mothers who have never been married. During the 1980s the employment rates of lone parents declined, and by 1990 only 41 per cent of lone parents worked (Clarke, Craig, and Glendinning 1996). This resulted in the vast majority of lone parents becoming dependent on means-tested benefits. Only a minority of lone parents receive payment from a former partner towards their own or their child's upkeep. Payments of benefits also differ, with separated and divorced mothers being likely to receive more benefit than lone parents.

The rapid growth of marital separation mainly through divorce has increasingly defined the role of the social worker in terms of preventing family breakdown and working with families who have experienced family breakdown (Aldgate 1997).

Families, women, and poverty

The principal causes of poverty during the 1980s were old age, sickness, and disability, which accounted for 60 per cent of the women who were on the supplementary benefit line. Some two-thirds of single women pensioners live at or below the poverty line, compared with about half the equivalent for men. Unemployment accounts for 20 per cent and lone parenthood 10 per cent of those women who live in poverty. Eight out of ten lone parents are dependent on an income-tested social security benefit which with child benefit and one-parent family benefit on average constitutes three-quarters of their income. Half of Britain's lone parents rely upon income support (DSS 1997).

It should also be remembered that social policy during the 1980s has exacerbated the desperate situation in which many women and children find themselves. The 1986 Social Security Act cut back rights to inherit a spouse's pension entitlements by 50 per cent. This rule differentially affects women since they are more likely to survive the spouse.

State policy does not take account of the way in which benefits are distributed within the household, yet women are less likely to have fiscal control within the family. A *laissez-faire* labour market has resulted in women commanding lower pay than men, whilst being more likely to be engaged in part-time and temporary employment. Women are less powerful than men with regard to occupational welfare and trade union politics and are also less likely to gain qualifications which enable them to achieve high-status jobs. Treatment of women by personal social services also results in women being discriminated against both as carers and as recipients of care (Taylor-Gooby 1991).

The family is seen by both Labour and Conservative parties as a form of social organization which could reduce expenditure on social care in a situation of increasing demand for social services. Marsland makes this position explicit when he argues that:

The family is the indispensable mechanism in the production of autonomous, self reliant personalities, capable of resisting the blandishments of welfare dependency. It is only in the context of loving support and rational discipline which the family offers—provided it is intact and functioning effectively—that children can be reliably socialised into the values and skills which social autonomy requires. (Marsland 1996a: 194)

The Labour government elected in 1997 sees the family as the mechanism which is central to the creation of social responsibility. The proposed 'parenting order' is significant and in practice would give the courts the power to 'Deal effectively with parents who wilfully neglect their responsibilities or need help in fulfilling them' (Home Office 1997: 2).

This takes the idea of enforcing good parenting one step further than the previous Conservative government. The assumption that the nuclear family is a supremely desirable social structure has worked to ensure that women are more vulnerable to poverty than men. Taylor-Gooby has argued that state policy generally stops at the front door and does not take into account the fact that most women have less control over the distribution of income than men. The state has not intervened sufficiently in the labour market to ensure that women are protected from low pay. The lack of help from state resources combined with lower pay is reflected in the lack of influence that women appear to have over trade unions' politics (Taylor-Gooby 1991).

For many years feminist critique has focused on the nuclear family as a source of women's poverty, dependency on men, discrimination within the labour market, and the exploitative relationships within the private domestic world of the home. Despite the belief and hope placed upon the family social workers are often confronted with a different reality. During the 1980s there was a substantial increase in the employment rate of married women whilst the employment rate for lone parents fell from 47 per cent to 42 per cent. These factors have created a situation in which the dependency of lone parents on means tested benefits has increased between 1981/2 and 1988/9 from £1.4 billion to £3.2 billion (Clarke, Craig, and Glendinning 1996).

The scheduled abolition of the lone-parent benefit in March 1998 will further exacerbate an already difficult situation.

The impact of poverty

Since the Second World War new opportunities particularly in the area of employment have opened up for women. This has been accompanied by greater income insecurity, since jobs on offer to women are more likely to be part-time and temporary. This combined with the persistent poverty experienced by single women has often trapped them within a cycle of domestic responsibilities and low-paid, low-status employment (Lewis and Piauchaud 1987, Gladstone 1985).

The recent detailed examination of income and wealth commissioned by the Rowntree Trust found that income inequality had grown between 1977 and 1990, reaching the highest level recorded since the war. There have according to this study been polar shifts between double-income families who are able to spend relatively little time with their children, and the poverty associated with lone parenting. In both cases children appear to suffer (Hills 1995).

Pressure groups concerned with child poverty have shown increasing concern over the tendency of government to cut benefits to poor families by as much as £200 million per year whilst an estimated £3.2. billion per year in benefits are unclaimed.

The increasing complexity of benefit rules and lack of access to advice and information leave many needy claimants unaware of the cash help available. Despite the government's stated aim of simplifying the system, it is hard to see how cuts on this scale can do anything other than render it more complicated and less accessible. An increase in poverty is the obvious consequence (Witcher 1996: 1).

Family poverty appears to contribute to parental anxiety and stress. Poverty is also considered by poor families themselves to have a profoundly negative impact on their lives (Magura and Moses 1984, Waterhouse and McGhee 1996).

The 1985 Housing Act effectively created a series of barriers over which applicants were forced to pass before the local authority needed to recognize its duty to provide secure and permanent accommodation (Burrows, Pleace, and Quilgars 1997). This policy is being pursued despite the rapid reduction of safe permanent housing options for women and children in the wake of policies designed to reduce council housing throughout the 1980s and 1990s. The research available does indicate that women will find it far more difficult to be accepted for rehousing unless they have the active support of housing advice agencies, or are represented by committed solicitors, which is time-consuming and expensive. In other areas the wait for rehousing even after acceptance can be very long (Hague and Mallos 1995). This policy effectively means that single parents and their children are no longer regarded as being housing priorities and have little hope of guaranteed permanency of accommodation. Seven child care charities launched a campaign to persuade the government not to repeal. The repeal was hastily constructed in a high-profile anti-single parent campaign, which was orchestrated by leading members of the then Conservative government (O'Hagan and Dillenburger 1995). This policy has had a direct impact on the ability of social workers to find accommodation for homeless women and children, many of whom will have been subjected to violence.

The Child Support Act

The imagery of the virtuous nuclear family and feckless single parent is reflected in the Child Support Act which came into effect in April 1993. The stated aim of this legislation was to ensure that parents honour their moral and legal responsibility, and strike a fair balance between the interests of the child and second families. Amendments to the legislation took account of expenditure levels of absent parents. All parents in receipt of income support, family credit, or disability allowance are now compelled to agree to the recovery of maintenance from absent parents and must co-operate with the Child Support Agency in tracing them. The only cause for exemption to this is if a lone parent has reasonable grounds to believe that tracing an absent parent could cause the lone parent or a child to suffer. All maintenance recovered from absent parents is deducted pound for pound from income support. All questions of contact between parents, children, spouse maintenance, and all issues concerned with property and cash settlements were to be dealt with by the courts (Clarke, Craig, and Glendinning 1996).

One of the stated aims of the Act is to ensure that fathers contribute to the maintenance of their children. Although women have been differentially affected by the harassment of CSA officers the agency has become an 'unmitigated disaster for women, children and fathers alike' (O'Hagan and Dillenburger 1995: 77). The 'Network against the Child Support Agency' has wide support from numerous pressure groups and national newspapers. There is little evidence that the Act results in absent parents meeting their financial responsibilities. In some cases the Act has brought about the end of informal benefits that were sometimes paid to the children whilst creating a deterioration in the relationships between parents and children (Clarke, Craig, and Glendinning 1996).

A recent study has suggested that for the majority of lone parents the Child Support Act has made no difference to their income. A significant proportion of families are worse off following the implementation of the Act. Some former partners have reduced the informal help they gave the family in response to the government's actions, which included contributions towards clothes, school expenses, Christmas and birthday presents. There has also been opposition to the formula by which maintenance liability has been assessed, which in some cases has led to substantial increases in maintenance payments.

Measures introduced since 1993 have been designed to alleviate some of these criticisms. The targeting of absent fathers already paying maintenance to children of former relationships appears to have resulted from the need to achieve savings in social security expenditure, by dealing with cases which would yield a considerable amount of maintenance. The Child Support Act has failed to meet its own performance targets. Only 52 per cent of lone parents are satisfied with its performance compared to 65 per cent, which is the target set by the Child Support Agency (Speed and Seddon 1995). Thus there is no indication that the new legislation has increased incentives to work. There are also wide variations in the interpretation of the mother's right to refuse to co-operate with the Child Support Agency as a result of legitimate fear and distress. Undue emphasis appears to be placed by agency support staff on the benefit penalty if lone parents fail to co-operate with investigations being made by the Child Support Agency.

Violence and the family

Domestic violence, which happens mostly to women and children, is one of the most common crimes against the person, making up one-quarter of all the reported crimes and half of the homicides committed against women each year (Dobash and Dobash 1980). The British Crime Survey of 1992 found that domestic violence was the most common violent crime faced by women. The desirability of the nuclear family as reflected in social policy and social work practice often distracts attention from the violence perpetrated against women in domestic situations. Although domestic violence against women does not occur exclusively in the nuclear family it is often the site of systematic long-term abuse which for many years was neglected by social workers.

In 1971 the first refuge was set up in Chiswick for the victims of domestic violence, and in one decade the numbers of refuges had increased to 200. The publication of Pizzey's *Scream Quietly or the Neighbours Will Hear* in 1974 had a powerful impact and did much to increase consciousness of the prevalence of domestic violence (Pizzey 1974). Most refuges provide safe accommodation for women and their children, advice, and support.

The ineffectiveness of the police to deal with situations relating to domestic violence and the increased publicity that the issue gained was instrumental in the setting up of a parliamentary select committee on violence in marriage which signalled in principle support for women's refuges (Dobash and Dobash 1992). The Domestic Violence and Matrimonial Proceedings Act 1976 and Housing (Homeless Persons) Act 1977 make some limited provision for victims of domestic violence. During the mid-1980s there was a reawakening of concern relating to the incidence of domestic violence. The need for a multidisciplinary approach in order to assist and prevent violence is essential. Yet the research indicates that practice in this area is uncoordinated, under-resourced, and lacking any clear sense of purpose (Binney, Harkell, and Nixon 1988, Edwards 1989, McWilliams and McKiernan 1993). The lowest rates of child abuse occur in households which are free from violence (O'Hagan and Dillenburger 1995). Important recent research has specifically linked the experience of domestic violence with the response of agencies such as social work. In a study of 484 women in Surrey, 31 per cent had suffered domestic violence at some point in their lives. Of these 48 per cent were disappointed with the police response, 36 per cent were dissatisfied with the social services, and 19 per cent were dissatisfied with their GPs (Dominy and Radford 1996). Legislation has had disappointing effects and does not assist in enabling women to remove violent men from the home. Judges appear reluctant to evict a husband from a home which is rented or owned in his name.

The full extent to which domestic violence occurs across class and cultural barriers is to a large extent unknown. Even in cases in which domestic violence is reported, police and social services are reluctant to interfere since domestic violence is still regarded as a personal problem. Many women are afraid to talk about assaults but are likely to suffer violence up to thirty-five times before they report it to the police. Women tend to try to deal with domestic violence in their own homes, and frequently blame themselves and attempt to change their own behaviour in order to suit their partner (Donnan 1991). Under-reporting of domestic violence is to some extent related to fear of the consequences in terms of court appearances and the involvement with the police. Domestic violence ultimately is not simply an example of breakdown of individual relationships but reflects a society in which the differential status accorded to men grants them the power to abuse women.

Although some probation work is being developed in domestic violence units, more focused attention should urgently be given to assisting women who need safe alternative accommodation, and protection.

Working with families

The 1989 Children Act omitted to take any account of domestic violence, at exactly the same time as other government departments were beginning to acknowledge the problem. Social policy and conventional social work wisdom has tended to reflect the view that children are best brought up by their families (Hague and Malos 1995). Such a policy emphasis on the family is reflected in child care practices, and serves not only to discriminate but to create professional forms of intervention which are in themselves abusive towards women. Although such abuse appears in many forms one of the most pervasive is the professional avoidance of men. This usually means professional complicity in structures and organizations which over-scrutinize women and fail to scrutinize men. The avoidance of men also extends to making no attempt to understand the significance of men in child care situations particularly where abuse is involved. O'Hagan and Dillenburger (1995) argue that the process of avoidance impacts at all stages of child care processes including referral, investigation, intervention, care proceedings, fostering, and long-term assessments. Social workers, they suggest, may avoid men for a number of reasons. They may genuinely believe that the man is irrelevant to a particular situation. Alternatively they may consider that men themselves are the principal cause of the women's difficulties, or may experience a personal repugnance towards men who act violently towards women. Avoidance may also stem from a lack of personal security in the presence of men, particularly those with a history of violent behaviour towards women and/or children. Social workers frequently avoid men blatantly by defining them out of the situation, relying on explanations given by other relatives. The consequent over-scrutiny of women particularly by lone parents constitutes in the words of O'Hagan and Dillenburger a form of 'abusive child care'. Avoidance of men also seriously affects the paramount task of protecting children against violence since only a partial assessment can be achieved in these circumstances (O'Hagan and Dillenburger 1995). Dominelli and McCleod conclude that

With the exception of a few social service departments, where as the results of the activities of individuals and groups attempting to raise feminist issues concerning child abuse in social services, feminists have still not applied a feminist perspective to the monolithic bureaucracy relating to the prevention and detection of child abuse which dominates social services field-work. (Dominelli and McCleod 1989: 125)

Conclusion

Social work is predicated on the centrality of the values associated with the nuclear family which dominate policy thinking. The nature of family life and its possible decline needs to be understood by those who work in the personal social services. In order for both social policy and practice to be more effective attention must be more directly focused upon the impact of changing family patterns. Policy is unclear as to the role of social work in assisting families to adjust to radical changes. Growing cohabitation and marital breakdown are realities which social workers face on a daily basis. Little will be achieved by exhorting individuals to live in family forms prescribed and recommended by government.

Exercise

Alice has been married to Ian, a 'financial consultant', for seven years. They have one child, Eleanor, aged 5, who attends the local primary school. Alice has returned to work for an advertising company where she had a career before giving up her job to look after Eleanor. Since her return to work difficulties within the marriage have developed, since Ian seems convinced that she is 'flirting with men'. Ian's drinking has increased to the point where he is consuming at least one bottle of wine each night after work. There is also strong evidence to suggest that he is drinking during the day since he does not appear to be sober when he returns from work. He has put continual pressure upon Alice to give up her job and have more children. Over the last eighteen months Ian has become violent towards Alice. During arguments, particularly when he has been drinking, he has kicked and punched Alice, and each time the attacks appear to have more intensity. On three occasions he has threatened to kill her. Following a particularly violent weekend Alice is physically unable to attend work due to the fact that Ian has punched her in the eye and pushed her down the stairs, leaving her with a damaged leg. Instead of going to work Alice has phoned a woman friend, who has suggested as she has on many previous occasions that she contact social services. Alice has been afraid to do this previously since she is fearful of Eleanor being taken into care. She now agrees to move away from the house to stay with her friend on a temporary basis, whilst Ian is at work, and contact social services for help. Her main argument for doing this is that she feels unable to guarantee the safety of her daughter in the house. She can no longer tolerate Eleanor being in a house in which violence and alcohol increasingly dominate.

Broad principles

In September 1994, social services committees approved the Social Services Domestic Violence Policy. These 'Good Practice Guidelines' have been produced to provide guidance to staff who are working with adults and children who experience domestic violence. They are summarized below.

- Domestic violence occurs as a result of a violent and abusive person who chooses to use violence to control.
- When women report violence they need to be supported in a sympathetic and sensitive manner. Social services departments must be aware that leaving an abusive relationship is often a long process. Staff should never make decisions for women.
- The aim of any intervention is to maximize the opportunities for women to take control of their lives.
- Staff should stress that the perpetrator of violence is responsible for violence. Staff should seek to reassure the woman that it is not her fault and that she is not alone.
- Breaches of confidentiality can have consequences for women including possible injury and even death. The whereabouts of women and children should never be discussed with the perpetrator, relatives, or friends. The whereabouts of women and children should not be disclosed to other agencies without the woman's consent, unless there is a statutory requirement for social services to do so in child protection cases. If staff need to pass information on to another member of the staff, this should be explained to the woman.

Social services employees must not under any circumstances put the perpetrator in touch with the woman and/or children who are fleeing violence. Even agreeing to pass messages establishes that staff know of the woman's whereabouts. This endangers her and the member of staff.

1. How can these guidelines be applied to the situation faced by Alice?

2. Consider how the guidelines might apply to the following groups within social services when considering how best to assist Alice:

> from the perspective of the emergency and duty team;
>
> from the perspective of the social work mental health team;
>
> from the perspective of staff in residential and day services;
>
> from the perspective of children's day centres;
>
> from the managerial perspective.

FURTHER READING

K. Clarke, G. Craig, and C. Glendinning (1996), *Small Change: The Impact of the Child Support Act on Lone Mothers and Children* (London, Family Policy Studies Centre) examines in detail the position of lone parents and the impact of the Child Support Act on family relationships. Family Policy Studies Centre and Joseph Rowntree Foundation (1997), *Single Mothers in an International Context* (London, University College London Press) gives a thorough overview of policy and practice related to single mothers with dependent children in a number of industrialized countries including the USA, Australia, Japan, Germany, Sweden, and Ireland. This edited collection also contains a useful chapter on the British example by the editors Simon Duncan and Rosalind Edwards. Some excellent material on the effect on changing distributions of income and wealth is contained in J. Hills (1996), *New Inequalities* (Cambridge, Cambridge University Press). A. Walker and C. Walker (1996) (eds.), *Britain Divided* (London, Child Poverty Action Group) contains some excellent chapters on housing, health, food as social exclusion, and a useful appendix documenting the policies which directly affected poor families between June 1979 and August 1996. The Department of Social Security has produced a full account of family credit, maintenance, and the barriers to work in a report by A. Marsh, R. Ford, and L. Finlayson (1997), *Lone Parents, Work and Benefits: The Family Resources Survey* (London, HMSO), which gives detailed information relating to the incomes and circumstances of 26,000 households. The report is divided into chapters on social security benefits, tenure, housing costs, assets and savings, carers, those needing care, and employment.

CHAPTER 11

Sexuality and Social Work

- The legislative background
- Social work services and sexuality
- Basis for good practice: practice guidelines

Introduction

Social workers in all settings are required to address questions related to sexuality, yet the subject receives comparatively little attention in the social work literature. Consequently on social work training courses it is a neglected area when compared with other areas which require statutory intervention, e.g. mental health, child care. Issues related to homophobia are often left unaddressed or insufficiently integrated into what are often seen as more mainstream anti-discriminatory concerns. This is particularly regrettable given that sexuality is a dynamic which is directly related to statutory intervention. Homosexuality can be defined as 'Sexual behaviour between people of the same gender and the people who engage in this' (Bremner and Hillin 1994: 9). Davies and Neal draw the important distinction between 'homosexual behaviour', which they define as having sex with someone of the same sex, and 'homosexual identity', which they define as seeing oneself as a homosexual.

The legislative background

Anthropologists have demonstrated that homosexual behaviour occurs in all cultures and is approved of in many (Davies and Neal 1996). Despite this, discrimination against homosexual people has been structured into society throughout history. The term has medical origins and has widely been regarded as an illness which can be cured.

The 1885 Criminal Law Amendment Act was intended to stop child prostitution by raising the age of consent for girls from 13 to 16 years. Labouchere introduced an amendment to the Act which resulted in homosexuality being outlawed, although few prosecutions were brought under the Act. The most famous prosecution to be brought was in 1895 against Oscar Wilde which ultimately led to his ruinous imprisonment. Homosexuality was increasingly medicalized during the nineteenth century with concentration being given to its causes and eventual cure. Such cures have included electric shock treatment, brain surgery, castration, biochemical therapies, and psychoanalysis (Davies and Neal 1996).

The report of the Wolfenden Committee in 1957 to some extent accepted the disease model but took the view that the function of law was not to intervene in the private lives of individuals, but rather to protect the public from injurious or offensive elements and to provide safeguards against exploitation of the vulnerable and innocent.

Ten years later the 1967 Sexual Offences Act made homosexual acts between consenting adults over the age of 21 legal. Other activities were still illegal for gay people but legal for heterosexuals. This included sex between those aged 16–21, soliciting in a public place, the procuring of homosexual acts which could allow two consenting males to stay overnight, or indecency between two men which could include kissing and hugging in a park (Ford and Robinson 1993).

The reaction against gay people was created by three principal factors:

- the new right political and ideological agenda which gave primacy to family life and the nuclear family—a theme which has appeared in relation to all aspects of social policy since 1979;
- the pandemic of AIDS which was presented by many arms of the media as a 'gay' disease;
- a media-created association between gay people and Labour councils and the teaching of homosexual preference to the young and unsuspecting.

This was reflected in section 28 of the 1988 Local Government Act. This legislation is mainly concerned with creating competition within local authority services. However, the Act states that it is illegal for the local authority intentionally to promote homosexuality, to publish material with the intention of promoting homosexuality, or to promote the teaching of the acceptability of homosexuality as a preferred family relationship, unless its purpose is treating or preventing the spread of disease (Local Government Act, section 28, in Bremner and Hillin 1994).

This effectively prevented an authority from promoting homosexuality or publishing material which might promote homosexuality. The notion that homosexual relationships were preferable to family life was also forbidden to be taught in schools. The inclusion of this section in the legislation produced an outcry from many organizations including the trade unions, Arts Council, Library Associations, the National Council for Voluntary Organisations, and most broadsheet newspapers (Bremner and Hillin 1994). In 1994 the age of consent was lowered from 21 to 18 following an amendment to the Criminal Justice Bill.

The guidance notes accompanying the Children Act 1989 explicitly lay down the responsibilities of social work agencies in relation to sex and sexuality. Section 7 volume iv of the guidance notes relating to the 1989 Act states that

The experience of being cared for should include the sexual education of the young person. This is absolutely vital since sexuality will be one of the most potent forces affecting any young person in the transition from childhood to adulthood. (iv (7). 107, in Bremner and Hillin 1994: 58)

The notes go on to emphasize the importance of giving guidance to young people on the use of contraceptives and taking cognizance of the needs of young people who are gay. The need for staff to have support in these areas is also recognized in the legislation (Bremner and Hillin 1994).

The policy reflects a number of shifts which have been directly related to political ideology. Following the moves to decriminalize homosexual activities in the late 1960s the attempt to define homosexual activity as deviant and aberrant was firmly in place by the late 1980s. In an account of legal problems faced by homosexuals, Dodd concludes that homosexuality and homosexuals are still perceived negatively in society and by many who administer the law. To refer to an individual as a homosexual in a court hearing can still be regarded as an attack on their good character. It should also be remembered that with regard to sexual orientation no specific legislation exists to make discriminatory behaviour against gay and lesbian people an offence, although ineffective legislation does exist in the case of gender and race (the Race Relations Act 1976, and the Equal Opportunities Act 1975). It can therefore be argued that:

The 1980s licensed oppression of lesbians and gay men. Clause 28 of local government legislation prohibited local authority employees from promoting homosexuality in their services. Clause 25 of the 1991 Criminal Justice Act unhelpfully and deliberately confused consensual homosexual offenses with offenses of sexual abuse, and placed more gay men at risk of being treated more punitively than ever by the courts. (NAPO 1993a)

Britain thus encourages a level of institutionalized judicial discrimination against gay and bisexual citizens which is greater than in any other member state of the European Union. In 1989, according to official Home Office figures, criminalizing men for consenting gay behaviour cost the taxpayer some £12 million and resulted in 3,500 prosecutions (Tatchell 1991).

Weeks (1986) has identified an absolutist position which conceptualizes sex outside the nuclear family as dangerous, disruptive, and antisocial. Social work seen from this perspective would encompass tight and authoritarian regulation of sexuality. In rejecting both classical Marxism and functionalism, Weeks argues that sexuality is moulded through complex and overlapping mechanisms which create domination, opposition, subordination, and resistance.

Instead of seeing sexuality as a unified whole, we have to recognise that there are various forms of sexuality: there are in fact many sexualities. There are class sexualities and gender specific sexualities, there are racial sexualities and there are sexualities of struggle and choice. (Weeks 1986: 41)

Such a view of sexuality is not reflected in social policy.

Social work services and sexuality

One of the most obvious features relating to the literature on social work and sexuality is its paucity. Given the undoubted levels of discrimination against gay and lesbian people, it seems surprising that more attention is not directed towards this area in terms of both training and practice.

All too often social workers collude with service users who perceive the 'problem' in terms of homosexual impulses. If these could be exorcised then the problem would disappear (Parry and Lightbown 1981, Davies and Neal 1996). Many homosexual service users still seek a 'cure' for homosexual feelings. The job of any counsellor or worker therefore is to assist in accepting a positive attitude towards homosexuality.

Coming out in the context of employment, including professional social work, may have a number of serious consequences. Local authority social work departments have failed to recognize lesbians as suitable for fostering and adoption. Social work can ignore the specific needs of lesbian women or locate lesbianism as central in all aspects of assessment. Both approaches result from prejudices and stereotypes and a failure to understand specific needs of individuals. Social work has a strong tendency towards the pathologization of homosexuality. It is vitally necessary for social work students to examine their own values and feelings towards homosexuality before they are equipped to work with gay people (Cosis-Brown 1993). The lack of research into this area can also be seen in relation to gay and lesbians in residential practice (Lloyd 1993).

Many social workers do not consider discussing sexuality unless it is raised by the service user (Robertson 1993). Generally, social work and sexuality take a low profile even in residential establishments for younger people (Bremner and Hillin 1994). Probation services tend not to have sexual orientation in their equal opportunities statements (Senior 1992). The rationale for this has never been clearly articulated.

The question of violence against gay and lesbian people also needs to be seriously addressed by social workers. In the USA, gay and lesbian communities have brought attention to the scope and consequences of violence. Activism in the USA includes the documenting of violent incidents, the establishment of crisis intervention centres, and the sponsorship of public education campaigns (Jennes 1995).

Basis for good practice: practice guidelines

- The helper must first have come to terms with her or his own sexual identity and feelings. The professional who claims never to have had homosexual feelings is rather like the psychotherapist who has never had dreams. Exploring and attempting to understand one's own sexuality is a prerequisite to working with gay people (Clark 1987).

- Workers must be aware of the anger felt by many gay people at the years they have spent suppressing emotions and suffering oppression.

- Workers must also be willing to work with gay people to combat the oppression against the latter which is structured into current social policy. This will involve the identification of gay stereotypes and the negative conditioning which is created by discriminatory language.

- Good practice involves facilitating gay people in forming their own groups.

- It is important to make the anti-discriminatory stance in relation to sexuality explicit at the outset of any such intervention.

- The availability of lesbian and gay information is an important aspect of practice with gay people.

- Homophobic assumptions made by colleagues and service users should be vigorously challenged at all levels (McCaughey and Buckley 1993).

- Policy and practice guidelines should be used to support this approach to anti-discriminatory work (Bremner and Hillin 1994).

- If an individual reveals HIV positive status their consent to have this recorded should be sought, if indeed it is thought necessary by the worker to record this.

- The distinction should be made between high risk as defined by HIV and high-risk behaviour. High-risk behaviour is defined by Bremner and Hillin as having unprotected penetrative sex. It thus becomes possible for a person who has protected sex with 100 different individuals to be safer than one who has unprotected sex with one individual. Information must be age appropriate and understandable.

Exercise

Garry was placed in local authority residential care at the age of 12 after his mother had died, and his father, an alcoholic, had been unable to care for him at home. Both events, the death of his mother and the cruelty and neglect he experienced as a result of living briefly with his father, had been extremely traumatic. Although Garry is doing better at school and has adjusted well to the residential establishment for the first two years, he finds that he is attracted to other young men in the residential establishment. He is afraid to discuss his feelings with any of the residential staff since they are all 'macho' and make jokes about 'queers' and 'fairies'. The hypermachismo atmosphere is dominated by sport. Until recently Garry had pretended to be interested in sporting activity, but feels unable to keep up the pretence for much longer, particularly since he is attracted to one particular young man who is also resident in the institution. If he comes out he fears bullying and physical violence, which he feels would be condoned by the male staff who 'hate queers'.

1. What are the legislative implications which are relevant to this case with specific reference to section 28 of the 1988 Local Government Act, and the 1989 Children Act?

2. What conflicts arise in the legislation which are exemplified in this case?

3. Construct some guidelines based upon the principles of good practice mentioned in the chapter which could apply to this situation.

4. What plans could be implemented by management in order that the situation faced by Garry did not reoccur?

FURTHER READING

D. Davies and C. Neal (1996), *Pink Therapy* (Buckingham, Open University Press) offers a clear and well-written guide to counsellors and therapists working with gay and lesbian bisexual clients. Much of the contents including the practice guidelines are applicable to social work. *Sexuality, Youth Work and Probation Practice* (Sheffield, Pavic, 1993) by Chris McCaughey and Karen Buckley also provides a clear and well-written guide to probation officers and those working in the area of criminal justice. J. Bremner and A. Hillin (1994), *Sexuality, Young People and Care* (London, Russell House Publishing and CCETSW) examines the practical and managerial issues related to sexuality and social work with younger people. Paul Mayho (1996), *Positive Carers* (London, Cassell) presents a readable account of the responsibilities and rights of individuals in the health care field which is increasingly relevant to social workers in multidisciplinary teams. The literature on HIV AIDS is now enormous, but a useful starting point can be found in J. Tavanya (1992), *The Terence Higgins Trust HIV/Aids Book* (London, Thorsons). Wallace Swann (1997) has written a useful guide to bisexual, transgender, and public policy issues, *Gay, Lesbian Transgender Public Policy Issues* (New York, Harrington Park Press). The policy examples given are from the USA.

CHAPTER 12

Children and Child Care

- The legislative background
- Neglect, abuse, protection, and social work services
- The problem of clarifying concepts
- The 1989 Children Act: collectivist or anti-collectivist?
- Media presentation of child care debates
- Adoption and fostering
- Services for black children
- Some debates within the research

Introduction

The prevalence of child abuse is estimated at being between two and four in every thousand, with one child per thousand under 4 years of age in danger of being severely injured (Waterhouse 1997). Such stark figures make professional intervention with children one of the most emotive areas in social work practice. This chapter explores the development of policy and practice in this area.

The legislative background

During the period of what is often referred to as the first industrial revolution between 1760 and 1830, there was no public regulation of the squalid, hastily erected living areas which surrounded the factories. Children were seen as a form of cheap labour, often working up to sixteen hours each day. In 1802, largely as a result of the work of Robert Peel senior, apprentice pauper children were restricted to twelve hours per day working whilst night work was banned. Pauper children were also given instruction in the basic three Rs. In 1819, due in no small measure to the efforts of the 'Grand Papa' of socialism, factory owner Robert Owen, the Factory Act restricted factory work to children over the age of 9 whilst children between the ages of 9 and 16 were not to work for longer than twelve hours each day (Ward 1970).

Stronger legislation followed in 1833 and 1844 by which time children were to spend half their time in schools. Dangerous machinery, which during the early years of the industrial revolution children had sometimes been required to clean whilst in operation, was to be properly guarded. This legislation was ineffective due to the fact that so much of it applied to the textile industry, whilst inspection during the nineteenth century was left in the hands of magistrates. Until 1836 proof of age was impossible due to there being no registration of births.

The work of the voluntary children's societies such as Barnardo's and National Children's Home was significant. Voluntary effort was often associated with organized religion, which also played a part in the evolution of services for children, in particular the revivalist evangelical movement, which called for the salvation of children.

At the same time some patchy improvements in services for children were seen, which were regulated by the 1834 Poor Law. In an attempt to discourage pauperism and save potentially recalcitrant young souls, separate accommodation for children was created away from the workhouse, with rudimentary schools being provided for some pauper children.

Cottage homes and foster homes were developed through the nineteenth century, although the range of occupations found for pauper children on leaving the care of the Poor Law was very narrow. The Poor Law Commission of 1905 reported that there were still some 14,000 children in workhouses, whilst an estimated 300,000 were receiving some form of outdoor relief. After 1850, other factors such as the growth of new technology gradually reduced the demand for child labour. Concomitantly this created homelessness amongst children.

One of the major problems in identifying neglect in the nineteenth century was the nature of child death. Infectious diseases like diphtheria claimed the lives of many children, whilst infanticide at that time was difficult to detect. In the nineteenth century children were regarded as threats to society mainly as a result of the fear of the possibility of crime (Dingwall, Eekelaar, and Murray 1984). In 1891 the Factory and Workshops Act raised the minimum working age to 11, and the Factory Act of 1895 restricted the number of hours per week worked by children under 13 to thirty, and abolished night work for the under-14s. By 1901 the minimum working age was 12. A brief period of economic upturn followed the First World War, but children's services, such as they were, became affected by the mass unemployment and the great depression of the 1930s.

Prior to the Adoption of Children Act 1926, parents could allow their children to be cared for by relatives, friends, or strangers without relinquishing parental rights or obligations. Under the 1933 Children and Young Persons Act, it was possible for parents to be prosecuted for ill-treating their children. Children who had been neglected or abused by parents were considered to be in need of care and protection. The impact of the Second World War, most obviously the effects of evacuation and the blitz, marked a watershed in the development of child care services.

In January 1945 Denis O'Neill died whilst in foster care as a result of neglect and ill-treatment. This led to the setting up of the Curtis Committee to enquire into the care of children in 1946. The resulting report focused on the absence of a single centralized authority with responsibility for children, the lack of properly trained staff in child care generally, and the sometimes excessively authoritarian regimes in some residential establishments for children. Concern was also expressed for children who had been evacuees, children in need of protection, juvenile offenders, adoptees, children in foster care, and chronically sick and disabled children. Recommendations were also made with regard to improvements in standards in local authority care although nurseries were found to be more progressive than other forms of child care. Although the report did not condemn conditions as being cruel, it emphasized the need for a proper code of conduct and for inspectors to enforce such codes in residential establishments for children. The Committee recommended that responsibility for 'deprived children' should be located within one government department and that local responsibility should be exercised by new children committees. In addition it recommended that those offering social work services to children (children officers) should be qualified. In 1947 the government accepted the recommendations of the Curtis Committee and began to act upon them.

The 1948 Children Act, with the National Health Service Act, (1946), National Insurance Act, and National Assistance Act (1948), constituted the cornerstones of the legislation which transformed the Beveridge plan into reality. The main principles of the 1948 Children Act included the establishment of local authority children's departments, a new emphasis on boarding out in preference to residential homes, restoration of children in care to natural parents, greater emphasis on adoption whenever appropriate, and responsibility for young offenders. Local authorities were given the duty to receive into care all people under the age of 17 years whose parents or guardians were unable to care for them. Authorities also carried out duties which were given to them under previous legislation including the supervision of children fostered for reward, the registration of adoption societies, providing information for magistrates on the background of children appearing in juvenile courts, and responsibility for children in 'remand homes' and approved schools. The establishment of a children's committee was made mandatory for local authorities, as was the appointment of children officers. The 1948 Act also specified that voluntary services were to be integrated into the national system of child care through inspection and registration. Further provision included the award of grants to voluntary homes for improvements in premises and equipment. A high priority was given to boarding out children whenever possible, although in instances where this was not possible they were to be kept in residential care.

The experiences of war had reinforced the idea that the family was a strong coherent social unit. This combined with a growing awareness that many parents failed to take adequate care of their children. The war had also left many families fatherless.

The dominant concern to keep the family together was further strengthened by a Home Office circular issued in 1950 which reiterated the importance of the family in child care. Thane has argued: 'The problems of children evacuated or separated by war conditions from their parents increased knowledge and concern among psychologists and others about childcare' (Thane 1982: 261). Such developing psychological interest had an immeasurable and lasting impact on the development of child care policy and social work practice which is still present today. The 1948 Act was supported by John Bowlby, whose ideas relating to the dangers of separating small children from their parents helped to create a family-centred approach which was shared by the social work profession. Closely related to this was the influence of the child guidance movement and a growing willingness of social workers to refer to primarily psychological knowledge (Hendrick 1994).

Throughout the 1950s something of a euphoria developed in relation to the possible impact of the 1948 Act on child care services. Hope for the future was also reflected in the growing role of social work in the area of child and family work. Such optimism was short-lived, with the incidence of increased juvenile crime, and the emergence of 'problem families'. The Ingleby Report of 1960 which resulted from such concerns recommended that a duty should be laid upon local authorities to protect children from suffering in their own homes, whilst local authorities were also given the power to carry out preventive work. Arrangements were to be made for the detection of families at risk, and local authorities were to be under statutory obligation to submit their schemes for the prevention of cruelty to children in their own homes for ministerial approval. Ingleby also recommended the commissioning of a study into existing services. Whilst the report clearly established a link between neglect, deprivation, and juvenile crime, the report was received with great disappointment from those who were concerned with children in trouble, since it lacked any sense of urgency. In many respects the report simply reiterated that juvenile crime was a serious social problem, and that the 'deprived child' was often involved in criminal behaviour later in life. A central policy aim, it was argued, should be the prevention and punishment of juvenile crime, a concern which was reflected in later legislation. The 1963 Children and Young Persons Act, although primarily concerned with delinquency, included a section which gave local authorities a duty to carry out preventive work. This Act also allowed children's officers to give material and financial aid to families, which further extended the role of social workers in a range of family experiences.

The 1969 Children and Young Persons Act, passed five years after the election of a Labour government, was based upon the Labour Party White Paper 'Children in Trouble'. This piece of legislation emphasized the importance of treatment over punishment (see Chapter 14 below). The 1970s represented a loss of direction in the area of child care and in welfare generally. The Houghton Report made a number of recommendations in 1972 which became the basis for the 1975 Children Act, which extended the rights of children through a welfare test. In deciding the future of a child, attention was to be given to the wishes of the child. It was also a duty of the local authority to provide comprehensive adoption facilities, whilst all adoption societies were to be approved by the Secretary of State. The introduction of a custodianship order was designed as an alternative to long-term foster care and allowed for application by a relative or foster parent for the legal custody of the child where adoption was thought to be inappropriate. Like the 1969 Act this legislation was not fully implemented.

With increasing awareness of child abuse came a concern that children should have stable homes and committed care. The impetus for this came from the work of Rowe and Lambert (1973), whose findings indicated that children were frequently disrupted within foster and adoption placements and that many could have returned home, whilst other children were being denied the possibility of any alternative long-term prospect of care. The 1975 Children Act, reflecting this concern, made it possible for children to be adopted without the approval of their natural parents. The legislation also enabled local authorities to pay allowances to facilitate the adoption of children in care.

Permanence entailed permanent separation and reinforced the notion of incompetent uncaring parents. More support for parents struggling to help their children in extremely difficult conditions was often required. Opposition to this measure to some extent came from the black community since permanence for their children had usually been achieved through placing black children with white parents.

The 1980 Children Act enabled a local authority to assume full parental rights for children who came into care with the voluntary agreement of their parents. Two years later the all-party Social Services Committee of the House of Commons undertook an inquiry into child care and reported in 1984 under the chairpersonship of Renee Short. The Short Committee was set up to examine the continuing debate relating to the rights of children, the growing dissatisfaction with the balance between the courts and local authorities in decision-making relating to children, and the movement from residential care to foster care. The concentration of the Committee was therefore focused on the relationship between the rights and responsibilities of parents and the state with regard to children, and the balance between courts and social services departments in mediating these. The report recommended a more positive attitude towards prevention by improving inter- and intra-departmental co-ordination. The Committee further recommended a clearer organizational commitment to prevention by raising its profile within social work practice. It also recommended the introduction of family centres for intensive social work with complete family units. There also, so it was argued, needed to be more understanding and research into preventive work in order to clarify where it should be concentrated for greater effect. It was also recommended that the long-term rate of supplementary benefit should be extended to unemployed families with children. There also appeared to be considerable confusion with respect to the responsibilities of social workers, courts, and the law. A recommendation was therefore made that the courts should make decisions relating to significant issues concerning long-term care, rights, and responsibilities, while social services should take day-to-day decisions about children. Concern was also expressed by the Committee in relation to the possible unsuitable use of place of safety orders, recommending that all such orders should be confirmed by a court within one week of being granted. The Committee argued for a working party to review existing law in order to create more coherence and clarity (Parton 1991). Research from the D.o.H. (1985) also confirmed that children were being admitted into care in an atmosphere of panic with increasing use of compulsory powers such as the place of safety order. The Review of Child Care Law reporting in 1985 followed the lead of the Short Report, emphasizing the importance of including parents in child care decisions as far as possible. Parton (1991) has argued that the principles of partnership, family support, shared care, respite care, maintaining links, and return to family were all given pre-eminence. The processes of reform which preceded the passing of the 1989 Act thus had a long gestation period. The Act was not simply a response to the Cleveland inquiry but had a far more detailed history.

A Review of child care law was established in response to the recommendations of the second report from the House of Commons Social Services Committee. The 1989 Children Act aimed to simplify and rationalise the committee (1983–1984) on Children in care (HC 360, 1984). No less than 12 informal consultation papers were issued by review in 1984–1985. The Report to Ministers Review of Child Care law was a further consultation document in 1985 and in 1987, a White Paper on the Law relating to child care and family services was published (Cm. 62, 1987) followed by the Children Bill. (Hallett 1991: 284)

Many commentators agree that in the area of child care during the 1970s and 1980s all roads appear to have led to the passing of the 1989 Children Act. The Children Act incorporated many of the ideas emanating from official reports and research which had developed throughout the 1980s, creating a new agenda and framework for child care practice. It set out a comprehensive child care system, including children who were disabled, in hospital, or in independent boarding schools, groups hitherto excluded (Packman and Jordan 1991). The Act also represented a change in the way in which children were approached by social services, placing parental responsibility, support for children and families, and partnership between parents, social services, and children centre stage. Custody, care, control, voluntary care, and access were abolished as was the place of safety order. Children who truanted were no longer to be committed to care, and criminal care orders were abolished. Local authorities under the Act were to implement partnership, parental responsibility, prevention, and protection (Pinkerton and Houston 1996). The protection of children from 'significant harm', a concept that has subsequently become highly contentious, and the welfare of the child were seen as being of paramount importance in family proceedings. Court orders were to be used as a positive step, whilst delay in court proceedings was also highly prioritized (Ball, Preston-Shoot, Roberts, and Vernon 1995).

Neglect, abuse, protection, and social work services

Parton identifies the Maria Colwell inquiry of 1974 as the starting point of popular interest in child abuse. Maria Colwell, one of a family of nine children, in 1971 had shown signs to neighbours and teachers of being traumatized and had been diagnosed as being depressed. The long-term plan of the social services department was to return Maria to her natural mother's parents. During the last nine months of her life some thirty complaints, including weight loss, physical injuries, and neglect, were made to various authorities about the treatment that Maria was receiving from her mother and stepfather. The family received visits during this period from a variety of social work agencies. In January 1973 Maria was killed by her stepfather.

The inquiry into the case was surrounded by the creation of a moral panic constructed around two principal failings. First, there was the failure of the social services to respond to reported abuse. Secondly, there was the apparent wish of social workers to return the child to what turned out to be a fatal situation within the family.

The report of the inquiry resulted in the creation of a new set of regulations and procedures implemented between 1974 and 1976 which created a far more sophisticated set of administrative guidelines for investigating child abuse. The main characteristics of these were Area Review Committees staffed by senior management staff, case conferences for front-line workers in child care, abuse registers, and manuals which were designed to assist in the detection of child abuse (Hendrick 1994). A Commons select committee set up in 1975 to consider violence in marriage had its brief widened to consider violence in the family. The Committee reported that the more violent forms of abuse were only part of a series of forms of neglect and violence which children were forced to suffer. The Committee found that more support for local agencies through rate-supported projects was required to prevent child abuse, as were adequate facilities for children under the age of 5, child minders, playgroups, nurseries, education for parenthood, and more training for social workers and police in detecting and managing abuse.

None of these measures prevented the incidence of similar scenarios developing in the 1980s. Jasmine Beckford (1985), Kimberley Carlile (1987), Tyra Henry (1985), Charlene Salt (1985), Reuben Junior Carthy (1985), and Stephanie Fox (1990) were all killed whilst in care of social services departments. The essence of the findings of the Beckford inquiry was that good social policy and social work practice demanded that the care, safety, and interests of the child were paramount over any professional desire to keep the family together. Social workers should be vigilant in removing children from potentially dangerous parents. The circumstances surrounding these deaths suggested that little had changed since the finding of the Colwell inquiry (Cm. 412, 1988). Too little had been done too late, which had resulted in the death of vulnerable young children.

User Groups

In 1987 the Cleveland 'affair', as it was to be called, focused attention on other criticisms of social workers and paediatricians in that they were using their powers to separate innocent parents from their children too hastily. Similar allegations were made in the press following the Rochdale and Orkney satanic abuse cases in the early 1990s. Following the Orkney child care investigation Lord Clyde in his report recommended that the European Convention on Human Rights of the Child should be taken into consideration in child protection (Asquith 1993). This was to have a considerable effect on the development of Scottish child care law, as reflected in the Children (Scotland) Act 1995 (Tidsall 1996). The Cleveland inquiry conducted by Lord Justice Butler-Sloss concluded that the central problems in child care practices resided in the lack of inter-agency co-operation, a theme which had also been present in the inquiries following the deaths of both Jasmine Beckford and Maria Colwell.

These central and recurring themes led to the apparently irresolvable dilemma faced by social workers and policy-makers. Inquiries into the Beckford (London Borough of Brent, 1985), Carlile (London Borough of Greenwich, 1987), and Henry (London Borough of Lambeth, 1987) cases indicated that social workers were not acting quickly enough to remove children from dangerous situations. Concerns addressed in the Cleveland Report (Secretary of State for Social Services, 1988) suggested that social workers acted too hastily (Parton 1989). These cases created a number of central contra-dictions which threw child care policy and practice into turmoil. In Northern Ireland the Children (NI) Order 1995 follows to some extent the example set by the 1989 Children Act in that it moves child care services away from monitoring and policing towards empowerment through partnership (Kelly and Pinkerton 1996). The Children (Scotland) Act of 1995 has several innovations which are not included in legislation relating to Northern Ireland or England. There is a statutory duty in Scotland specific-ally to recognize disability in service plans. The Scottish legislation introduces an ex-clusion order for an alleged abuse (see Tisdall 1996 for a full account of the current policy and practice issues in Scotland).

Residential care for children has also been subject to considerable scrutiny following a number of crises which developed following the abuse of children whilst in residential care. In 1989 the 'pindown' phenomenon became public when an adolescent girl in local authority residential care was found to have been confined to one room for a long period, whilst also being deprived of education and forms of sensory stimulus. It emerged that the practice had been carried out between 1983 and 1989 and involved 132 children aged between 9 and 17 years. The report into the Staffordshire pindown incident stressed that staffing levels had been poor, and training inadequate.

Similar problems of unqualified, inexperienced staff, and lack of clear objectives, were held responsible for the brutality which occurred at the Ty Mawr residential establishment in Wales. In 1991 Frank Beck received a life sentence for some seventeen counts including attempted rape, buggery, and other forms of assault, whilst being officer in charge of a number of Leicestershire children's homes between 1973 and 1986. In all these instances

148

Line management of facilities and heads of homes tended to be ineffective or non-existent. Line managers also had a minimal if any direct contact with units and so were in no position to observe malpractice assuming of course they recognised it. Adequate complaints systems were not in place. Homes were often trying to achieve objectives that were probably beyond them, so that unacceptable practices seemed attractive as a way of establishing order. (Berridge and Brodie 1996: 185)

A number of initiatives taken in the main by the Department of Health followed the residential care crises. These included, significantly for practice, two reviews of residential care in England and Wales which focused upon the importance of staff training (see Berridge and Brodie 1996).

On the one hand the 1989 Children Act reaffirmed in official polemic at any rate the determination of the state to protect the child from danger and the rights of parents simultaneously against undue interference in family life through consensual techniques, partnership being the most obvious conceptual tool. This tendency, however, to some extent is countered by an increased emphasis on regulatory supervision or what Parton calls legalism, which is 'The ethical attitude that holds moral conduct to be a matter of rule following and moral relationships to consist of duties and rights determined by rules' (Parton 1991: 194).

Legalism in child care is focused upon the relationships between professionals, service users, parents, and children. The rule of law from this perspective takes precedence over other considerations. Thus social work activity involved in the creation of a consensual form of partnership, whether it be between voluntary and statutory agency, parent and child, parent and parent, is seen as requiring legal scrutiny. A vital focus of the 1989 Children Act was to make social workers more accountable, parents more responsible, and transfer responsibilities to the courts. Underlying legalism was the resurgence of dangerousness in child care; like the disease model, this reflected a belief that dangerous individuals and families can be detected and isolated. Such an approach seeks to balance competing concerns from both the child rescue and the family rights lobbies (Woodhouse 1995). The concept of dangerousness has been combined with the disease model to create a recent major professional preoccupation with risk and risk analysis. If the characteristic of the actual or potential abuser can be identified the incidence of the problem can be predicted and prevented, so the argument goes. The role of the researcher and practitioner is to identify risk factors and characteristics associated with potential cases of child abuse. Social work textbooks have also tended to focus upon the development of checklists and warning signs for social workers in this area of practice. The Department of Health, drawing on the disease model, has devised typifications of abuse. Physical abuse occurs when there is bruising, burns or scalds, or a bone injury. Although these indicators often occur normally in a child's life, non-accidental injuries show in slightly different ways and are often accompanied by unconvincing explanations. Neglect occurs when the carer fails to meet the basic needs of the child, including when a child is left alone, unsupervised, and is often associated with a failure to thrive. Emotional abuse occurs when there is a lack of affection and love.

Sexual abuse occurs when an adult or older child uses a child for their own sexual gratification.

The concern with risk is understandable following the tragic child care events of the 1980s and 1990s. However, the domination of risk could undermine the urgent need for positive support for vulnerable families (Dartington Research Unit 1995). Checklists are usually constructed from research studies which have examined the characteristics of abusing parents or from the experiences of professionals. This approach is based upon studies of populations who have actually abused their children rather than studies of populations as a whole. Thus such a lack of control possibly gives a skewed and inaccurate picture. Furthermore studies which have been written by practitioners can concentrate on the severity of the abuse, the assessment of the parents, and parental co-operation with the agency. Action based upon such material should be taken with care since parents often complain of being labelled by agencies, whilst parental co-operation is an extremely difficult criterion to apply and can lead to discriminatory forms of practice (Kelly 1996).

Despite increasing practice specialism, considerable research effort, and the extremely high profile of this area of policy and practice, a number of fundamental issues appear to undermine efforts to intervene successfully in family life in order to promote the safety and well-being of children. Despite the 1989 legislation there is still considerable uncertainty as to what constitute the child's best long- and short-term interests. The balance between the parent and the state, and between men and women, as well as questions relating to accountability, appears to be still unresolved (Parker 1995). The crucial concept of partnership might if clung to with excessive zeal lead children into high-risk situations. On the other hand partnership might be deployed to mask coercive social work action (Kaganas, King, and Piper 1995). This leads to a further unresolved question as to when children are best protected by separation from their parents and when not. The methods whereby children can best be protected from significant harm are still unresolved. Recent evidence indicates that developments in social policy have increased the likelihood of the influence of structural factors such as ill health and poverty. Such factors may be directly relevant to the incidence of child abuse. The knowledge upon which child care practice is based appears to have been subject to swings in intellectual commitment and flawed methodologies.

The problem of clarifying concepts

The manner in which the legislation has emerged strongly suggests an unsatisfactory conceptualization of fundamental concepts which have grounded policy and the operationalization of concepts in practice. Child abuse, or child protection as it has been more latterly described, has focused media and public attention more clearly than any other issue in social work on the relationship between policy and practice. Despite the complex development of policy in this area since the Second World War there still remains some confusion over what constitutes abuse.

Dingwall has suggested that the definition of child abuse is so wide as to encompass most problems which can have a detrimental effect on the child (Dingwall 1989). Parton (1989) argues that the lack of a clear definition reflects the 'rudimentary' level of research into child abuse. Such a lack of clarity can also be seen in the wide variation in the reported incidence of child sexual abuse. Some evidence suggests that the studies which have been carried out into the prevalence of abuse suffer from fundamental methodological problems and could result in a gross underestimation of the incidence of abuse.

One of the results of the findings of the various inquiries following child care traged-ies was the perceived need to reconstitute the concept of child care to form the notion of 'child protection'. This was accompanied by the official broadening of the notion of child abuse to include neglect, and physical, sexual, and emotional abuse. A number of models of abuse appear to have emerged in the literature. It is useful then to examine some of the ways in which the concepts have evolved and been reflected in policy and practice.

The influential 'disease model' was developed in the late nineteenth century and was based upon ideas designed to fight infectious diseases (Giovannoni 1982, Armstrong 1983, Parton 1989). This model assumes that child abuse is attributable to a particular disease which has an onset phase, known duration, and impact on all parts of the body. In some cases death can result. Having established the knowledge relating to the disease it is necessary to intervene in order to prevent the disease and identify the population which are most at risk.

Despite the existence of the disease model there was a relative absence of concern relating to child abuse from 1900 to the 1960s. Instead there was a widespread belief within child care circles that physical injuries to children were most usually accidental.

The 'battered baby' model developed by Henry Kempe in 1962 referred to a clinical condition in young children who had received serious injury, and was closely identified with subdural haematoma, a pooling of blood under the skull, and evidence of broken or healing bones. In 1962, following the publication of Kempe's paper, there was a rapid development of studies which sought to define how best to deal with the neglect of children (Swann, 1993). By 1976 Kempe had abandoned his original term for the more generic notion of 'child abuse' and 'neglect'. The subsequent rediscovery of child pov-erty occurred due to the convergence of a number of factors. The women's movement had begun to influence the field of child care (Parker, 1995). Such a form of analysis seriously questioned the assumption that the family was a safe haven for children and ultimately the best place for children to thrive and develop. This ran parallel with the development of a civil liberties movement which concentrated critically on the extent and nature of state intervention into the private lives of people. In the field of child care this enabled a number of lobbies to gather in strength including the National Associ-ation for One Parent Families, Justice for Children, and the Children's Legal Centre.

Another influential lobbying group was PAIN (Parents Against Injustice), which had helped to frame some of the parents' rights issues eagerly pursued by the media following the Cleveland affair (Parton 1991).

The Seebohm Report resulted in local authority social services departments becoming better staffed with increasing numbers of qualified social workers—a 25 per cent increase between 1972 and 1974 and another 50 per cent by 1980. Although the impact of training in this and other areas of social work is open to some debate, Parker has argued that formal social work training raised awareness and the possible warning signs of potential abuse to children (Parker 1995).

The 1989 Children Act: collectivist or anti-collectivist?

The 1989 Children Act represented important elements of a new conceptual framework for the development of social work with children. The fundamental premises upon which the 1989 Act is based and subsequent developments in practice have fuelled further debates.

The introduction of internal markets and competitive principles has been one of the most significant developments in the delivery of social services in Britain since Beveridge. Hallet has argued that the 1989 Children Act marks a distinctively different approach to the market. Whilst the community care legislation represents a residualization of state activity, with social service departments becoming enablers rather than direct providers, the Children Act is less residualist, and indeed envisages an expanded role for the state in the provision of services. Part III of the Act, as Hallett argues, lists a range of new local authority services to children including the identification of children in need, support of children, links with families, and expanded day care of children. Notwithstanding this, the Children Act does rest on the belief, as was the case with earlier legislation, that children are best looked after by their families.

Alaszewski and Manthorpe also argue that the 1989 Children Act and the 1990 community care legislation emanate from different traditions in social work. The former is based upon the social worker's role in protecting children, acting as an advocate, and participating in legal proceedings. The community care legislation related more to the old welfare departments with an emphasis on the allocation of scarce resources, and the administration of services (Alaszewski and Manthorpe 1990). The Act is surprising in that it does not appear to move towards a residualization of the local authority care as has been the case with community care practice since the passing of the 1990 NHS and Community Care Act (Packman and Jordan 1991). In a study of the community care arrangements in twenty-five authorities Lewis and Glennerster report problems in treating children within the framework of the purchaser and provider split. Work with children has tended to remain separate, which reflects the partnership and prevention preoccupations within the 1989 Children Act. This may well result in the development of ever more specialist children services (Lewis and Glennerster 1996). Thus in some respects the Act appears to differ from more recent trends in social policy formulation, tending towards a more collectivist approach.

While not seeking to overemphasize the importance of the apparent social demo-cratic elements in the 1989 Children Act, other tendencies are more consistent with anti-collectivist themes which have come to dominate policy and practice. The gov-ernment is not prepared to provide extra resources for implementation of the new approach. It appears that the policy shift from providing and funding as envisaged by Beveridge and Seebohm, to one of enabling, subsidizing, and regulating, which have been the hallmarks of practice and policy development, will be as evident in child care practice as it is in work with disabled and older people (Parton 1991).

The place of parental responsibility does mark an important innovatory feature of the Act. Eekelaar (1991) describes two aspects to the concept of parental responsibility. First, there is responsibility in the sense that child care belongs to the parent rather than the state. The second is responsibility in the sense that parents have duties towards their children. The basic ideology underlying this pivotal feature of the legislation is that parents left to their own devices will fulfil their own parental obligations possibly with a little unobtrusive assistance. This could be seen as constituting a retreat by the state, and an endorsement of the principles of *laissez-faire* individualism and self-sufficiency, the twin guiding principles of new right political ideology.

Parental responsibility is inextricably linked to the idea of partnership between state and parents. Although the term 'partnership' does not appear in the Act itself, in several places it is present in government guidance to the Act: 'Partnership with parents and consultation with children on the basis of careful joint planning and agreement is the guiding principle for the provision of services within the family' (Thorburn, Lewis, and Shemmings 1995). Underlying the idea of partnership is the liberation and empower-ing of the responsible parent. Kaganas, King, and Piper (1995) point out, however, that there are two serious obstacles to partnerships. If workers cling too rigidly to the notion of partnership and the responsible parent, it could put children at risk. On the other hand the language of partnership might be used as a form of rhetoric to mask the coercive power that authorities have over families judged to be irresponsible.

In a recent study of 220 child care cases which reached child protection conferences, only 2 per cent of family members were considered to be in full partnership with the local authorities. In the same study 14 per cent were described as participating to some considerable extent. This proportion was unchanged if only the main parents were in-cluded. Some 7 per cent of the main parents in the study were considered not to have been involved at all (Thorburn, Lewis, and Shemmings 1995).

Following the 1989 Children Act the notion of significant harm marks the boundary between state intervention and family life. Harm legally refers to ill treatment, which can be physical, sexual, emotional, or social impairment of health. Significance turns upon what health or development can be expected for the particular child. Before any care or supervision order is made by the courts they have to be satisfied that harm or the likelihood of harm is attributable to the current care arrangements of the child. Minor shortcomings in care should not give rise to the possibility of compulsory proceedings. 'Significant' therefore means substantial, considerable. The concept has been subjected to considerable judicial interpretation for instance in deciding what is significant relative to a similar child and deciding whether particular legal thresholds have been crossed (Hardiker 1996).

Media presentation of child care debates

The role of the media in socially constructing public consciousness about social work issues with possible consequences for policy formulation has been previously discussed. The circumstances surrounding the setting up of the Barclay Report in 1981 and the reformulation of CCETSW's Paper 30 in 1995 in the aftermath of the political correctness débâcle in the 1990s are important examples of the intense interest of the media in social work issues. The possibility that the media are able selectively to focus and represent social work issues in a way that ultimately manufactures public opinion and influences the development of social policy has to be considered.

Populist new right critics of social work and other forms of media attention may have drawn attention to social work in the early 1980s and been connected to policy developments during the early days of the Thatcher government. Many of the debates around the child care incidents of the 1980s provided a further opportunity for the various arms of the media to both orchestrate and define debates within social work practice. There would appear to be little doubt that every opportunity was taken by particular arms of the media specifically to utilize child care in order to present a negative view of social work, whilst linking the issues with wider, more constant tabloid themes. The most obvious popularized image was of the social worker as the hapless incompetent agent of socialism interfering with the nuclear family unit. The manner in which child care is presented by the media is more complex than simply a reactionary, simple-minded, sensational press attempting to damn all forms of state intervention into the private domain. Aldridge (1994) describes the media presentation of social work as being akin to the practices of some restaurants, highly sensitive to the relationship between a known cuisine and the market. Recipes never emerge in the same way on more than one occasion, with this year's delicacy being relegated to boring the next.

The media showed great interest in the child abuse cases with a clustering of intensely covered cases in the mid-1980s, most notably Jasmine Beckford, Kimberley Carlile, and Tyra Henry, whilst other cases like Reuben Carthy and Charlene Salt which occurred during a similar period received little press interest. A number of themes appeared to run through the media coverage of the child abuse cases according to Aldridge. The place of the family in child care was central to the ways in which contradictions within child care practice were presented by the media. Press criticisms of the professionals involved in the Cleveland affair appeared to reflect the traditionally held view that the family was intrinsically the rightful site of child care.

Another important aspect of the child abuse cases is the racial one. The Cleveland affair enabled social workers to be represented as agents of an authoritarian state, whereas in other cases, e.g. Beckford, they were presented as weak dupes, easily fooled by wicked people.

For the right-wing press Aldridge argues that 'race' is not alone the determining factor in deciding that a particular case is newsworthy. In the Reuben Carthy case it was impossible to tell that both defendants were black.

In the high profile trials race is in part a complex surrogate for other items on the press agenda. One is the racial dimension of the demonised loony left. Another is the search for the deviant, undeserving, dangerous minority at whom the strong state can legitimately direct its control measures. (Aldridge 1994: 67)

Parton has argued that the bill preceding the passing of the Children Act was presented as a policy to prevent the abuse of parents' rights rather than the rights of children and received surprisingly little media attention, possibly due to the complexity of the issues (Parton, 1991).

Adoption and fostering

Adopting was introduced to Britain in 1926 and is generally regarded as being a successful institution. However, despite the enormous amount of research that has been carried out in the area, as Ryburn has argued, there is a great deal which is unknown. Although the majority of adoptees are satisfied and well-integrated members of society (Triseliotis 1991), there is some evidence to suggest that adoptees are over-represented in the group of population experiencing mental health problems. Ryburn has argued that there is a close association between poverty and adoption and indeed all forms of substitute care for children. She argues that historically most adoption orders have been the result of consent being given by parents who have no alternative due to material deprivation. One significant growth area envisaged in the 1993 White Paper on adoption is inter-country adoption. Ryburn argues that the current policy adopted by government fails to acknowledge issues like the sale of children and that the inter-country adoption trade is only open to those who can pay.

Intercountry adoption can never offer an effective solution to global inequalities which are at the heart of the massive and escalating problems of child poverty, homelessness and abandonment in less well developed countries. (Ryburn 1996: 204)

Judicial statistics indicate a drop in the number of adoptions from 22,500 in 1974 to 6,326 in 1996. Half of the adoptions in 1994 were stepparent rather than stranger adoptions. Possible explanations for this include the greater use of contraception, abortions, extra-marital cohabitation, and the growing acceptance of single parenthood (Barton 1996). Ryburn argues that adoption has always been a cheap alternative form of child care and has been utilized at the expense of other possible approaches including more support for the children's own family. Since it is so cheap to operate its future is assured (Ryburn 1996).

With regard to foster care, most children experience short-term placements, although not much is known about how children themselves experience fostering arrangements (Sellick 1992). Far more research has been carried out into residential care but has concentrated on special provision. Residential establishments for children with emotional and behavioural difficulties vary tremendously in their approaches (Grimshaw and Berridge 1994).

Approaches to adoption have changed since the early 1970s, as adoption has increasingly become central to the permanency movement (Fox-Harding 1991). Previous practices, which used adoption to create new permanent attachments in cases where attempts to return children to their natural families had failed, are now largely discredited. Although the 1989 Children Act recognizes the importance of kinship, the number of compulsory admissions to care has increased markedly. The number of children who were committed to care and subsequently adopted has shown a 35 per cent increase between 1988 and 1991. The number of contested adoptions could be as high as 75 per cent (Ryburn 1996).

One of the central aims of the 1989 Children Act was to make the boundary between support at home and away from home more permeable. This has been largely successful due to the greater use of respite and short-term placements. Access to services appears to have become confined more to families with children at risk, a problematic finding given the difficulties in defining which children are at risk and which are not. The approach also excludes many needy children. This situation has been exacerbated by resource constraints.

Services for black children

Research evidence dating from the end of the Second World War suggests that black children are treated differentially within the child care system, and that a process of black family pathologization is blamed for the disproportionate number of children who have been taken into care by social work departments since 1948 (Ely and Denney 1987). Numerous other studies indicate that black families suffer from material hardship, which is likely to produce tensions in child care, whilst social work agencies have been quick to stigmatize black families (Gill and Jackson 1983, Small 1984, Fletchman-Smith 1984).

In more recent research into services for black children in the public care system, Barn (1993) concluded that developments were both encouraging and discouraging. Black children are more likely to be placed in racially and culturally appropriate settings than was previously the case. Regular contact between black children in care, and the efforts of residential care services to move from a Eurocentric framework to an anti-racist mode of working, are also apparent. The employment of black workers appears to have moved beyond tokenism. Most black children entering care now do so on a voluntary basis. On the more pessimistic level, black children are still significantly over-represented in care, entering care twice as quickly as white children, and are still more likely to be made the subject of a compulsory care order. Preventive work is less likely to be undertaken with black families. Social workers' negative perceptions of black families can lead them towards a 'rescue mentality' which is frequently applied to black families. Some children were also inappropriately placed in situations where their cultural needs were not met. Black children also had a slim chance of being placed at home on trial. Despite the 1989 Act there is a lack of partnership between social workers and black parents. Overall, Barn concludes that black families experienced a qualitatively different form of child care service, which in essence is inferior to that experienced by white service users.

At the stage of admission into care social services departments need to improve their practices to conduct assessments in order to take account of the effect of racism upon the lives of black service users. The ability of social workers to negotiate practice goals with black families will improve the effectiveness of the service on offer. There also needs to be more recruitment of black foster parents, with particular attention being paid to the employment of black residential workers. Also the participation of children in decision-making processes is vital. Jackson has demonstrated that racism also affects the manner in which child protection practice operates. Black children have many of their rights and privileges denied them, and their abuse has not been recognized due to ignorance and racism on the part of social workers (Jackson 1996).

Barn, Sinclair, and Ferdinand, in a study of 196 children looked after or supported by three different local authorities, found that financial hardships faced by local authorities made service provision to black families 'patchy' and 'incremental' (Barn, Sinclair, and Ferdinand 1997).

Some debates within the research

Studies of child abuse constitute one of the larger areas of social work research and it will not be possible to present an adequate picture of current knowledge in the space available in this section. It is important to point out that despite the amount of work that has been done in this area compared with some other user groups, no clear picture emerges as to the aetiology of child abuse. Studies conducted during the 1960s and early 1970s were largely clinical in nature, and suffered from vague definitions of abuse, and control groups were very rarely used. Later studies have cited a variety of factors, not necessarily associated with each other, including larger families, families with closely spaced children, families with young children, single-parent families, families under stress, poverty, marital discord, social isolation, poor health, low birth weight, and illness in infancy (Cohn 1983).

Overall different research appears to produce lists of poorly defined and sometimes contradictory characteristics which the social worker is meant to utilize in practice (Parton 1989: 63). Latterly, although researchers have attempted to improve their research methods, it is still difficult to see any conclusive correlation between particular factors and different types of abuse (Parton 1989).

Research in the 1990s appears to have been more concentrated around the workings of the 1989 Act, services for children at home, in the community, children looked after away from home, and services for children after they have left accommodation or care (Hill and Aldgate 1996). Much of the time spent in case conferences is devoted to the detail of abusive incidents, whilst honesty, reliability, and open communication have been shown to be important ingredients in enabling families to co-operate. The vast majority of children who are subject to child care procedures stay at home. There is a need to shift emphasis from investigation to family support (Audit Commission 1994). Nationally there has been a trend away from compulsory care placements towards voluntary accommodation, which marks a contrast to tendencies which developed in the 1980s. Research does suggest that distressed parents value respite care for children (Bradley and Aldgate 1994). Thorburn also emphasizes the importance of matching the social work method with the requirements and wishes of the family. Keeping the family involved and giving clear information as to what may happen and the powers available to the agency is seen as an effective way of approaching child protection work (Thorburn 1997).

Conclusion

Child care appears to have become dominated by a number of what would appear on the surface to be conflicting influences. In this chapter the impact of poverty and adversity in general on children needs to be recognized by policy-makers and social workers (Waterhouse 1997). Since the death of Maria Colwell subsequent inquiries into other tragedies have demonstrated the urgent need for a nationally co-ordinated system of child care which improves inter-professional collaboration.

Exercise

The following case study shows how work with particular user groups overlaps, in this case mental health and child care services.

Chris, now aged 28, was born in a large Midland town and has a 10-year-old daughter, Alice. She has an ageing mother who lives locally but otherwise lives an isolated existence. She attends a community centre attached to the local psychiatric hospital having now made a number of serious attempts on her own life. Social services involvement goes back over a seven-year period. Following violence from Owen (Alice's father), Chris contacted social services and moved into a women's refuge when Alice was 3. On leaving the women's refuge Chris obtained a flat on a large council estate and lived independently with Alice. The relationship between Chris and Owen continued fitfully with Owen moving into the flat for short periods. These attempted reconciliations usually ended in violence being perpetrated against Chris and frequently required police intervention. Owen moved to another part of the country and was killed in a car accident. Following this incident Chris became depressed and was prescribed anti-depressants by her GP. One year later Chris was admitted to hospital having taken an overdose. Alice, now aged 6, was temporarily placed with her grandmother. For some years after the overdose Chris appeared to cope well, although the flat was in a state of disrepair. Chris's mental health appeared to deteriorate. When Alice was 7 Chris made a further attempt on her life, and was compulsorily detained in hospital under section 2 (twenty-eight-day assessment) of the 1983 Mental Health Act. Alice on this occasion due to the increasing immobility of her grandmother was placed with foster carers. On being discharged from hospital, Chris attempted to remove Alice from the foster carers and the police were called, which resulted in Chris being charged with breaching the peace. After a report from the psychiatrist to social services stating that Chris was well enough to look after Alice, the two lived independently in the flat. In the months that followed Alice was admitted to hospital on two occasions following accidents in the home, and concern was expressed by social workers as to whether Chris could establish an appropriate routine within the flat which was safe and secure for Alice. Following a further incident in which Chris was again compulsorily detained under section 2 of the 1983 Mental Health Act, social workers made a decision to instigate initial care proceedings should Chris attempt to remove Alice from foster care again. After Chris's discharge a decision was made to keep Alice in foster care for a five-week period in order that a comprehensive assessment could be completed.

Initially Alice was accommodated under section 20 of the Children Act which stipulated that the local authority had a duty to provide accommodation as Chris was temporarily prevented from doing so. Following the assessment a care order was applied for and granted in respect of Alice under section 31 of the 1989 Children Act on the grounds that she would suffer significant harm and that: 'The harm or the likelihood of harm is attributable to (1) the care given to the child or likely to be given to the child if the order were not made' (part IV, section 31, 2 (b) (i)).

The order lasts until the child is 18 unless discharged, and gives the power of parental responsibility to the local authority together with in this case the parent, who retains her right to exercise any aspect of her parental responsibility so long as it is not in conflict with the plans for the child made by the local authority. The local authority has a primary duty to promote the welfare of Alice by regularly reviewing the written care plans with reference to specific guidance related to the Children Act 1989. The plan should be implemented by a key worker and take into account the wishes and feelings of the parties involved whilst paying attention to local resources and cultural and ethnic factors. It should also be ensured that all parties are aware of the purposes and nature of the intervention and objectives of the plan. Copies of the plan should be sent to all parties and areas of dissent should be recorded (Children Act 1989, vol. iii Guidance and Regulations). A care plan was constructed which would seek permanent placement for Alice. The family placement team were commissioned to find an appropriate placement. Alice was to have once-weekly contact with her mother.

Questions

1. What are the major problems involved in implementing a care plan for a child under these circumstances? How can social policy appropriately address these problems?

2. How appropriate is the idea of a permanent placement for Alice in this case?

3. How can partnership between the local authority, Alice, and Chris best be achieved?

4. How is it possible to understand and act upon the wishes of the child in this case?

FURTHER READING

D.o.H. (1995), *The Challenge of Partnership* (London, HMSO) and J. Thorburn, A. Lewis, and D. Shemmings (1995), *Paternalism or Partnership? Family Involvement in the Child Protection Process* (London, HMSO) emphasize the practices which appear to be most successful in creating effective partnership in child care practice. Dartington Social Research Unit (1995), *Child Protection and Child Abuse: Messages from Research* (London, HMSO) summarizes some of the most recent major pieces of research which are relevant to good social work with children. M. Hill and J. Aldgate (1996), particularly in part i of their book *Child Welfare Services* (London, Jessica Kingsley), specifically address developments in policy research and their relationship to good practice. Chapters in K. O'Hagan (1996) (ed.), *Competence in Social Work Practice* (London, Jessica Kingsley) give useful summaries of developments in child protection, the 1989 Children Act, and residential child care which are specifically related to CCETSW's 1995 competency requirements. *Racism and Child Protection* (London, Cassell) by Valerie Jackson (1996) provides a recent and readable introduction to the issues raised by racism in child protection work. R. Barn, R. Sinclair, and D. Ferdinand (1997), *Acting on Principle* (London, British Agencies for Adoption and Fostering/Commission for Racial Equality) explore the histories of 196 children looked after or supported by three different local authorities.

CHAPTER 13

Mental Health Policy and Services

- History and legislative development
- Causes of mental illness
- Community care policies: the practice backdrop
- Dangerousness and social work
- The impact of current policies and practices on services users
- Effectiveness of community services
- Mental health, ideology, and social work practice

Introduction

Mental health is one of the most contentious issues in social policy and social work practice. It is also an area which is endowed with numerous accounts charting the development of policy and practices in mental health services (Jones 1960, 1988, Busfield 1986, Bean 1986, Pilgrim and Rogers 1993). This chapter will describe the development of practice in relation to policy shifts, and examine some of the current debates which link policy with practice.

History and legislative developments

Private 'madhouses' were first established in the seventeenth century, with real growth following the restoration of 1660. By the eighteenth century confinement of mentally ill people in private 'madhouses' had become firmly established with numbers of public asylums peaking in the mid-nineteenth century (Busfield 1986). From that point the number of public asylums also rapidly increased. The charitable or voluntary hospitals which had emerged throughout the eighteenth and nineteenth centuries were intended more for so-called 'curable' cases.

Before the nineteenth century no separate provision was made for pauper 'lunatics'. Those considered dangerous were occasionally confined to private or voluntary 'mad-houses', but in the main they were kept within the poorhouse or given outdoor relief. A parliamentary select committee between 1815 and 1816 catalogued deficiencies in the existing provision including overcrowding and excessive constraint. The first specific legislation relating to mentally ill people was enacted in 1714 and 1744. These measures made parishes liable for the cost of keeping mentally ill people in private 'madhouses' or voluntary asylums. Legislation of 1774 made it necessary for a certificate to be gained before a private 'lunatic' was admitted to hospital. In 1828 the Madhouse Act repealed the 1774 Act, setting up a centralized and improved system of inspection and licensing of madhouses. Data for the number of mentally ill people before 1844 is inexact. By 1889 there were over 17,000 pauper lunatics, defined as persons of unsound mind, in workhouses. The number of mentally ill people in private madhouses reached its peak in 1848 whilst numbers of people confined in public asylums increased rapidly during the second half of the nineteenth century (Busfield 1986). The history of social work involvement or its equivalent in compulsory admission can be traced to the Poor Law when relieving officers had duties to remove patients to workhouses or the asylum. In so doing they acted alongside clergymen, churchwardens, and constables (Bean 1986).

The Lunatics Act of 1845 established a permanent regulatory commission which was charged with the inspection of all types of asylums. Licences were to be granted by magistrates. A further Act of the same year made it a legal requirement for counties and boroughs to create their own public asylums. The number of such institutions increased after the legislation from twenty-four to eighty-seven by the turn of the century. In 1853 legislation made it possible for inmates of private licensed madhouses to remain as voluntary residents if they had been previously certified. This was soon extended to those seeking readmission who had been certified within the previous five years. From 1857 private madhouses in Scotland could admit patients for a period of six months with one medical certificate confirming mental illness. With the break-up of the Poor Law relieving officers gradually became 'authorized officers' (Bean 1986).

The 1890 Act introduced the necessity to issue medical certificates in every certified case, other than when an order had to be made urgently. All detention orders ceased to have an effect at a specified time, although they could be renewed. The Act was in many respects a reflection of three dominant currents in nineteenth-century thought. First, it reflected the dominance of legalism and the legal profession emanating from a desire to strengthen legal safeguards. Secondly, it reflected custodialism, given the custodial character of the asylum. Thirdly, the idea of detention and isolation from the community was seen as providing a form of protection to the individual (Jones 1960).

At the turn of the century these themes were further developed within mental health policy. The 1913 Mental Deficiency Act gave local authorities the right to detain mentally disordered people or 'deficients', as they were called at this stage, in institutions or colonies and to grade them as 'idiots', 'imbeciles', or 'feeble-minded'. The Act allowed the use of segregation not as a method of protecting the vulnerable, but as a strategy for protecting society against 'the deficient', who were defined as a corrupting influence. This according to Williams was justified through scientific methods which underlay a growing interest in the Eugenics movement. This view of the world incorporated the assumption that inherited characteristics of degenerates could be identified and classified, and that birth control and sterilization could improve racial quality. The Eugenics movement enjoyed the support of many prominent welfare reformers including Keynes and Beveridge (Williams 1996a).

In 1926 the Macmillan Commission advocated a more medical approach to the treatment of mentally ill people, drawing a clear distinction between detention and treatment. The Mental Treatment Act of 1930 introduced voluntary admission, whilst also adding temporary and certified admission. A person could be admitted temporarily for up to six months if they were unable to express their willingness or unwillingness to enter the 'asylum'. The Act also created a change in nomenclature whereby an 'asylum' became a mental hospital, whilst lunatics became patients. Local authorities were also required to make appropriate arrangements for outpatient psychiatric treatment. The transformation from the 1890 Act which concentrated on legalism to the medically oriented therapeutic approach, according to Busfield, can be attributed to other changes which were occurring. First, there was the development of ideas and practices related to psychiatry. Increasingly private psychiatric patients were treated outside hospital. Secondly, the Macmillan Report advocated the treatment of symptoms at an early stage, whilst the Poor Law was based upon the principle of deterrence. The Poor Law emphasized the saving of money; the Macmillan Report advocated the expansion of mental health services. Thirdly, the Macmillan Report also gave greater emphasis to non-residential forms of care, whereas the Poor Law had focused on relief (Busfield 1986).

As the 1930s and 1940s progressed there were new developments in treatments and approaches in the treatment of people with mental health disorders. Various forms of shock therapy were introduced, including insulin coma therapy in the 1930s, electroconvulsive therapy, lobotomy, and psychotherapy. There were also major developments in psychopharmacology, particularly in the use of tranquillizers, and the development of psychotherapy.

The 1940s and 1950s also saw new attempts to develop psychotherapy 'therapeutic communities', separate units usually of not more than 100 patients within larger hospitals. Implementation of the Beveridge plan integrated mental health services within the new National Health Service. In 1948 the National Health Service took responsibility for psychiatric and what were then referred to as subnormality hospitals under the regional health boards, whilst local authorities retained responsibility for community mental health services such as they were.

In 1957 a royal commission on the law relating to mental health and mental deficiency (the Percy Commission) recommended care in the community for the mentally ill as offering more humane and cost-effective care than long-term care in a psychiatric hospital (Brown 1985). The 1959 Act was concerned with definitions of mental disorder, the administration of hospital and community services, and procedures for the admission and discharge of patients. The psychiatric hospital retained central responsibility for the care of mentally ill people. The 1959 Mental Health Act defined mental disorder as mental illness, arrested or incomplete development of mind, and psychopathic disorder. Patients under this legislation could be admitted with a view to treatment informally without fear of detention. Compulsory admissions were of three basic types. First, there was the order for observation for up to twenty-eight days (section 25); secondly, for treatment for up to one year (section 26); and thirdly, in cases of emergency, a section 29. Admission was usually made on the recommendation of two medical practitioners, although in the case of an emergency it could be on the initiative of a friend, relative, or mental health officer with the agreement of one doctor.

In many geographical areas generic social workers were required to do stand-by duties which could involve them directly in emergency admissions under the Act, even when they had little specialist knowledge of mental health procedures. Social workers operating as mental health officers were issued with warrants. Local authorities varied regarding the extent and nature of training that was provided. In some areas social workers had to have additional training whilst in others this was not the case. Following the support for the generic principle enshrined in the Seebohm Report, the 1959 Act reflected the belief that a qualified social worker had the necessary knowledge and expertise to make decisions related to compulsory admission, and required no extra formal training.

The weaknesses of the Act began to emerge and fears began to surface that social workers were possibly supporting some compulsory admissions which constituted miscarriages of justice. As specialization in other areas of social work began to develop there was a growing realization that it was unrealistic to expect a qualified social worker to be an expert and indeed safe in all areas. It became apparent that social workers were often woefully ignorant of the law in specific areas of practice. This applied particularly in the case of social workers involved in mental health compulsory admissions. The Act also set up the Mental Health Review Tribunals to which appeals against continued detention could be made.

The Mental Health Act of 1959 put great emphasis on the importance of informal treatment and community care. One of the recommendations made by the Percy Commission which was never implemented was the earmarked grant for the development of non-medical services such as training. Two years later the then Minister of Health, Enoch Powell, announced that over a period of fifteen years the number of hospital beds devoted to the mentally ill would be halved. This represented the closure of some 75,000 beds. He hoped that the remaining beds would be for the most part located within general and not psychiatric hospitals. In 1959 the Mental Health Act created the need for a structure which encouraged hospitals to create a more co-ordinated way forward (Allsop 1995).

Underlying this approach lay two conflicting policy concerns. First, there was anxiety about the state of the mental hospitals. Secondly, and possibly more importantly, there was growing concern as to the increasing expenditure incurred by NHS services. On the surface a commitment to humanity and welfare was the stated concern of Powell's speech, whilst the cutting of beds policy had its roots in an ideological conflict between collectivism and anti-collectivism (Whitehead 1992, Jones 1988). Despite the fact that there was little real incentive provided by the government, many hospital adminis-trators and psychiatrists began to initiate community care policies. Changes in pharma-cology also shifted the emphasis away from containing people in institutions to the use of long-term medication in the community.

As the practical implications of the Act unfolded, criticism came from most quarters including the Royal College of Psychiatrists, MIND, the National Association for Health, MENCAP.

The Act defined the powers of the Mental Health Review Tribunals in a limited manner, most of their activities being concentrated on the patient's discharge from detention. Criticism also centred around the composition of tribunals, which tended to reflect almost entirely a medical model which the 1959 Act sought to create (Anderson-Ford and Halsey 1984). Tribunals were also criticized for the infrequent opportunities that patients had to make application to them, whilst some patients under restriction orders had no right to apply. Legal aid was not allowed within the tribunal system, whilst the powers of the tribunals were restricted to the discharge or reclassification of patients. A tribunal was therefore legally bound to direct a discharge if the patient under the terms of the Act was no longer considered to be mentally disordered. The 1959 Act did not concern itself with the legal rights of the patient. The tendency towards the *ad hoc* power of the medical profession could result in the incarceration of patients sometimes for long periods. The 1959 Act made the medical practitioner the key pro-fessional in making application for compulsory admission (Pilgrim and Rogers 1993).

The publication of the hospital plan in 1962 proposed the creation of new and large district hospitals which might include services for mentally ill people. Despite this, during the 1970s admissions to mental hospitals continued to rise, whilst two forms of distinct treatment were emerging. Short-stay wards were intended for those who were in hospital for shorter periods of possibly weeks or days. There were also more intense forms of treatments of longer duration for more chronic long-stay patients, although many patients on the 'back wards' did not receive treatment.

Following the revelations of maltreatment of psychiatric patients in hospitals, and calls from prominent patient-centred organizations including MIND for the rights of people with mental illness to be respected, a review of the law was put into place. This resulted in the passing of the 1983 Mental Health Act, which marked a further move towards legalism. It was a prescriptive Act, tying the professionals down to procedures designed to prevent abuse. In its final form it represented an uneasy compromise between the civil rights concerns of MIND and what the DHSS lawyers thought it possible to achieve by law (Jones 1988: 39).

Mental illness as a generic concept is not defined in the 1983 Mental Health Act, but categories of mental disorder are delineated. Severe mental impairment is defined as a state of arrested or incomplete development of mind which includes severe impairment of intelligence and social functioning. This is associated with abnormally aggressive or seriously irresponsible conduct. A psychopathic disorder is defined in the Act as a persistent disorder or disability which results in abnormally aggressive or seriously irresponsible behaviour or conduct.

Section 5 of the Mental Health Act allowed for application for compulsory admission to be made on a voluntary basis. Section 2 provides for short-term compulsory admission for assessment whilst section 3 allows detention for treatment for a period of up to six months. In order for compulsory admission to be undertaken there must be grounds to believe that an individual is suffering from a form of mental disorder which could put the safety of the individual and others at risk. Under the 1983 Mental Health Act, an approved social worker is an officer of a local social services authority appointed by the authority as being competent to deal with compulsory admissions. The main responsibilities relate therefore to application for admission for assessment, treatment, assessment in cases of emergency, and admission to guardianship. A code of practice (D.o.H. 1993) now exists which requires all those assessing for possible admission under the 1983 Act to take all relevant factors into account in order to ensure that whenever possible all appropriate alternatives to compulsory admission are considered. The code of practice is also intended to ensure that all action is in compliance with the legal requirements of the Act.

The guardians' role is essentially related to caring for those who are unable to look after themselves. Under the 1983 Act the guardian has three specific powers:

1. to require the patient to live at a place specified by the guardian;
2. to require the patient to attend specified places at specified times for medical treatment, education, training, or occupation, although there is no specific power to enforce treatment;
3. to permit the approved social worker the right to gain access to patients (Bean 1986).

The 1983 Act has been described by Anderson-Ford and Halsey as a

Series of amendments to the 1959 Act—most significantly in relation to the rights of the patient, the powers of tribunals, the Mental Health Commission, and powers and duties of approved social workers. (Anderson-Ford and Halsey 1984: 15)

The Mental Health Commission was charged with the responsibility for instituting procedures for second opinions, particularly for those refusing ECT treatment, also having major responsibilities for hospital visits, and investigation of complaints.

The 1983 Mental Health Act enables a mentally disordered person to be taken out of the prison system at the remand, sentencing, or post-sentencing stage. Under section 35 of the Act, a court must be satisfied that the defendant is not suffering from any form of mental disorder as defined by the Act. Offenders can also be taken out of the prison system whilst serving their sentence due to mental illness, but returned to prison if they recover sufficiently during their sentence.

One of the major problems with regard to the Mental Health Commission is that it deals primarily with patients who are formally detained.[1] Patients who are in the community are frequently at most risk. Patients also experience great difficulty in gaining information relating to procedures for supporting their applications for discharge.

The 1995 Mental Health (Patients in the Community) Act makes provision for certain mentally disordered persons in England and Wales who are receiving care and supervision after leaving hospital, and provides for the making of community care orders in the case of mentally disordered patients in Scotland. The main provisions of the Act relate to supervised discharge from hospital for treatment. The patient may be required to reside at a specific place. Supervision is the responsibility of the supervisor and the responsible community medical officer. Supervision in the community is normally for six months, renewable for a further six months and then a year at a time thereafter.

Causes of mental illness

Huxley has argued that, although female rates of mental illness exceed male rates, when drug dependency and antisocial personality are taken into consideration greater parity is found. Black people are also over-represented in involuntary hospital admissions, although the disproportionate number of black people in the mental health system is diminished if class is taken into consideration. Unemployment, social class, and life events appear to have had a substantial effect on the six million psychiatric diagnoses which are made by GPs each year. At the beginning of the 1990s mental illness was responsible for the loss of 71 million working days (Huxley 1997).

Community care policies: the practice backdrop

In a television interview with Melvyn Bragg shortly before his death, playwright Dennis Potter accused the then Conservative government of using terms like 'community care' 'When they mean close that costly thing and put that madman onto the street'. However

[1] Section 117 of the 1983 Mental Health Act also made some community provision for patients who had been the subject of treatment orders.

severe Potter's judgement might be, his description encapsulates the fears that many social workers and mental health service user groups articulate at the use of terms like market welfare, mixed economy of care, and competitive tendering in the area of mental health social work and practice.

The closure of psychiatric hospitals and the transfer of mental health services into the community has been driven by a number of forces, some of which constitute recurring themes throughout this book:

- the wastefulness and destructiveness of collectivist approaches (Marsland 1996a);
- the failure of the welfare state to eradicate poverty through social security and other systems (Spicker 1993);
- the move in many European countries, most notably Italy, towards deinstitutional-ization. Many European governments by 1990 had devised programmes for shifting provision from the public to the voluntary sectors (Tomlinson 1991);
- the concept of normalization which originated in relation to those with physical and educational impairments and encapsulates the idea that people with mental health problems should be treated in the same way as all other members of society (Jones 1988).

Although the compulsory admission into hospital is an aspect of social work practice which receives great attention in the literature and on social work training programmes, of far greater importance to most long-term users of mental health services are community services.

Community services

We will see later how the larger welfare landscape is dominated by the 1990 NHS and Community Care Act which raises fundamental policy issues related to citizenship and rights (Chapters 15, 16, 17). There are currently two specific approaches to policy which are designed to assist individuals with mental health problems in the community: the care programme approach and the mental illness specific grant, which will now be considered in greater detail.

Care programme approach

The 'care programme approach' policy initiative is intended to provide arrangements for continuing care in the community of people who have severe mental illness. It em-phasizes the importance of assessment planning and co-ordination of services whilst also reflecting concern for those who fail to receive services because they fall through the care net. In the official words of the Department of Health, the care programme approach seeks to create 'systematic arrangements' agreed with social services authorities for assessing regular supervision of staff. The care programme approach (CPA) bears some strong similarities to the care management approach advocated by Griffiths in 1989, in that a worker is responsible for assessing needs, creating a care plan, and directing its implementation. However, CPA differs from care management in that it is exclusively directed towards those with mental health problems, and is implemented by the health authority. Table 13.1 shows how CPA services are divided into three broad areas, home-based, day, and residential care. The existence of the two initiatives which both aim at giving care in the community has brought about some confusion. The source of these two care approaches gives rise to differing perceptions, with CPA working within a medicalized framework with a strong emphasis on describing psychiatric conditions and symptomology from a scientifically classified standpoint, and the personal social services model which traditionally has attempted to conceptualize mental health problems from a variety of perspectives, locating the causation of mental health problems with other wider social problems like poverty. This difference of approach has led to some difficulties in professional collaboration. This was recently emphasized in an extensive report prepared by the Social Services Inspectorate which called for more interagency agreement, improved joint working, shared information systems, and service delivery through integrated community mental health teams (D.o.H., Social Services Inspectorate 1997).

Table 13.1. **Types of CPA services**

	Acute/emergency	Rehabilitation/continuing care
Home based	Intensive home support. Emergency duty team. Sector teams.	Domiciliary services. Key workers. Care management.
Day care	Day hospitals.	Drop-in centres. Support groups. Employment schemes. Day care.
Residential	Crisis accommodation. Acute units.	Ordinary housing. Unstaffed group homes. Adult placement schemes. Residential care homes. Mental nursing homes. 24-hour NHS accommodation. Medium-secure units. High-security units.

Source: Department of Health (1993), in Sharkey (1995: 29).

There have also been some delays in implementing this policy, with lack of specific direction as to how the policy was to be implemented (Braye and Preston-Shoot 1995).

The mental illness specific grant

This source of finance was first made available from April 1991 and is intended to encourage local authorities to expand the range of services to mentally ill people in the community. The funding intended to finance 70 per cent of the costs of additional services for the mentally ill in the community is specifically earmarked for that community care function. An inspection carried out after the first year of its operation indicated that the ring fencing of specific resources meant that mental health projects did not have to compete with other priorities, which to some extent avoided delays. Projects generally were responsive to the needs of individuals and appeared to be having a beneficial impact on service users (Nocon 1994).

Dangerousness and social work

Frequently the closure of psychiatric hospitals and the development of community services for mentally ill people is connected with the concept of dangerousness. The assumption that dangerousness is linked to certain types of disorder is contentious.

Pilgrim and Rogers have argued that the emphasis in the media on dangerousness is actually unwarranted. The overwhelming majority of people designated mad are

Perplexing, but they are harmless and docile and do not constitute a threat to anyone around them. However, the unpredictability of those deemed to break social expectations without an intelligible reason then fuels fantasies of threat in others. (Pilgrim and Rogers 1993: 190)

One of the greatest problems for social workers specializing in mental health care is that the rapid rundown of psychiatric hospitals from 69,000 beds in 1983 to 45,1000 in 1992 has not been matched by a corresponding growth in local authority private or voluntary sector accommodation. The growth in available places for the same period has been 7,026 beds although there has been a rapid increase in the numbers of places in day hospitals and day centres (Mohan 1995). Following revelations about ill treatment of people with learning difficulties at Ely hospital in the late 1960s, media coverage of mental health issues followed a recognizable pattern. Nursing staff, usually male nurses on 'back wards', would be accused of cruelty or ill treatment by relatives or former friends of staff. This would be followed by an inquiry under legal chairmanship, and conclusions relating to specific allegations. In some cases the allegations were proved and criminal charges would on occasion follow (Jones 1988). Media interest in the case of Ben Silcock, a user of mental health community services who in 1992 was severely mauled after climbing into the lions' enclosure at London Zoo, led to the Department of Health reviewing its procedures for care of mentally disordered people in the community in 1993. Three important recommendations followed the Department of Health Review.

- There was to be a tightening up of arrangements for the discharge of people considered to be a danger to themselves or others.
- Key workers were to be appointed for each person with clear responsibilities and accountabilities for supervision of services and treatment. Such key workers would normally be psychiatric nurses.
- Health authorities as in the case of CPA would be the lead responsibility.
- From October 1994 hospitals and community health units were to set up registers for seriously mentally ill people who had been discharged to live in their own homes (Sharkey 1995).

These measures appear to have had little impact on the quality of service provided for mentally ill people.

In a social work text which reflects the competency-based approach to social work practice, Campbell acknowledges concerns about those with mental health problems who may take their own lives, or the lives of others. This should constitute

An important aspect of the student's assessment. It is therefore important that she/he is aware of a knowledge base which can support skills in assessing such risk—past history of mental disorder, a history of chronic social disorganisation. The immediate circumstances of risk in the client's life, including evidence of recent disruptions to close relationships, debilitating life events, verbal or written expressions of intention to commit suicide, access to alcohol, drugs or firearms, indicate high risk. (Campbell 1996: 77)

Whilst some would argue that risk assessment in mental health situations should be similar in quality to risk assessments in all fields of social work, the risks involved in compulsory admission should not be underemphasized. Following compulsory admissions the likelihood of further admissions is increased, since the service user's support networks in the community may collapse. Social and legal status is significantly reduced, while the admission itself may be therapeutically ineffective. The risks of admitting to hospital have to be carefully balanced against the dangers of not admitting (Fisher, Newton, and Sainsbury 1984).

Ramon argues that the degree of certainty involved in risk-taking within mental health cases is at a lower level when compared with the risks that social workers take in other areas of practice.

While this implies the possibility of creative use of existing knowledge, it may also mean opting for the safest option, even if this implies a further reduction in a person's quality of life or his/her future potential for living. (Ramon 1992: 93)

The impact of current policies and practices on service users

Homicide and suicide are sometimes issues within mental health work, and concern has recently been expressed in relation to the apparently increasing suicide rate amongst mentally ill people. This gave rise to the Boyd Report on Homicide and Suicide which examined 39 killings. Two-thirds of these involved deaths of members of the patient's own family. The report also examined 240 suicides and 740 suspected suicides by mentally ill people in the first ten months of 1995. Of the suicides, 53 were in-patients, 154 outpatients, and 33 patients discharged within the previous year. Two-thirds of the 240 suicides were men, half were unemployed, and one in ten was black. Two of the 39 homicides were carried out by in-patients, and 36 by patients who were officially in contact with community psychiatric units. Some 16 of the perpetrators of homicide were said to be suffering from schizophrenia (Brindle 1996*a*).

In their response to the Boyd Report, the pressure group Sane argued that the links made by the inquiry between the inadequate resourcing of community care and dangerous situations involving mentally disordered people highlighted a breakdown of accountability within the mental health services. The position adopted by Sane is that the government must acknowledge that inadequate resourcing of community care can precipitate death (Sane 1996). Sane also carried out research into high-risk mental health patients with whom they had contact. This revealed a high degree of dissatisfaction with the treatment of those who are at grave risk of suicide who do not receive the care that they require. Sane concluded that people discharged from psychiatric hospitals at high risk of suicide were left to 'fend for themselves'.

The Department of Health responded by denying evidence of increased number of homicides and suicides, arguing that they were spending upwards of £2.4 billion each year on mental health. In addition the government argues that a new mental health challenge fund will increase spending by £20 million whilst the mental illness specific grant for local authorities is to be increased by £11 million to £58.3 million in 1996/7 (D.o.H. 1996).

The debate relating to resourcing was refuelled when Andrew McCulloch, formerly a Department of Health assistant secretary with responsibility for mental health policy, argued that in some areas funding on mental health services needed to be doubled. He regarded the closure of psychiatric hospitals without adequate community care resources as only 'half a policy'. Severely damaged and distressed people cannot be left to fend for themselves. 'Oceans of need are unmet', especially in inner cities (McCulloch 1996). Since coming to power the Labour government is currently reviewing policy in this area. Such debates relating to need and resources have taken on an almost ritualistic form with pressure groups arguing that more resources are needed and the government of the day arguing that they are providing the highest possible level in a situation of finite resources. What is particularly significant is that mental health users have not yet gained sufficient rights to have their own perspective taken seriously.

Effectiveness of community services

Despite the powerless position which they occupy it would appear that users of mental health services can derive some benefits from deinstitutionalization and care in the community. A number of American studies of people with mental health problems suggest more positive than negative outcomes for service users treated in the community, although there is considerable diversity and ambiguity in patterns of service delivery (Cnaan 1994).

In the UK it is unclear as to whether the progress made by service users is attributable to a particular approach to care or whether changes would have occurred anyway. Some would argue that the only way to ensure that social work intervention, and not extraneous circumstances, has been instrumental in creating change is through the use of randomized controlled trials (MacDonald and Sheldon with Gillespie 1992). This requires that one group receiving the form of care under review is compared with another group not receiving the particular form of care. It is also vitally important for such controlled groups to be randomly selected. The North East Thames Regional Health Authority study examined the closure of five major psychiatric hospitals and concluded that the closure was not initiated in order to cut costs. The political origins of the closure ranged from a genuine desire to improve the positions of marginalized groups, to more accurate targeting of resources, and the pursuit of geographical equity within the NHS. The research also suggested that the resettlement process had produced a greater level of service satisfaction than had hitherto been the case in the psychiatric hospitals.

Problems identified by the study included the fact that hospital practices tended to permeate community care facilities in 'asylum-like' facilities in community homes. Service users were offered little choice in the types of accommodation and activity on offer. Carers and users tended to be consulted rather than actively involved in the decision-making processes relating to the type of services on offer. The study also noted that greater knowledge of community networks could bridge the gap between consultation and genuine service user power. Hospital users can benefit from use of the same support and advisory services in employment and recreation as other citizens (Tomlinson 1991).

It now appears to be widely accepted that great improvements can be achieved in the quality of life for long-term users of mental health services within the community when compared with institutional care. Petch in an extensive study of community health projects in Scotland (1992) concludes that supported accommodation in the community can enable individuals with a considerable history of mental health problems to live in security within the community. She goes on to argue that this has positive effects on the quality of life for the whole community.

In a comparative study of public, private, and voluntary residential establishments for the mentally ill, Oliver and Mohamad found that hostels which were intended for residents with relatively high levels of independence tended to have the lowest levels of material comfort. Group home residents exercised most influence on their living situation and enjoyed the greatest levels of comfort. Boarding-out residents enjoyed least independence, family contacts, and external contacts. Overall well-being was enhanced by living in the community (Oliver and Mohamad 1992).

Studies of local mental health community care projects indicate a possible way forward for a democratization within the mental health services. In an attempt to broaden the involvement of both users and carers within the Hereford and Worcester area, a project was developed working with older mental health users. Networks of carers and users in the community were developed in which issues were identified by carers, users, and social workers. Joint commissioning of services appears to be a promising development, with attempts being made to incorporate the users' standpoint within service contracts and service providers. Users and carers have been involved in providing input into joint training events shared by health and personal services personnel. Carers are involved as lay inspectors of social services registered with a brief to ensure that the residents' and relatives' views are gathered. Despite the obvious achievements of such projects difficulties still remain. They include the differing perceptions of staff in health and personal social services as to what is meant by carer involvement. This is partly accepted by the health authority perceiving itself as a planning service for the general population, whilst staff from the personal social services see themselves as assessing the needs of individuals. The researchers argued that there was a need for continued monitoring of services, more open sharing of information, and clearer definitions of how people wish to involve themselves (Goss and Miller 1995).

In a study of the experiences of psychiatric service users Pilgrim and Rogers reached the conclusion that the 1983 Mental Health Act does not appear to have created any improvements to patients' rights, but has produced a new layer of state-funded professionals, namely the Mental Health Commissioners and second opinion doctors (Pilgrim and Rogers 1993). Infringements of rights within the mental hospitals which occurred in Rampton in the 1970s were repeated a decade later in Ashworth.

Other writers reiterate this theme in that mental health service users continue to possess few tangible rights whether they are in hospital or in the community. There also appears to be a significant degree of local variation in the interpretation of sections of the Act. All this leads towards a haphazard and differentiated level of after care provision (Barnes, Bowl, and Fisher 1990).

These and other problems have given rise to a mental health users' rights movement, which has led to the creation of patients' councils both inside and outside hospital, users' forums, and advocacy schemes. Users in some areas are being used as evaluators and researchers (Ramon 1992). We will see in the last part of this book that although such developments are to be welcomed, they tend to represent attempts at providing access and information rather than genuine attempts to address dominant power relations. Such initiatives fail to conceal a massive and usually unquestioned power imbalance between those medically defined as mad and the professionals who work within mental health services. Estimations as to the proportions of mentally disordered persons incarcerated within prisons appear to vary from study to study. Such estimates will also be subject to the variations of both methodology and definitions of mental illness. Some studies suggest that somewhere in the region of 20 per cent of prisoners might be suffering from some form of mental disorder whilst the number of offenders described medically as psychotic could be as high as 9 per cent (Bean 1986). Gunn in a more recent study has placed the number of mentally disordered offenders at 37 per cent (Hudson, Cullen, and Roberts 1993). Only a small proportion of those sentenced whom Gunn identified as suffering from mental health problems are transferred to psychiatric institutions. The Reed Committee found little exact data on the numbers of social services staff who were working with mentally disordered offenders. The Reed Committee recommended that local authorities should consider designating a senior officer to be responsible for the overall development of work with mentally disordered offenders. The Committee also recommended that social and probation services should work more closely together (Reed 1992).

Mental health, ideology, and social work practice

The medical model continues to dominate social work practice and policy within the mental health field. The medical approach to psychiatric illness has been summarized by Jones (1988) who argues that it is situated within the realm of diseases which frequently have a biochemical base and can be conquered by biochemical means. Forms of mental illness are as amenable to medical treatment as other organic diseases such as cholera.

Campbell argues that the adoption of the medical model ultimately leads to a more effective and better quality of service for the user. The social worker should utilize the medical model 'Because it seems to provide an epistemology which apparently strengthens practice judgements and helps demonstrate capacity to work as an effective member of the organisation' (Campbell 1996: 76).

CCETSW in its guidance to qualifying courses requires qualifying Dip. SW students to 'Demonstrate a basic understanding of psychiatric diagnoses, causes, symptoms, and treatments, and be basically familiar with the psychiatric vocabulary' (CCETSW 1994b: 13). This will enable them to 'recognise when people are becoming mentally ill'. A good grasp of psychiatric classification will enhance multidisciplinary working and solve the client's problems (Campbell 1996). Symptomology and fluency within psychiatric discourse are seen as being essential to effective practice with mentally ill people. Little attention is given to doubts about the 'scientific status' of psychiatrically based judgements since the need for a medical basis to mental health practice now constitutes an accepted orthodoxy. One possible reason for this is the eminent adaptability of the classificatory models utilized in psychiatry to the checklist approach of competencies which infuses social work assessment and training (CCETSW 1995). Nellis has powerfully argued that

Definitions of competence are therefore unlikely to be neutral, but will reflect both the increasing ascendancy of employer interests in education and training institutions, and the more managerially defined forms of practice now required in most public sector organisations. The competence movement should in fact be seen not as an autonomous 'vocational' development, but as both the consequence and counterpart of the expansion of corporate management in these organisations. (Nellis 1996: 13)

The monolithic and highly regulated view of mental health practice which has arisen from the competency movement raises major concerns which will now be explored at greater length. First, the supremacy of the medical model itself will be critically considered. Secondly, the use of technical forms of psychiatric language in social work practice will be discussed. Thirdly, we will consider the contradictions which emerge from policy in relation to practice. Fourthly, new forms of managerialism and the supremacy of organizational requirements will be discussed. Finally these issues will be drawn together in relation to some of the themes which have already been explored in the book.

The medical model

Psychiatrists have a peculiar amount of power within the British mental health system even though the medical treatment of mental illness has been much criticized by writers on both sides of the Atlantic. One of the best-publicized critics is Thomas Szasz, who saw mental illness as being located within the realm of myth. He writes:

The mythology of psychiatry has corrupted not only our commonsense and the law but also our language and pharmacology. To be sure, as are all corruptions and confusions, this is not imposed on us by conspiring or scheming psychiatrists; instead, it is simply another manifestation of the deep seated human need for magic and religion, for ceremonial and ritual, and the (unconscious) expression of this need in what we self-deceivingly think is the science of pharmacology. (Szasz 1974: 11)

The classificatory and organic edifice upon which the psychiatric model is built is undermined by Szasz's assertion that mentally disordered people have problems in living which are not medical. This then leads Szasz towards an overarching critique of institutionalized and community-based psychiatric care.

Laing (1967) developed a similar critique from a British perspective although the two forms of analysis are distinct. Laing's overwhelming concern has been to make intelligible the self-expression of people designated as suffering from mental disorders. What is regarded as mad or not mad is socially and not organically constructed. Schizo-phrenia becomes not a form of mental illness but an authentic experience. Such a brief account of this position does no justice to the case put forward by a group of writers who collectively developed the anti-psychiatry model (Jones and Fowles 1984).

Claims that madness is manufactured by a form of professional discourse are in many respects problematic and can be viewed partly as the product of the late 1960s and early 1970s when texts which made fundamental attacks on established institutions were bestsellers.

Radical critiques of psychiatry, although exaggerated and selective in the kind of evidence used to support arguments, are more than polemical artefacts. The explora-tion of such ideas should be inextricably linked to discussions of policy and social work practice since they constitute the basis for a fundamental questioning of the distribu-tion of power in mental health practice. Such concerns are sadly lacking in the 'tick box' ethos which now dominates social work and social policy.

The issue of language

Inextricably linked to the issues of professional power is the second problem, which is an unquestioning approach to the use of medical language and terminology, which, as we have seen, is now emphasized as an essential attribute in modern mental health practice.

There is a critical relationship between quasi-technical psychiatric language and power which has been overlooked in the endless search for new forms of evaluating 'quality' and competence indicators in social work. Psychiatrists are influenced by advice given on patients in formal assessments made by nursing and social work staff and diagnoses made by GPs.

Depending on the GP's ability to detect disorder and the nature of the diagnosis, the patient may then be referred to a psychiatrist, and then based on her assessment, be referred to a psychiatric hospital. The model gives central place to the role of the GPs and consultants in mental health care, presenting the former as the crucial gatekeepers whom patients must normally pass. (Watters 1996: 112)

Crucial to the understanding of this gatekeeping process of which social workers are a fundamental part are all forms of technical language and discourse. Discourse mediates between meaning and the sentence and is constructed by service users, psychiatrists, and social workers. Analysis of discourse enables the diversity and complexity of mean-ings in relation to professional practices to be critically examined. The important point here is that different levels of meaning are present both within words used and beyond. This applies as much to psychiatric discourse as to other forms of professional and non-professional discourse. Stenson (1993) identifies a number of forms of professional social work discourse. First, the citizen exchange form is negotiated and consists of talk amongst equals. Secondly, hierarchical discourse involves the service user adopting the position of story-teller providing information for scrutiny to the gaze of the public authorities. This is then translated into the official form of discourse which can be seen in reports and formal assessments. Thirdly a 'rhapsodic' form of discourse is described in which there may be recurrent motifs in the argument which are stitched together. Here themes of discourse run in a thematic progression from A>B>C>D. Although these themes might be tenuously related there is no continual proposition which runs through the discourse. Such thematic dispersal presents the reader with a series of gaps which are intertwined with each other creating what Foucault (1972) referred to as interplays of differences, distances, substitutions, and transformations. This can be seen in the following extract from a pre-sentence report on a black male youth which purports to find no 'rational' explanation for criminal behaviour.

He threw a drain grid through a shop window on each occasion and stole watches and items of clothing from displays. I gather that some of these goods were recovered. The defendant adds that they are items he neither wanted or needed and can offer no explanation for what he says are spontaneous acts of folly. (Denney 1992: 128)

Here it can be seen that themes are dispersed throughout and not organized in any progressive or deductive sequence. Specific mention of the drain grid serves to dramatize the offending act, while the recovery of the goods could lessen the effect of the offence. The offender did not need the goods and therefore the form of behaviour being described takes on a bizarre character. The last part of the sentence leaves room for the possibility that the subject of the report has understood the nature of his own actions, but is framed somewhat unconvincingly given what has previously been said about the subject of the report. Here possibilities are presented by the social worker which permit the activation of incompatible themes and the establishment of the same themes in different groupings within the sentence. A number of differing forms of discourse operate within social worker–service user and psychiatrist–patient relations. Rodger has also perceptively argued that there is no one single professional discourse within social work but a variety of negotiated forms of discourse which emerge from encounters between individual social workers, service users, and psychiatrists (Rodger 1991).

In other words a social worker may give one explanation of a service user's behaviour verbally, perhaps in interview, whilst feeling unable to express her- or himself as fully or possibly as critically in a formalized report or case conference at which a psychiatrist is present, where a medicalized form of discourse will dominate.

In its guidance to programmes on the question of mental health CCETSW is cognizant of such tensions. Although not expressing this in terms of competing forms of discourse, CCETSW acknowledges the point in terms of differing perspectives within mental health work.

One such tension faced by social work educators may be between advocating learning from and about models and perspectives adopted by those directly involved in working with mentally ill people other than social workers and advocating a predominantly 'social perspective' model. In fact good social work practice recognizes and works creatively with a range of approaches and models, against the background of social work values and perspectives, while accepting the tension between them (CCETSW 1994*b*: 10).

Implementing such a pluralistic form of practice is fraught with fundamental difficulties. The adoption of the medical classification of depression by social workers serves as a useful example. Distinctions between endogenous and reactive depression are frequently employed by social workers and probation officers in explaining the behaviour of service users. For reasons which need yet to be fully explored in the literature, reactive depression appears to be associated with offending behaviour in a way in which endogenous depression is not. Also the distinction between the two forms of depression as used by social workers is far from clear. Having a depressive label attached to a service user particularly on medical records can possibly affect future assessments by social workers, and even a service user's future job prospects. Thus the distinction between concepts which purport to have a technical and precise meaning and causality of differing conditions appears to vary from individual to individual and situation to situation. CCETSW claims that classifications of mental disorder can be jointly reached by social workers and psychiatrists and be precise, scientific, and relatively unproblematic. This proposition would seem to be at least questionable. What is more likely to emerge is complex combinations of self-evident truths, 'common sense', and psychiatric terminology. Yet, as Heidegger has argued, common sense is based upon an appeal to the 'self-evident nature of its own truths' (quoted in Worral 1990: 19).

Despite this, the use of quasi-technical language by social workers brings with it an authority which implies that professionals have shared meanings as to what constitutes concepts such as depression and schizophrenia. The usefulness of the work of such critics as Szasz and others is that it moves beyond a quasi-professional form of discourse, enabling mental health professionals to think about the possible implications of the (often imagined) specificity of such terms.

One of the dangers of the current emerging social work and social policy orthodoxies is an unquestioning acceptance of psychiatrically dominated discourse in that official definitions of an individual's condition are not as specific as the exactness of science suggests. It is to some extent an easy option for training organizations such as CCETSW to utilize scientific discourse in their search for certainty within the minefield of social work competence. Whilst CCETSW at least formally recognize the possible interrelationships between definable mental illnesses and wider structural factors such as racism and sexism, they fail even to acknowledge the overarching dominance of medical models of mental illness in their guidance to students. In order for the rights of mentally disordered persons to be respected, it is necessary that social workers fundamentally question meanings that are ascribed to the behaviour of individuals in ways which medical personnel are either unwilling or unable to do. Such an ability could be regarded as a core competency. One of the most helpful ways of regarding psychiatric discourse is not to eliminate it or reject it, but, as Oliver argues in the field of disability in which similar arguments apply, 'There is no such thing as the medical model of disability, there is instead, an individual model of disability of which medicalisation is one significant component' (Oliver 1996: 31).

The contradictory role of the social worker in mental health work

To some extent the role of the social worker in compulsory mental health detention has been created by trial and error, or, as Bean puts it, largely by accident (Bean 1986). This is reflected in the complexity of the role of social workers, particularly in the implementation of the 1983 Act. Prior has pointed to the development of four contradictions within the role of social workers under the 1983 Act which are not recognized in the official advice given to social workers wishing to specialize in mental health work.

- The Act indicates that the social work role contains a professional opinion and recommendation which requires a certain level of training and expertise in mental health work. According to Prior the legislation gives similar powers to the nearest relative, who has no training, and who is also expected to be objective about the patient.
- Whilst making an application for hospital admission the approved social worker is expected to consider less restrictive alternatives, which are possibly community based. Under the community care purchaser and provider approach the social worker is acting as purchaser and provider of services simultaneously.
- Social workers act on behalf of the patient whilst also acting to protect the public from unnecessary risk. Can the social worker be both a carer and a controller simultaneously?
- The final contradiction concerns the concentration of specialist training in one area undertaken by the approved social worker whilst in other areas of mental health work particularly in the area of community care training appears to have been comparatively neglected. Thus Prior is forced to ask whether training resources are being used appropriately given the relatively small amount of work carried out by the ASWs compared with other areas of mental health work (Prior 1992).

It would appear to be misguided for social work practitioners simply to follow the latest managerial imperative whether it be multidisciplinary work or CPA without asking fundamental questions. Four obvious questions appear to flow from the previous discussion which link social policy with social work practice.

1. How do the aims and objectives of current mental health policies provide specific benefits for mental health service users?

2. Can recent developments in mental health policy and practice be seen as justifying the economic imperatives of a particular form of ideology?

3. Do current policies reflect a genuine desire to break down stigmatizing labels and improve the quality of life for mental health service users in the community?

4. Is intense resource restriction within community care of the mentally ill always the most cost-effective approach in the long term?

The terrain of debates within the field of mental health reflects the policy positions which constantly re-emerge. The collectivists want continued expenditure on in-patient and outpatient care with a concomitant increase in taxation if necessary. Living a 'normal' life in the community is a basic substantive right of citizenship.

The new right whilst incorporating the concept of dangerousness and enforced detention for a proportion of patients saw uncontrolled expenditure on mental health as profligate and ultimately as driving increasing numbers of people into the under-class. Translated into practical policies it could be argued that when demand for mental health services outstripped supply the anti-collectivist solution was not continually to increase the supply of services, but to reduce the demand. Mental health services could not be rationed in quite the same way as other services for a number of reasons. Users of mental health services were seen as being potentially 'dangerous' not only to themselves but to others. They also posed a political danger in that particular cases, such as that of Ben Wilcox, gave the appearance that community care policies for mentally ill people were dangerous and at breaking point.

The political solution to this problem was to change the nature of the demand by dissipating it into the community. This was justified on the grounds of being a more cost-effective way of providing mental health services, whilst giving the appearance of offering all the advantages of normalization over long-term institutionalization.

Managerialism and the supremacy of the organization

We have seen in Part I of this book and in this chapter how good practice is being officially defined within terms created by the requirements of organizations, policy-makers, and managers. Pollitt (1993) has powerfully argued that managerialism has come to take an increasingly prominent part in the policies adopted by British anti-collectivist governments during the 1980s and 1990s. To privatize, or cut mental health services completely, is perceived as being dangerous and electorally problematic. 'The only remaining political option, therefore, is to improve the productivity of these services, so that there [*sic*] quality can be maintained or even increased while the total resources devoted to them is held down' (Pollitt 1993: 48).

Good management therefore becomes for Pollitt the 'acceptable face of right wing thinking'. This is particularly salient in the case of mental health where the concept of dangerousness has been so effectively used by the media to construct moral panics about mentally disordered people. Officially, as we have already seen, the requirements of the organization appear to take precedence over all other things. This is despite the fact that, as Pilgrim and Rogers have argued,

One can safely say that there is a general consensus about moving from a system of warehousing people in large Victorian asylums to 'care in the community'. However, over and above this global objective, there appear to be few agreed principles about the look of a post institutional world. (Pilgrim and Rogers 1993: 55)

Managerial practices have failed to create anything like coherence in their approach to mental health policy since the nineteenth century. Social workers to some extent have been caught in the ebb and flow of ideological debates and managerial whim. Both these tendencies can operate at different levels. Some local authorities have never accepted guardianship orders, for instance (Bean 1986), whilst all local authorities have been forced to respond to initiatives such as CPA.

Conclusion

There are two ways of viewing community care policies for mentally ill people depending on the ideological perspective which is adopted. It can be seen as a desperate, fragmented, confused, and under-resourced attempt to cope with mentally ill people. Alternatively it can be viewed as the inevitable result of attempting to combine a humanitarian concern for the mentally ill with a cost-effective market-led approach which has due regard to the rights of the taxpayer. This leaves the social worker to some extent in an ambiguous position. Evidence would seem to suggest that if properly resourced care in the community for the mentally ill can bring qualitative advantages over institutionalized care. Proper resourcing requires the allocation of resources to be diverted from other essential welfare budgets. The social worker therefore is always attempting to create qualitative improvements in a situation of constant and unrelenting budget restriction. An overemphasis on monolithic categorizations of competence can divert attention from this central contradiction which social workers face on a daily basis. The 1983 Mental Health Act with all its manifest weaknesses has provided the basis for a structure which addresses what has become a worryingly fluid role for the social worker. However, despite the emergence of an optimistic consensus surrounding the 1983 Mental Health Act, mental health practice has manifestly failed to recognize mental health service users as people of worth.

Rogers and Pilgrim in an important analysis of mental health policy in Britain have argued that policy-makers face three problems in the future. First, at the political level central government has failed to provide adequate supportive social policies to ensure citizenship for people with mental health problems. Secondly, at the level of service delivery there has been a resistance from clinical professionals who have conceptualized their work in terms of hospital-based practices. Thirdly, at a cultural level citizens, mental health professionals, and politicians have failed to break free from the discourse which dominated mental health over a century ago. 'Hospitals need to be left behind conceptually as well as physically by all parties as we enter the twenty first century' (Rogers and Pilgrim 1996: 202).

In order to improve practice and related policies, adequate resources must be targeted to maximize the efficiency of community care, whilst the prediction of dangerousness needs to be improved.

Exercise

Basing his work on an extensive reading of the literature on case management of the chronically mentally ill in the USA, Cnaan (1994) argues that case management has a number of drawbacks. These can be summarized as follows.

1. For service users to benefit, care must have no time limitations. This means that services will be expensive and grow exponentially in order to be effective.

2. Evidence suggests that care management is most effective for most difficult service users. Cost makes it necessary to reserve the best care for the most challenging service users. Less difficult service users are cared for by less well-qualified personnel.

3. Demographic factors play an important part in the way in which service users utilize care management. Age, 'race', and gender are related to service use.

4. Case management tends to be highly professionally directed.

5. Case management can overload case managers. This creates a difference between official expectations and reality.

6. Case management largely ignores the service users' relatives and friends.

7. Case managers spend considerable time on administrative tasks.

8. There is little continuity in care-giving.

9. Case management is often viewed as a way of providing basic services by less-qualified workers.

10. The use of para-professionals as case managers may further segment service delivery systems.

11. Case managers are sometimes lowest in the professional hierarchy.

12. It is not clear to whom case managers owe their allegiance, the service user or the agency.

13. Case management is not necessarily cost effective.

14. It is unclear what team work means in case management.

15. Case management is currently the most fashionable form of practice although its purposes are unclear to many professionals.

16. Case management cannot be a substitute for the necessary supporting infrastructure of services.

Which of the points mentioned by Cnaan do you think are applicable to the care programme approach currently being used in the UK?

Can any lessons be drawn from the American experience which might improve mental health services in the UK?

Case study

Karl has a long history of mental illness and at the age of 30 has been described by a psychiatrist as a 'long-term schizophrenic', having spent a number of spells as an in-patient in a psychiatric hospital throughout his twenties. With the help of a community mental health team Karl had been stabilized in the community. Karl left his council flat in a large city to live with his mother in a quieter rural setting. Disagreements soon broke out between Karl and his mother which resulted in him moving back to his own flat. On returning home he found that the flat had been burgled and considerable damage had been done. In addition he had large outstanding rental debts and was in danger of eviction.

What partnerships would be appropriate in this case between other professionals and family members in developing appropriate support for Karl?

What would be the basic requirements of a care plan which would be appropriate for Karl?

FURTHER READING

D. Crepaz-Keay, C. Binns, and E. Wilson (1997) examine the involvement of survivors of mental health services in the provision and evaluation of services in *Dancing with Angels* (London, CCETSW). R. Olsen (1984) (ed.), *Social Work and Mental Health: A Guide for the Approved Social Worker* (London, Tavistock). This provides a good account of the requirements of the 1983 Mental Health Act. D. Tilbury (1993), *Working with Mental Illness: A Community Based Approach* (London, Macmillan). Tilbury provides a clear explanation of community mental health practice. P. Bean and P. Mouser (1993), *Discharged from Psychiatric Hospitals* (London, Macmillan/MIND). D.o.H. (1993), *Code of Practice: Mental Health Act 1983* (London, HMSO) provides an essential framework for understanding the current arrangements for the care of people who are mentally ill. D. Tomlinson and J. Carrier (1996) (eds.), *Asylum in the Community* (London, Routledge) is an empirically based account of how the concept of asylum can be provided outside hospital. A. Rogers and D. Pilgrim (1996), *Mental Health Policy in Britain* (London, Longman) provide an impressive critical introduction to mental health policy and practice issues.

CHAPTER 14

Working with Offenders

- Historical developments in policy and practice
- Social work practice and prisons
- The victim's perspective
- The probation service: markets and effectiveness

Introduction

Crime is a central political issue which has often been used as an indicator of the moral state of the nation. Yet even to include a discussion of the criminal justice system in a book with social work in the title would for some appear to be controversial in the late 1990s. Its inclusion is justified for a number of reasons. First, developments in welfare work throughout the nineteenth and twentieth centuries have had influence on the course that social work practice has taken. Secondly, even though probation training has been removed from generic social work education in an effort to make probation work appear more punitive and more akin to police work, social workers are daily confronted with issues which relate to crime. This constitutes an important justification for the inclusion of social work in a discussion of penal policy. This chapter pays attention to the way in which social work in the criminal justice system has developed, and the way in which the treatment of offenders and crime has been constructed as a crisis.

Historical developments in policy and practice

Before 1775 prison was used fairly sparingly as a form of punishment, sentences generally being short and confined to those who had been found guilty of fraud, rioting, or manslaughter. Most usually for arson, murder, and highway robbery the punishment was death.

Nineteenth-century crime: policy and trends

In the nineteenth century penal policy treated adults and children alike. The reasoning underlying this was that the law existed to punish and not to reform. In 1814 within one day five children between the ages of 8 and 12 were charged with petty larceny (Morris and Giller 1987).

In 1816 the building of a national penitentiary was begun; it had a harsh regime, and this heralded a new austere period in British penal policy. At the Coldbath Fields House of Correction silence amongst the inmates was introduced during the 1830s along with the use of the treadmill and a basic diet. Transportation was finally abolished in 1853 and more specialist forms of imprisonment began to emerge. The convict service was established in 1850, which included specialist prisons for public works, a prison for juveniles, and a convict prison. By the mid-nineteenth century incarceration had become the major sanction for adult offenders.

In 1847 the Juvenile Offenders Act allowed magistrates to hear cases of petty larceny. In 1855 the Criminal Justice Act extended these powers to adults who were charged with similar offences. The Prisons Act of 1877 transferred the power of judges to the Home Office and created the Prison Commission. The Gladstone Report of 1895 proposed that more attention should be paid to the moral responsibility of prisons, and placed reform before deterrence. The resulting legislation of 1898 introduced a new system of classification which separated younger from older prisoners.

A new era in penal policy

The period between the Gladstone Report and the beginning of the First World War marked an increase in the range of sanctions available to the courts. These included probation in 1907, borstal training, and preventive detention. Also at this time juvenile courts were introduced which had jurisdiction over children under the age of 16. Preventive institutions were also created which were less vigorous than the borstal system. The development of the concept of alternatives to prison and diversion from prison for certain offenders began to emerge, although by the twentieth century the prison stood at the centre of the penal system (Garland 1985).

Post-Second World War
developments in criminal justice

Following the Second World War the 1948 Criminal Justice Act was introduced by the Labour government, at the point at which the welfare state was being constructed. This

Act appeared to represent a drift into further law and order, with the introduction of punitive detention centres which were designed to create a 'disciplined' environment for the young offender. Also the notion of abolishing capital punishment was abandoned in 1948, whilst the minimum age for imprisonment was reduced from 16 to 15 (Brake and Hale 1992, Gilroy and Sim 1985). Although similar ideas were echoed in the 'short sharp shock' which heralded the 1982 Criminal Justice Act the measures advocated in 1948 illustrate the point that authoritarian forms of state intervention cannot exclusively be associated with Conservative governments.

In the years following the Second World War the numbers being imprisoned increased rapidly. Between 1955 and 1964, after levelling off in the beginning of the 1950s, the prison population doubled (Maguire 1994). The Criminal Justice Act of 1961 gave the power to juvenile courts to impose prison sentences on adolescents without remitting to the Crown Court (Pitts 1988). This presented a major increase in the power of magistrates (Farrington 1984). The Criminal Justice Act of 1967 brought about the introduction of parole at a time when the size of the prison population was rapidly increasing. The same piece of legislation introduced the suspended sentence which by the 1970s was the second most used sentence for adult males in the Crown Court. The Act also formalized the status of probation committees and probation areas. The 1967 Act also introduced provisions for juries to convict by a majority rather than a unanimous verdict, and following the Mountbatten and Radzinowicz Committees tightened up prison conditions for long-term prisoners.

The Kilbrandon Committee (1964), which had been set up to examine juvenile crime in 1964, made a distinction between juvenile offenders and those in need of care and protection. The Committee recommended that the needs of the child should be assessed in the light of the fullest possible information.

The 1969 Children and Young Persons Act aimed to substitute non-criminal proceedings in place of criminal procedures for children aged between 10 and 14, whilst encouraging a more liberal use of care proceedings and voluntary agreements between parents and social workers. It was believed that this would enable forms of treatment to be devised without resorting to the courts. The Act also included mandatory consultation by police with social services before the prosecution of 14–17-year-olds, and the introduction of care orders which in some cases gave power to vary the disposition of the courts. The courts were also able to intervene if it was shown that the child's home circumstances were unsatisfactory (Morris and Giller 1987).

Some critics of the Act argued that it failed to offer children the protection of the law, and rendered them vulnerable to excessive intervention and incarceration which was justified as being a form of 'treatment'. The Children and Young Persons Act was also a compromise and to some extent built upon a contradiction in that it promoted both diversion from and the provision of welfare in courts. Further, it perpetuated these competing policy positions in the way in which juvenile offending was dealt with by the criminal justice system. The formality of adjudication in the courtroom was retained whilst there was an increased emphasis on social welfare (Gelsthorpe and Morris 1994:

965). In 1970 the incoming Conservative government made it clear that they had no intention of implementing it.

The 1972 Criminal Justice Act, later amended by the Powers of Criminal Courts Act 1973, empowered probation committees to provided day training centres, probation hostels, and other establishments for the rehabilitation of offenders. The Act also in an attempt to discourage custodial sentencing made it necessary for the courts to consider a social inquiry report before imposing a custodial sentence on any individual under the age of 21 and on those over 21 who had not served a period of imprisonment. The Act also saw the introduction of community service orders which allowed offenders to undertake unpaid work for up to 240 hours. Community service was to be supervised and organized by the probation service. Day training centres were introduced where offenders were required to attend for up to 60 days for non-residential training.[1]

The 1977 Criminal Law Act reduced the right of defence lawyers to challenge jurors, and removed the right of jury trial for a number of offences. Under the same Act a coroner no longer necessarily had to have a jury when investigating a sudden or violent death (Brake and Hale 1992).

Following a number of high-profile disturbances in prison during the 1970s, the prisoners' rights movement developed, in conjunction with a further rise in prison numbers and the threat of industrial action by prison officers. In 1979 the Committee of Inquiry into the United Kingdom prison services under the chairmanship of Lord Justice May reported (the May Report). The May Committee introduced the notion of positive custody which was meant to create a prison environment in which prisoners could be responsive to the demands that would be made upon them in the wider society. Such a wide-ranging approach did not gather widespread support, and the thrust of the campaign within prisons has been for improved basic conditions and rights (Newburn 1995).

With regard to juvenile justice Gelsthorpe and Morris argue that two opposing trends can be seen throughout the 1970s. There was an increase in punitive dispositions and custodial disposals in particular. This was combined with an increased use of diversion. Paradoxically there was also a decline in the use of welfare-oriented disposals (Gelsthorpe and Morris 1994).

Towards a law and order society

It was with the election of the most anti-collectivist government since the war in 1979 that the changing authoritarian nature of the state appeared to be expressed through penal policy.

---

[1] In Scotland the Social Work (Scotland) Act of 1968 introduced welfare tribunals staffed by lay people. Within this system children's hearings are concerned only with disposition (Gelsthorpe and Morris 1994).

We are now in the middle of a deep and decisive moment towards a more disciplinary, authoritarian society. This shift has been in progress since the 1960s; but it has gathered pace through the 1970s and is heading, given the spate of disciplinary legislation now on the parliamentary agenda, towards some sort of interim climax. (Hall 1979: 3)

Popular modes of media communication had constructed a crisis the only remedy for which was a populist demand for more law and order.

In a society dominated by authoritarian populism even to raise the question of welfare rights and civil liberties was described by Hall as tantamount to declaring oneself a subversive (Hall 1979). The 1980 White Paper 'Young Offenders' set out the proposals which were later to constitute the 1982 Criminal Justice Act. This Act reflected the call from the then Home Secretary William Whitelaw for the 'short sharp shock'. Detention centres were to have more vigorously disciplined regimes with minimum sentences being shortened to twenty-one days and maximum lengths to four months. Imprisonment for under-21s was abolished, and former borstals became youth custody centres. The length of the youth custody order was fixed by the sentencing court although there was the possibility of remission on parole. The minimum youth custody sentence was four months and one day, although magistrates and juvenile courts could impose sentences between the minimum and six months. Although the policy marked an intention to make sentences shorter it marked a break with the short-lived welfare model seen in the 1969 Children and Young Persons Act.

The 1988 Criminal Justice Act included a new sentence for those over the age of 15 in a young offender institution and separate detention centres ceased to exist. These were now amalgamated with youth custody centres to become young offender institutions. Courts were given the right to decide the length of sentence although the location of the institution in which the sentence was to be served was determined by the Home Office.

The 1991 Criminal Justice Act represents what Cavadino and Dignan call 'punitive bifurcation'. This twin-track strategy represented a situation in which sentencers although losing a little discretion over their sentencing practices, could increase sentences for violent and dangerous offenders on one hand, while sentencing more property offenders to non-custodial sentences. Those guilty of the most serious offences should go to prison for 'a long time'. All offenders, the Act states, should be punished for the 'gravity of their offences'. Before imposing a custodial sentence, the courts should be satisfied that the seriousness of the offence warrants custody. Punishment should whenever appropriate be in the community with the possibility of probation being combined with other penalties like community service through the 'combination order' (Home Office 1990a).

The stated aims of the Act also reflected a more centralized role for the probation service. The new approach was ostensibly designed to create a more coherent framework for sentencing offenders. Probation was to be combined with other forms of disposal and the courts should have powers to make curfew orders, possibly reinforced by electronic monitoring. Community penalties should be easier to enforce, with three

clear stages of enforcement consisting of warning, administrative action by the probation officer, and recall to court.

Prisoners, it was argued, should spend at least half of their sentence in prison, which
replaced the previous position whereby prisoners were expected to serve at least one-
third of their sentence for sentences under one year. The White Paper called for more
scrutiny of parole applications made by long-term prisoners convicted of further
imprisonable offences. The White Paper also recommended that the courts may order
that for any new offence the outstanding period of the prison term be served in addition
to any new sentence (Home Office 1990*b*).

Against a climate of successive moral panics and constructions of crises within the
criminal justice system especially about juvenile offending crime, there was a predictably punitive reaction to some of the amendments and more progressive (i.e. more
equitable) elements of the otherwise punitive Criminal Justice Act 1991. The main
amendments to this Act have been those concerned with sentences now taking fuller
account of all associated offences and previous behaviour, and the principles under-
pinning the unit fine system being compromised. If one adds to that the government's
policy statements and proposals about toughening up prison regimes, introducing
secure training centres for so-called persistent juvenile offenders, the increased use of
custodial remands, and an ever increasing adult prison population, the trend towards a
greater authoritarianism is apparent.

The 1993 Criminal Justice Act reversed some of the most important measures contained in the 1991 Criminal Justice Act. The 1993 Act enabled sentencers to take into
account any previous offences when deciding the seriousness of the offence. The 1993
Act also removed the system of unit fines, replacing it with what was described as a more
flexible system in which seriousness and financial circumstances are taken into consideration.

The 1994 Criminal Justice and Public Order Act created secure accommodation for
12–14-year-olds, whilst increasing the grounds for refusing bail. The Act also allowed
inferences to be drawn from the use of the right of silence, and the introduction of a new
offence of aggravated trespass (Newburn 1995). The Act also allows curfew order
provision to be introduced on an area-by-area basis (Vass 1996).

The 1994 Police and Magistrates Courts Act is widely regarded as further centralizing
the control of the Home Office over the police, enabling the Home Secretary to set objectives for policing and requiring police authorities to perform targets for measuring
the achievement of police authority functions. The set of objectives and targets will be
constructed annually by the Home Secretary. The Act also creates centrally devised
forms of financial control over police budgets.

Social work practice and prisons

Although recently challenged by the Home Office as cost ineffective, social work is conducted in prison establishments through the probation service. Probation officers in prisons currently undertake a variety of tasks linked to resettlement of offenders, problems arising whilst sentences are being served, liaising with families, and preparation of reports for the parole board and other bodies.

The justification for increasing the use of prison and increasing the prison population to unprecedented levels is that 'prison works'. In examining the evidence which underlies this proposition, including Home Office research over some twenty years, Vass finds such an assertion to be 'At best inconclusive and, at worst, riddled with methodological flaws' (Vass 1996: 159).

The victim's perspective

Social workers frequently work not only with the perpetrators but also with the victims of crime. The rise of victims' interests is a reflection of the broadening function of the criminal justice system as a whole. A number of legislative and administrative changes dating from 1970 have added more restorative justice services to the existing retributive and rehabilitative criminal justice functions. We have seen earlier in this chapter that these include restitution schemes, mediation, and reparation schemes particularly in the 1980s, and an increased emphasis on compensation payments and victims' interests. The latter has expressed itself for example through victim surveys (Hough and Mayhew 1983), the continued expansion of victim support schemes, and the publication of the Victims' Charter (Home Office 1990c).

The 'Victims' Charter', subtitled 'A Statement of Rights for Victims', contains a guide to good practice and not legally enforceable rights. It emphasizes the importance of keeping victims informed of due process of law, sentencing, and compensation possibilities. Its very existence is symbolic of the rise in interest about victims' needs. Resource implications about, for example, rights to a certain level of service or information are not addressed. A victim's right to home visits by a victim support worker will cost more than the victim travelling to a local centre for help and advice. Accounts of victims having no reserved place in the court and in some cases being forced to queue with other members of the public for a seat in the public gallery are not uncommon. Another approach that has been piloted is to incorporate the victim's view directly in probation officers' pre-sentence reports, although the purpose of this approach has not always been clear. Another recent measure taken by the government regarding the introduction of impact statements is meant to ensure that the courts are aware of the effects of particular crimes on victims. This forms the basis for the construction of a new victims' charter. In addition every victim should be told by the police if the offender is caught, cautioned, or charged and any other significant development in the case. The probation service will also tell a victim when someone sentenced to life imprisonment or a serious sexual or violent crime is to be released (Travis 1996).

Any charter for victims will be judged on the degree to which it is implemented, not on its intentions however worthy they might be. The extent to which police, court, and probation practices have changed, or should change, in relation to victims' needs is also the subject of continued debate. The needs of victims have been identified and minimum standards of service for victims are recommended in the Victims' Charter, but in most cases legally enforceable rights across the board remain elusive. Zedner's (1994) claim that the place of victims in the criminal justice system has been transformed from 'forgotten actor' to 'key player' is somewhat exaggerated, although victims appear to be increasingly valued members of the cast.

The probation service: markets and effectiveness

The case for more punishment and the increasing importance of the market can be seen from a number of perspectives but by far the most often used justification for more punishment is the ineffectiveness of welfare in dealing with criminals. The probation service and other state-financed welfare organizations are presented by the new right as hopelessly ineffective, wasteful, and useless. The probation service, like other social work services, has been subjected to the idea of market testing in the belief that the market can regulate and create efficiencies which the state-run and -delivered services cannot deliver. Commercial involvement in criminal justice services can, so it is thought, create more responsive, efficient, and economic service.

The case for more authoritarianism and punishment is fuelled by fears of the emergence of a new rabble, and a moral breakdown. Murray identifies the increase in crime, along with illegitimacy and the economic inactivity of working-age men, as being symptomatic of the emergence of a new underclass. Murray claims that violent crime has increased by 40 per cent between 1987 and 1992. The message from the new right is clear—helping criminals does not appear to stop them so why help them more? The first problem centres on the meaning of effectiveness. The current policy trend towards oversimplification, social control, and law enforcement, and the current desire of politicians to define probation as a law enforcement agency, has led them to regard effectiveness simply as the relationship of a particular approach to the reduction of crime as measured by conviction or reconviction rates. There are numerous problems in using what would appear to be an obvious yardstick. Populations are regionally different in respect to age structures, criminal histories, and offending patterns. Reoffending may also measure the effectiveness of policing and policing strategies in particular areas. A comparative appraisal of the different form of intervention and their effectiveness in preventing reoffending is further complicated by the fact that few studies deal with offending histories. Some have argued that a defendant's criminal history and current living situation outweigh the type or length of any intervention determining the likelihood of reconviction. With regard to juvenile crime the Home Office has identified a number of processes as influencing desistance from crime; they are:

- dissociation from offenders;
- forming stable relationships and having children;
- acquiring a sense of direction. This is created mainly through taking responsibility, forging relationships, and establishing a more structured way of life;
- understanding the consequences of crime (Home Office 1995).

In putting the family at the centre of the process of enabling young people to desist from crime the idea of family group conferences, originating in New Zealand, would, the Home Office argued, possibly be effective. FGCs are in practice linked to the youth court attended by the young offender, members of the family, the victim, an advocate for the young offender, a police officer, and a social worker. Decisions in the form of action plans are ratified by the youth courts. Sanctions available include reparation, formal apologies, community work, and undertakings to attend school and not associate with co-offenders. Thus for the Home Office two of the most significant traits associated with juvenile offending, truancy and association with criminal peers, are built into the response to offending whilst a central part is played by the family, the most powerful influence on offending. Petersilia and Turner (1992) in the United States have described most intensive probation supervision training as involving combinations of weekly contacts with the probation service, unscheduled drug testing, strict enforcement of community service, and the attachment of severe conditions to probation orders. The failure of intensive probation to create any positive results in the UK in the 1970s has not discouraged the government at various points from reactivating the plan (Vass 1996). Von Hirsh has argued that intensive probation can create substantial deprivation depending on the type and level of community sanction. In order for a community sanction to have any level of acceptability it should be consistent with the dignity of the offender (Von Hirsh 1990). Another approach has been taken by theorists who advocate an evidence-based approach to devising practice with offenders. In her review of appropriate methods for developing 'effective' probation practice MacDonald argues that there are two sorts of research which probation officers should utilize:

1. the research which helps us to understand why people offend;
2. the research which concerns strategies that are most effective in reducing offending.

Such attention to empirical evidence would according to MacDonald indicate to policy-makers that the recently revived 'short sharp shock' is not effective, and that young people concerned tend to enjoy it (MacDonald 1994).

Raynor to some extent supports this view, arguing that examination of a large number of studies indicates that the most promising directions for the probation service appear to be located within a number of clearly defined areas. First, programmes should be targeted and designed for offenders who are at high risk. The focus should be on characteristics and circumstances which have contributed to their offending, not simply on offending behaviour. Programmes should be highly structured in order to be effective. Expectations must be explicit in order that people understand exactly what is expected of them. Effective programmes require committed and effective management and appropriately trained staff (Raynor 1996).

Conclusion

Debates within criminology have now challenged official versions of crime, and could inform the probation service on its future role. If considered thought is to be given to how social work can be related to crime reduction, policy-makers must move beyond the calls for tougher punishment towards a more evidence-based approach to working effectively with offenders. Without some grasp of the relevant theory and empirical research one can only fall back on the oversimplistic 'commonsense' explanations and crude prescription (Nellis 1996). Probation officers and those who work with offenders should have the ability to challenge dominant calls for more punishment with the need for structured intervention which directly challenges offending behaviour.

Exercise

Practice and perspectives in criminal justice

Probation practice has been linked to various perspectives which have inflenced the development of penal policy since the war. King (1981) and Davies, Croall, and Tyrer (1995) have summarized a number of perspectives which have occurred and sometimes recurred within the criminal justice system:

- the due process model;
- control theories of crime;
- the rehabilitative model;
- the bureaucratic efficiency model;
- the denunciation and degradation model;
- the power model.

Due process

Due process encompasses the idea that the defendant has rights including the presumption of innocence, the right to a fair and impartial trial hearing, equality before the law. Probation practice and social work practice in the courts constitute a fundamental part of due process.

Control theories of crime

Control theories of crime direct attention towards the notions of right and wrong. From this perspective parental supervision and discipline may also be linked to criminality. The logical form of work which results from this approach is casework, which as we have seen in relation to mental health has the power to define reality within the treatment process. The control approach is also reflected in the idea that the purpose of the criminal justice system is essentially to reduce and prevent crime. Police and prosecution services have supremacy within the system as crime fighters. Recent developments in policy have emphasized this approach. Control theories have had considerable influence on policy-making within the area of probation. The implementation of electronic surveillance and curfews as methods of punishing offenders in the community were both measures included in the 1991 Criminal Justice Act.

The rehabilitation model

This model effectively replaced the treatment model and gained dominance during the 1960s and 1970s. It emphasizes the importance of taking into consideration social factors which impinge on crime, the diversion of young offenders from the courts, the importance of counselling, and the involvement of social workers and probation officers at the sentencing stage. Punishment and direct control here take on a lower profile. Such an approach was reflected in the Children and Young Persons Act of 1969. The concept of rehabilitation was to be relatively short-lived, losing ground in the 1980s and 1990s to pragmatism and the reassertion of control.

Bureaucratic efficiency

Here the importance of speed and efficiency, the independence of the criminal justice system from politics, the minimization of expense and conflict are emphasized. The development of pragmatism dominated the criminal justice system for two decades following the collapse of the rehabilitative model, and became the major influence on the development of penal policy.

Denunciation and degradation

This is an elaboration on social control. Public shaming serves the important function of reinforcing dominant social values. It is exemplified most clearly by Pitts when in his discussion he invokes the prescription of the ex-Chief Constable of Greater Manchester, James Anderton, who recommended penal work camps where

Through hard labour and unrelenting discipline they [young offenders] should be made to sweat as they have never sweated before and remain until violence has been vanquished by penitent humiliation and unqualified repentance. (Pitts 1988: 43).

The 'power model'

This approach emphasizes the alienation of the defendant, the social class differences between those who are judging and those who are being judged, and incorporates a variety of Marxist forms of critique. Such accounts embrace the idea that definitions of crime are socially constructed by agencies responsible for crime control, the police, and the courts, who are ultimately the primary definers of crime.

The purpose of this exercise (Table 14.1) is to examine the relationships between the values which underlie policy and the way in which both values and policy relate to possible forms of social work practice with offenders. Identify the core practice implications, values, and policies which characterize each model.

Table 14.1. **Exercise**

	Due process	Control	Bureaucratic efficiency	Denunciation, degradation	Power model
Practice					
Values					
Policy					

Case study

Karl, aged 21, lives alone in a flat on a large council estate in London. He performed poorly at school but has been employed from the age of 17 in a variety of jobs including supermarket work and car cleaning for short periods. His parents separated when he was very young and he has few social contacts. Most of his offending has been petty and has been associated with theft from shops. He is prone to depression, and most of his offending appears to have been associated with anger. He has been subjected to a probation order which was completed without breach, and community service. He has reoffended and faces the possibility of a short prison sentence if convicted.

What possible forms of intervention might be effective for Karl?

How would we measure the effectiveness of intervention?

Which model of intervention would be most helpful to Karl?

FURTHER READING

M. Davies, H. Croall, and J. Tyrer (1995), *Criminal Justice: An introduction to the Criminal Justice System in England and Wales* (London, Longman) provides a clear basic descriptive account of the criminal justice system in England and Wales. M. Maguire, R. Morgan, and R. Reiner (1994) (eds.), *The Oxford Handbook of Criminology* (Oxford, Clarendon) provides a weighty and substantial account of theoretical debates, written by leaders in the particular specialism discussed. The book examines crime and causation, crime control and criminal justice, and social dimensions of crime and justice. M. Cavadino and J. Dignan (1992), *The Penal System* (London, Sage) provides a well-written and much used account of many of the issues raised in this chapter. They direct particular attention to the notion of crisis and criminal justice. T. Newburn (1995) *Crime and Criminal Justice Policy* (London, Longman) also provides a clear and concise account. T. May and A. Vass (1996) (eds.), *Working with Offenders* (London, Sage) provides recent debates within the probation field.

PART III

Markets: Welfare and Practice

CHAPTER 15

Competition and Community Care

- The emergence of community care
- Aims of community care

Introduction

The origin of the term 'community care' in the UK can be traced to 1930 when it was used to describe provision for the 'mentally handicapped' to live outside hospitals whenever possible. The term 'case management' was first used in the USA to identify potential service users in the community (Payne 1995). Weil (1985) moved the concept from client identification towards individual assessment and diagnosis which more directly linked clients to service implementation, advocacy, and evaluation. The model adopted by the Department of Health in 1990 formalized the notion of care management to include the determination of need through assessment, care planning, implementing, monitoring, and reviewing. Thus case management was defined in 1985 as 'A set of logical steps and a process of interaction within a service network which assure that a client receives needed services in a supportive, effective, efficient and cost effective manner' (Weil 1985: 2).

Service brokerage, a notion which has gained influence in the development of policy and practice in the UK following the NHS and Community Care Act, originated in the independent living movement of Canada. The essence of brokerage can be described as having three basic components:

- Service brokers are independent of all agencies who provide services.
- The broker helps clients in deciding what support they need.
- Brokers are accountable to service users (adapted from Sharkey 1995).

The emergence of community care

The transformation of case management into care management within the British context occurred when care management was adopted by the Department of Health in 1989. Payne describes care management in terms of an activity which links community social work, social care planning, and counselling. The notion of care management as used by the Department of Health in 1990 emphasizes the importance of using available resources cost effectively and maintaining the independence of people by enabling them to live in the community, thus minimizing the effects of disability and illness. The term also now officially embodies the respectful treatment of users, equal opportunities, the promotion of individual choice, self-determination, and partnership between users, carers, service providers, and organizations representing them. Payne comments that this reflects the American interpersonal focus of case management, the production of the welfare approach developed by PSSRU, and also the advocacy and user participation approach deriving from care in the community projects (Payne 1995).

Although the genesis of the terms 'care management' and 'case management' as distinct concepts is important, Huxley has argued that case management has a long-established history of use and evaluatory research whereas the notion of care management is less well defined (Huxley 1993). It can be argued that the term 'care' has been adopted as a euphemism for 'case' in order to avoid the offence which can be given by describing people as 'cases'.

The official aims of care in the community following the 1990 NHS and Community Care Act can be summarized as follows:

- providing services to enable people to live in their own homes whenever possible;
- making service providers support for carers;
- providing proper assessment of needs and good care management with individual care plans;
- promoting the development of a flourishing independent sector;
- making providers of services more accountable;
- securing better value for money by introducing a funding structure based upon an internal market (adapted from D.o.H. 1989c).

The stated aim of this policy was to create a system which would lead to a needs-led, high-quality, co-ordinated community care service, providing choice for the service user. The mechanism for creating this was the internal market, operating within a mixed economy of welfare, in which local authorities would purchase service from a variety of competing service providers, some of whom were located within the state sector while others were voluntary, and most importantly the introduction of private service providers.

In 1992 central government imposed a rule which effectively meant that 85 per cent

Table 15.1. The relationship between policy and practice in community care

Policy		Practice
Providing services to enable people to live in their own homes whenever possible.	C A R E I N	Individual service planning (ISP) an integral part of service. Concentrate on assessment–screening–selection–monitoring–review–reassessment–case closure (Challis and Davies 1986).
To enable service providers to support carers.	T H E	Take account of preferences of carers and users.
To provide proper assessment of needs and good care management with individual care plans.		Allocate responsibility assessment for service plans. Care manager's role.
To promote the development of a flourishing independent sector.	C O M M	Collaboration skills. Information skills.
To make providers of services more accountable.	U N	Costing and budgetary skills.
To secure better value for money by introducing a funding structure based upon an internal market.	I T Y	Market-making skills. Networking skills.

Source: Adapted from D.o.H. (1989a, 1989c).

of new money allocated to community care had to be spent on private and voluntary organizations. The idea behind this policy was to expand the independent sector. Table 15.1 shows how both policy and practice are related to community care.

Conclusion

It can be seen that care management, with its emphasis upon individual, needs-led service planning, constitutes the basis for current practice. New skills, including market-making, costing, information skills, and collaboration skills, were also required to be developed. The development of community care was also dependent on the creation of a healthy internal market. Some commentators argue that community care planning had the potential for developing an opportunity for revitalizing the joint planning processes between health and social services. Moreover, the clarification of the planning role could enable health and local authorities to define their specific areas of mutual concern. The plans also offer the potential for establishing joint planning and information systems (Hudson 1992). The opportunity for more comprehensive planning and real consultation with users offered the hope of more economical and responsive forms of community care (Nocon 1994). An examination of the emerging reality of the policy in practice raises fundamental questions as to whether it is possible for this approach to live up to the great expectations of its advocates.

Exercise

Compare the following case before and after the implementation of the NHS and Community Care Act.

Before the community care legislation

Following a routine operation for a hip replacement the orthopaedic surgeon recommended that Mrs C, a widow who lived alone, be discharged to a residential home due to her immobility and confusion. Mrs C had only one daughter who lived some three hours' drive away and was unable to offer support to her mother. The daughter and hospital social worker spoke to the consultant in the hospital, who advised that residential care was the best option given that Mrs C was 82 years old, and that the possibility of her making a full recovery to any degree of acceptable independence was remote. An assessment by an occupational therapist was not thought necessary given the circumstances.

After the NHS and Community Care Act

Mrs C was operated on for a routine hip replacement and her case was discussed at a multi-disciplinary meeting. Occupational therapists, physiotherapists, doctors, and care managers were present. The consultant, having regard to Mrs C's physical state and confusion, recommended residential care on a long-term basis, given that Mrs C was 82 years old and her chance of making a full recovery to any degree of acceptable independence was remote. The care manager questioned this recommendation and requested a number of assessments including occupational therapy and a psychiatric report. Mrs C's daughter felt that her mother would prefer to go back to her own home with her neighbours and friends. As Mrs C recovered from the operation she became less confused. With home care, and the support of her friends, neighbours, and occasional visits from her daughter, she was able to live back in the community.

1. The different outcome may have been brought about by a number of influences; what are they?
2. In what respects did changes in community care policy affect the outcome for Mrs C?
3. Construct an appropriate package of care which would have assisted Mrs C and her carers.

FURTHER READING

Malcolm Payne (1995) provides a good introduction to community care and care management in *Social Work and Community Care* (London, Macmillan). P. Sharkey (1995) examines the emergence of community care in less detail; he gives some helpful case examples whilst paying particular attention to anti-discriminatory issues in *Introducing Community Care* (London, Collins). R. Means and R. Smith (1994) offer a scholarly account of the research into the development of community care policy and early indications as to its effectiveness in *Community Care: Policy and Practice* (London, Macmillan).

CHAPTER 16

The Impact of
Community Care in Practice

- Emergent models of practice
- Some positive indicators
- Some criticisms of the policy in practice
- The creation of market conditions
- Networks
- Collaborative planning and implementation
- Carers
- The voluntary sector and community care
- Assessing strengths and weaknesses

Introduction

Many of the chapters in this book have shown that the post-war welfare state has not been free from criticism, most notably from those whom it was ostensibly designed to assist (Oliver 1996). By the mid-1970s and following the election of the first Thatcher government a new conventional wisdom was developing which sought to demonstrate the need for a review of the approach to the delivery of state-controlled welfare policies. It can be argued that the solution which was offered by the Conservative government in the shape of internal markets represented a radical departure from the ideas enshrined in the Beveridge Report. Others have sought to demonstrate that such claims are exaggerated. This chapter examines the impact of the community care policy on care managers, social workers, and people who use the personal social services.

There are a number of preliminary comments which need to be made. First, judgements of current research in this area must be interpreted with considerable care, given the relative recency with which the welfare reforms have been implemented. Many of the research projects now published were conducted in the early days of policy implementation and do not reflect the current reality in practice. Moreover, they are often local studies which lack randomized controls and have been severely criticized from methodological standpoints.

Secondly, increasing financial stringency in public spending and local government, and the resulting organizational uncertainty may well have affected the implementation process. Thirdly, given the complexity of the new arrangements in differing geographical locations, it would seem difficult to draw any general conclusions from examinations of the policy in action in any particular geographical areas at this stage. Fourthly, there is a problem of defining what constitutes an outcome in relation to community care policy.

Outcome can be understood in terms of the 'Impact, effect or consequence of a service or a policy' (Nocon and Qureshi 1996: 7). Outcome also implies the need for more specific measurement which 'Must involve either a change in state, or the prevention of a deleterious change which could have happened without the services' (Nocon and Qureshi 1996: 11). Outcomes must also reflect definitions of appropriate community care outcomes as defined by users and carers.

Emergent models of practice

There is little doubt that the implementation of community care will require social workers to develop new skills, whilst a new professional group—the care managers—has emerged. Collaboration skills are required by those who work within the community care system. Collaborative tension is described well by Hughes who argues that:

Much of the official literature has defined an administrative model of community care which implicitly limits the role of practitioners to assessing need and arranging services provided by other people. The role of the care manager in particular is seen as essentially technical and administrative, managing the interface between user choice and resource availability. The care manager's role *vis-à-vis* the user within this model is one of ensuring provision. While the care manager will need to use professional skills to assist the user to articulate preferences and negotiate with providers to secure the best fit to meet need and demand, the care manager has not been predefined as a potential service provider herself. (Hughes 1995: 105)

Hughes goes on to argue that such a limited technocratic role restricts the role of the social worker and in the context of working with older people represents ageist attitudes (Hughes 1995). This restriction and diminution of role can lead practitioners towards a sense of being confused, deskilled, and demoralized. At the same time case managers have reported being isolated with little opportunity for peer group cooperation.

Government thinking on the role of the care manager has been less than clear. Research would suggest that to some extent the social workers' fear of complete deskilling as care management emerged could have been exaggerated. Although the work of the care manager is not purely mechanistic, a number of trends have appeared which do point to a changed role. Care managers tend to spend more time with heavily dependent service users, and there is less time available for care managers to counsel service users. Tasks overall have tended to become practical, although care packages can also be extremely complex. The administrative tasks required to create a care package combined with the co-ordination of the various parts of the package have become far more prominent in care management than was the case in social work. In many areas generic teams of social workers based in geographical locales have been replaced by a diversity of professional multidisciplinary teams. The generic term 'care manager' is also applied to those without a social work qualification, which has made the status of care management an issue with some social workers attempting to hold on to the title 'social worker'. The work of team leaders is also focusing far more upon budgets than on practice issues (Lewis and Glennerster 1996).

The required skills for care management include:

- the provision of adequate care to meet basic needs where individuals are unable to do so for themselves;
- the offering of opportunities to participate in life-enhancing activities, pursuits, and occupations in a way that recognizes clients as having rights to an enjoyable and fulfilling life;
- the teaching of skills which lead to greater independence and control over the living environment (Seed and Kaye 1994);
- the development of basic rights to service which include control over choice of food and clothing, safety in all aspects of life, and good medical treatment. People should be enabled to make new social contacts and have control over their own budgets.

Quality of life is inextricably linked to community involvement and the development of social relations. Needs-led assessments, according to Seed and Kaye, mark a move from a concentration on such concepts as suitability and readiness to one on developing opportunities. All packages of care are meant in theory to be arrived at through agreement, resulting in the client having an enhanced quality of life.

If the process of assessment is also to include an element of costing, social workers must have more clearly defined areas of knowledge relating to specific medical and disabling conditions, community facilities, and individual and community networks. The development of a rights approach to social work, more negotiating skills in the development of care packaging, and a greater appreciation of the competing interests that develop when attempting to construct individually tailored care packages will also be required from the social worker.

Cambridge has noted a number of diverse forms of emergent practice which have followed the implementation of the 1990 NHS and Community Care Act including:

- peripatetic case management involving senior local authority social work staff, some of whom have health authority backgrounds;
- multidisciplinary case management involving joint health and social services teams. Here case managers either retain or separate line management to a joint management committee. Team members have their own caseloads with specialist inputs;
- multidisciplinary teams solely within the health service, with accountability to the health authority;
- quasi-brokerage case management using individualized funding arrangements and some budget control by users;
- semi-independent case management outside the public sector with responsibility for case management held by voluntary interagency support and care staff (Cambridge 1992).

Differing authorities have moved at different rates in creating the purchaser/provider split. The enthusiasm with which community care arrangements have been embraced in different areas also makes overall assessments of the impact of the policy complex. Some authorities took a reactive approach to the changes, implementing the policy by instigating an assessment process and community care plan. In other areas policy did not develop until senior managers were convinced that the purchaser/provider split would benefit users. Other more enthusiastic authorities moved swiftly, seeing the legislation as another step to privatization which was both inevitable and welcome (Lewis and Glennerster, 1996).

Given all these qualifications a number of common threads emerge from the published studies which need to be considered when examining the implications for practice. Some of the studies which indicate positive benefits for service users also indicate a number of common problematic practice ramifications.

Some positive indicators

Whilst there was a good deal of scepticism prevalent in the years leading up to the implementation of community care policies, there were some hopes for the future expressed. In the UK the work of Challis and Davies, particularly their evaluation of community care projects in Thanet, greatly influenced policy-makers at the Department of Health in the late 1980s.

Challis and Davies (1986) examined almost 100 frail elderly people in the community who had reached the stage at which residential accommodation was becoming a likely possibility. Experienced social workers were given reduced caseloads and a decentralized budget. Social workers were able to purchase services and construct packages of care which seemed most appropriate to the needs of the older person. The costs of such purchased care were set at a rate which was one-third cheaper than residential care. There was a mixture of care provided ranging from informal care by relatives, semi-formal care, e.g. a day visitor, and some services provided by the local social services department. The experiences of the older people were compared with a similar group who were recipients of the traditional genericized form of local authority social work service.

The results were dramatically positive, with admissions into residential care being halved and the incidence of death within a year being substantially reduced. All this was achieved at a lower cost when compared with the previous system of service delivery.

The work of Challis and Davies was criticized from a number of perspectives. It has been suggested that the most complex cases were filtered out of the study. This meant that the complex reality of a social worker's caseload was not fully represented in the study. Although this scheme was an apparent success with older, frail people the question must be asked as to whether it would have been equally successful with other user groups.

To some extent these criticisms have been countered by other studies which claim positive benefit for service users. In an important study of over 200 people with learning difficulties five years after leaving residential establishments and moving into the community, Cambridge, Hayes, and Knapp (1994) found that care management had provided a co-ordinated service in response to need. Joint working and service arrangements between health authorities and social services had been introduced, with some NHS responsibilities being transferred to local government and some joint commissioning. Service commissioning tended to involve purchases from the voluntary sector rather than the private sector. 'Good quality services', according to what is described by the authors of the research as 'widely accepted criteria', had been set up whilst community services were generally described in favourable terms by service users. Positive developments had occurred in that new skills had been learned in the community.

Although there were some criticisms, for example of growing gaps in accountability, and few innovations in the development of checks and balances, they conclude:

From our involvement with the twelve services included in the evaluation, we know of no reasonable basis on which to challenge the policy of care in the community for people with learning disabilities, who would otherwise be long term hospital residents. In fact most people with learning disabilities are demonstrably better off living in the community than in hospital over the short and long term period. (Cambridge, Hayes, and Knapp 1994: 105)

Services had avoided the worst failings of neglect, victimization, and marginalization which are often associated with care in the community policies by the media.

Means and Smith have argued that one of the positive achievements of care in the community policies has been the emphasis on user involvement which has opened up the debate relating to empowerment and user involvement. Although it has been a slow process, pockets of 'innovative practice' have emerged from the reforms, including more examples of community care planning, development of partnerships in neighbourhood centres, and developing relationships between housing managers and care managers (Means and Smith 1994, Thornton and Tozer 1995). Tinker (1994) reports albeit in a tentative manner examples of positive collaboration in the delivery of services resulting from the community care arrangements. These can be summarized as follows:

- collaborative work, particularly in the provision of sheltered or extra-sheltered housing;
- collaboration in research, with researchers gaining access to more than one agency;
- examples of joint commissioning such as projects sponsored by the Social Services Inspectorate and the NHS management executive in Hampshire, Lewisham, and Oxford;
- training, for example in Cardiff where the housing department's community care team has helped to introduce a programme of interagency workshops (Tinker 1994).

There is evidence to suggest that between 1991 and 1993 opinions within local authorities changed in favour of markets in the delivery of social services. In a three-year period enthusiasm for the potential offered by markets became far more prevalent. It is now far less common for local authorities to be hostile to the concept of the mixed economy of welfare, and a form of 'market pragmatism' has evolved. The same study also appeared to suggest that profit maximization was not the main driving force behind the independent sector provision of services (Wistow, Knapp, Hardy, Forder, Kendall, and Manning 1996).

Some criticisms of the policy in practice

Despite some optimistic pictures of community care policies criticisms have been made from a number of directions. The major concerns so far expressed emphasize some of the central contradictions which underlie the policy:

- the lack of power and in some cases further disempowerment of particular groups within a policy which was proclaimed as offering greater needs-led user involvement;

- a possible overemphasis on informal networks;
- problems of collaboration in planning and implementation;
- the role of carers;
- demand outstripping the availability of services.

The creation of market conditions

A number of basic criticisms have been made of internal markets in the delivery of health and community care services. Such criticisms are reflected in the proposals made by the Labour government in December 1997 to abolish fund-holding GPs. The notion of cream-skimming means effectively that the less severely disabled are creamed off since they are less costly service users. This creates a rump of the most severely disabled people in the public sector, which will have a negative effect on staff morale (Le Grand and Bartlett 1993). Walker (1993) argues that evidence from the USA indicates that competitive choice in welfare may reduce user choice. The increasingly residual role of local authority will make it difficult to sustain the policies which have been made in the area of anti-discriminatory practice, since the market will create a situation in which the local authority has little influence over the terms and conditions of day-to-day service delivery in contracted agencies.

The internal or quasi-market itself is a source of bureaucracy and restricts the ability of service users to make choices about their services. Service users for instance do not have a choice in selecting their care manager. Carers do not have a real choice as to whether they wish to care for an ageing or disabled relative. Given the restriction on resources the care manager will become a gatekeeper rather than a professional who constructs through negotiation between purchaser and provider an appropriate package of care. The stated aim of giving increasing choice sensitivity is limited by the rationing of resources. Thus in Walker's view competition can only increase the power of the 'bureau professionals'. There is little new in these arguments and it is difficult to sustain the argument that markets *per se* are responsible for these negative outcomes. Social work to some extent was bureaucratic, and clients had little choice over the selection of their social worker. Carers have never had a real choice as to whether they wished to care, and resources have always been restricted.

One of the basic requirements for the mixed economy of welfare to work is that there should be a variety of service suppliers in order that the market can operate on a basis of purchasers having choice. Early findings indicate that there is a paucity of alternative suppliers of services, particularly in domiciliary and day care. The lack of potential providers could be explained by a number of factors including uncertainty about the patterns of future demands, small profit margins, and the difficulty of recruiting suitable staff. Voluntary organizations, thought to be a vital source of provider services, are involved in community care planning in a somewhat piecemeal and patchy manner (Common and Flynn 1992).

A study of twenty-five local authorities found that insufficient attention was given to the analysis of potential markets. Staff focused more upon current usage of providers rather than the mapping of future purchasing in relation to need. Transaction costs, or the costs of implementing the internal market, are an important yet neglected area of research and development. Block contracts buy services at an agreed price regardless of whether the services are used. Spot contracts are linked directly to individual service users and constitute one part of a package of care. Block contracts offer economies of scale and more certainty to providers, whilst restricting choice to individual service users (Wistow, Knapp, Hardy, Forder, Kendall, and Manning 1996). In order to attract more potential suppliers the contracting process needs to be simplified.

Even in areas in which markets are emerging little choice was being offered to service users and carers. Access to services was controlled by professionals and the contracted-out service was often simply a replacement for the service which had been previously supplied by the local authority.

Central to the success of the internal market of care is the question of adequate resources. A number of indicators would suggest that the centrality of an optimal level of resource is essential for the system to operate with any degree of success. One crucial indicator of the success of the policy is the degree to which it is possible for hospital patients to be discharged into the community. Bed blocking, a phenomenon which occurred before the days of community care, is still occurring in three-quarters of local authorities. In one local authority recently researched 178 beds were occupied by people awaiting discharge into the community. This is one clear indicator that demand appears to be outstripping supply of services. This has been recognized by the government who in December 1996 launched a challenge fund to health and social service authorities which would ease the bed blocking situation (Brindle 1996b).

Networks

One of the practical effects of the community care proposals is the emphasis which is placed upon the development and utilization of networks in the creation of individualized service plans. Informal care utilizes networks which have been created other than those that are associated with the official agencies like local authorities. The Barclay Report identified the extent to which networks play a vital part in care provision. Wenger (1994) has described a number of forms of network which exist in relation to her studies of older people in the community. 'Family dependent support networks' focus on local kin whilst locally integrated support networks are composed of family, friends, and neighbours. Local self-contained networks are composed of less frequent and more distant relationships with local kin and informal networks. Wider, community-focused support networks are active relationships with distant relatives with relatively few local contracts. Private restricted support networks occur where there are no local kin and minimal contact with others in the local community.

Collaborative planning and implementation

Official policy guidelines have constantly emphasized the importance of joint planning between health authorities and social services departments in order to ensure that plans are complementary (D.o.H. 1991a). The objectives of community care policy were that there should be no encumbrances to service provision created by boundaries between social care and health care. Community care was seen as an opportunity for co-ordinating services, whilst retaining the idea that health care needs would be provided for by the health authority and social care by local authorities (D.o.H. 1989a). Collaboration should occur at a number of levels between carers and users, providers and purchasers, and most obviously between health authorities and local social services departments. Some evidence would suggest that most progress has been made in the area of joint planning. Community care plans in some areas are being made jointly between local authority social services departments and health authorities. Such findings must be treated with some caution since the contents of plans are not a reliable indicator of outcome for service users (Wistow and Hardy 1994). In some areas there has been some imagination in joint planning of community care whilst other plans reveal minimal involvement by health authorities. Frequently community care plans appear to resemble commitments of specific resources rather than stating specific realizable objectives.

Although some 90 per cent of local authorities seem to be consulting with the voluntary sector this appears to occur following the preparation of the community care plan. Some representatives from voluntary organizations feel marginalized within the consultation process (NCVO 1992). There appears in many areas to be a lack of clarity as to the respective roles of the health and social services departments (Wistow, Hardy, and Leedham 1993). The reasons for poor collaboration are complex and relate to both policy and practice.

Problems of collaboration are further complicated by financial constraints. The financial responsibility for care is often shunted between health and social care agencies in an attempt to avoid spending. The situation is made more complex by the developing internal market within health care which could result in in-patient care being prioritized. A further difficulty results from policies which provide a means-tested social services system and a National Health Service free at the point of delivery.

Nocon concludes that the experience of joint working between health and local authorities has been variable whilst collaboration is 'fraught with difficulties'. He argues that a change in working culture must be established whilst care managers themselves must be aware of the need for a multi-agency approach (Nocon 1994).

Carers

Formal care is provided through the organized health and social agencies with reference to current legislation. Ungerson has recently described six settings in which carers work. 'Traditional formal carers' such as nurses and care assistants deliver care which is funded largely out of public expenditure. 'Mixed economy formal carers' work for non-profit-making organizations and receive possibly slightly lower pay than those carers in the formal traditional way. 'Volunteer carers' are linked to some form of social service delivery organization but are likely to be unwaged. 'Personal assistant carers' are usually employed by the user of the services. They are recruited through local and sometimes international labour markets. They are paid and sometimes employed on a live-in basis. 'Informal carers' are generally the kin of the person being cared for living in the same household as the care recipient. Unwaged, the carer may be in receipt of state benefit, and possibly receive money from the care recipient, e.g. disability living allowance or attendance allowance (Ungerson 1997).

Men appear to be more involved with caring for a spouse whilst women are more likely to care for non-spouses (Baldwin and Twigg 1991). The experience of people who become carers usually involves a loss of income and restricted employment opportunities, a negative affect on physical health, lack of privacy, low likelihood of receiving services in their own right, and gender differences in the response of agencies, with domiciliary support being more likely to be given to men than women users (Braye and Preston-Shoot 1995).

There are no clear arrangements designed to ensure that the needs of carers are taken into consideration. The overriding assumption in both the community care legislation and the Griffiths Report is that the family should be the primary source of care. Some families can provide good support while others supply the worst form of support. The policy also fails to take into consideration the conflicts of interest between those who are cared for and those who care (Qureshi and Walker 1989, Walker 1993).

Means and Smith identify the failure to take the views and wishes of carers into consideration as one of the glaring weaknesses of the community care legislation. The rhetoric of the community care legislation is seen in terms of helping carers to assist others rather than enabling them to make any real choice as to whether or not they wish to care in the first place. In order for any real choice to be made some alternative would have to be provided.

Access to public subsidy for people to live in independent sector residential and nursing homes is now through care managers so it can be argued that it has become easier for the state to discourage people from giving up their care responsibilities. (Means and Smith 1994: 227)

The possible effects of the 1995 Carers (Recognition and Services) Act, which effectively gives the right of an independent assessment of carers' needs, have yet to be fully researched.

The voluntary sector and community care

Another important feature of the new arrangements for the delivery of community care is the role of the voluntary sector in service delivery. Many community care voluntary organizations are enmeshed in local statutory decision-making networks, and most would hope to retain their role as pioneering new service developments working alongside the statutory sector. The voluntary health care sector is considerably smaller and a relatively minor provider of health care. The UK voluntary and health sectors have received considerable support from both central and local government. The voluntary sector was seen by the last government as providing a further source of competition along with the private sector in the mixed economy of welfare. The trend from residential and nursing home care to domiciliary services raises the possibility of voluntary organizations moving into respite care and the support of carers (Knapp 1996). The voluntary sector can be seen as being more cost effective, flexible, and less 'politically correct' than the bureaucratically dominated local authority services. Innovation, openness, and the development of the active participation of users, carers, and other citizens are the hallmarks of the voluntary sector. With increasing numbers of government contracts these features of the voluntary sector, if they ever existed, could be under threat. Flexibility could be compromised through the imposition of standardized contracts. In time these will simply become inflexible agreements between sectors. As Deakin has argued,

The other side of the coin of clarity is inflexibility, both in the definition of tasks and their discharge. The need to monitor and continuously review the achievement of service standards may result in the creation of new forms of bureaucracy as impenetrable and immutable as the older ones. The penalties for failing to meet standards may inhibit innovation. 'Commercial confidentiality' may obstruct users' access to crucial items of information about the service they wish to use. (Deakin 1996: 119)

Deakin goes on to argue that the introduction of contracts may also favour larger organizations at the expense of smaller, community-based providers who cannot accept the level of risk which may be involved in entering a contractual arrangement (Deakin 1996).

Other research indicates that voluntary organizations have experienced some difficulties in dealing with local authorities, with new service agreements leading to long and protracted negotiations. Although the new community care structures have led to greater professionalization in the voluntary sector, lines of accountability have become complex. Voluntary organizations which now have a principal line of accountability to the purchaser of the service also fear that their advocacy and campaigning role could be detrimentally affected (Lewis and Glennerster 1996).

In short, despite the envisaged extension of the contribution of the voluntary sector's role in the delivery of community care service, relatively little is known about its effectiveness. Moreover, the development of the contract culture could inhibit some of the most innovative voluntary organizations from developing further.

Assessing strengths and weaknesses

A central issue in considering the impact of the market-based community care approach relates to the measurement of success. Different interest groups in all policy initiatives will have their own version of success from their own perspectives. Cost minimalization may represent success for managers, but this might be achieved at a cost to service users (Hoyes and Means 1993).

Table 16.1. Potential strengths and weaknesses of community care policies

Potential strengths	Potential weaknesses
1. More choice created by market.	Users lost in gap between purchasers and providers (Le Grand and Bartlett 1993, Oliver 1996).
2. Efficient division of resources within the internal market (Challis and Davies 1986).	Wastefulness (Davies, Bebbington, and Charnley 1990).
3. Innovation, creativity (Means and Smith 1994).	Lack of accountability (Cambridge, Hayes, and Knapp 1994).
4. Devolved authority and budgets (Glennerster, Matsaganis, and Owens 1994).	Inequalities in redistributing resources (Glendinning and Bewley 1994, Institute of Race Relations 1993, Jadeja and Singh 1993, Mullen 1992, Langan 1990).
5. Lowering costs of care.	Scant attention to needs of carers (Walker 1993, Means and Smith 1994).
6. Information systems providing greater choice.	Insufficient attention to method of information gathering and giving (Baldock and Ungerson 1994, Wistow, Knapp, Hardy, Forder, Kendall, and Manning 1996).
7. Consultation and co-operation (Lewis and Glennerster 1996, Wistow and Hardy 1994, Tinker 1994).	Confrontation—increased tendency of care managers to restrict access to resources (Meetham and Thompson 1993).
8. Partnership between providers and purchasers.	Problematic collaboration (Glendinning and Bewley 1994, Hoyes and Lart 1992, NCVO 1992, Nocon 1994, Wistow, Knapp, Hardy, and Allen 1994, Lewis and Glennerster 1996).
9. Market responding to stated needs.	Paucity of suppliers of services (Common and Flynn 1992).
10. Developing quality and cost-effective services.	Prioritization of costs over quality (Meethan and Thompson 1993, Jowell 1991).
11. Direct cash payments leading to greater empowerment (Morris 1993, 1997).	Cash empowerment could create insecurity and deregulation (Ungerson 1997).

Conclusion

This chapter has shown that opinion is divided as to the possible impact of community care policies since the 1990 NHS and Community Care Act. The implementation of the policy has been achieved at a minimal political cost to the government. The demands put on authorities have been less than feared and on the whole the community care policy has been received positively by most social service staff because it was seen as having a potential for producing better, more responsive, user-led services (Lewis and Glennerster 1996).

The stated aim of care in the community policy was to transform and extend the social work assessment process to encompass a range of options which would be available to care service users. Assessment now officially includes social background, health, service user views and preferences, support needs, resource implications, the main carer's perspective, and a review of existing formal and informal support networks.

The distinction between health and social care may be a false one since the boundaries are often difficult to draw. The needs of people do not always fall into neat administrative divisions. The emergence of the care manager who is likely to have a background in one of the health professions further complicates the issue. At present care managers represent a complex amalgam of multidisciplinary training and professional experience and lack any single professional identity. Given the differences between social work training and the training offered to health professionals, it is not surprising that multidisciplinary relationships present difficulties and challenges.

Crucial to the success or failure of all these developments is the gap between policy rhetoric and the reality of care management. The overarching problem which links all the apparent difficulties is that need constantly outstrips available resources. The internal market will not create resources neither will it necessarily produce a system which provides higher standard services at a lower price.

Exercise:
assessing strengths and weaknesses

The potential strengths and weaknesses of the community care approach can be summarized as follows.

Potential strengths of current community care policies

1. Pockets of 'innovative practice' community care planning; development of partnerships between housing managers and care managers (Means and Smith 1994).

2. Local authorities being forced to examine their own in-house services in creating criteria which are necessary for contracting services to service providers in the voluntary and private sectors.

3. Joint community care plans (Wistow and Hardy 1994). Joint commissioning, e.g. Social Services Inspectorate and the NHS management executive in Hampshire, Lewisham, Oxford, and Wiltshire. Training initiatives, e.g. interagency workshops (Tinker 1994).

4. Co-ordinated, effective, economical service in response to needs (Challis and Davies 1986).

5. Care-managed services described favourably by service users (Cambridge, Hayes, and Knapp 1994).

6. Flexible use of budgets enabling more reactive relevant services to emerge.

7. The possibility that GP fund-holders could lead to increased efficiency, more responsive consultants, direct access to services like pathology, shorter waiting lists, consultants holding surgeries in GPs' premises.

8. Potential for greater voluntary sector involvement which could lead to more innovative and less bureaucratized practices.

9. Direct payments to service users for purchase of services.

Some possible weaknesses of community care policy in practice

1. Variation in forms of consultation (Glendinning and Bewley 1994).

2. Growing gaps in accountability, few innovations in the development of checks and balances (Cambridge, Hayes, and Knapp 1994).

3. Greater control of services through care managers (Means and Smith 1994, Meethan and Thompson 1993, Jowell 1991).

4. Assessment often being unlikely to be understood and participated in by service users (Baldock and Ungerson 1994).

5. Scant attention being given to the needs of black people and potential contribution of black voluntary organizations in the White Paper 'Caring for People'. Power to recover costs of community care problematic, for many black elders are without pension eligibility and can contribute little to the cost of care (Institute of Race Relations 1993, London Group on Race Aspects of Community Care 1993, Mizra 1991, Jadeja and Singh 1993).

6. Possible greater burden on women as carers increasing inequalities experienced by women (Land 1991).

7. Questions of quality and equal opportunities not being adequately addressed (Glendinning and Bewley 1994, Martin and Gaster 1993).

8. Disabled people, especially those with sensory or learning disabilities, being least likely to be involved in planning (Glendinning and Bewley 1994).

9. Possible restriction of GP services to patients of non-fund-holders (Mullen 1992).

10. Possibility of markets creating inequalities, which could reduce choice (Walker 1993).

11. Cream-skimming: the less severely disabled being creamed off since they are less costly. A corollary of this is the possible effect of the less eligibility principle as resources diminish and demographic changes create even greater demands on resources.

12. A paucity of alternative suppliers of services particularly in domiciliary and day care services (Common and Flynn 1992).

13. The failure to take into consideration the conflicts of interests between carers and cared for (Qureshi and Walker 1989, Walker 1993).

14. Lack of clarity as to the respective roles of the health and social services departments. Voluntary organizations' involvement, a vital source of competition, is piecemeal and patchy (NCVO 1992, Nocon 1994, Wistow, Hardy, and Leedham 1993).

15. Community care plans resembling commitments of specific resources rather than stating specific realizable objectives (Salter and Salter 1993).

16. Users themselves not being consulted (Glendinning and Bewley 1991, Hoyes and Lart 1992, Martin and Gaster 1993).

In what respects can community care reforms be seen as an improvement on the previous system of service delivery?

In what ways does the role of the social worker change following the community care reforms?

Can you add any points to either of these lists?

FURTHER READING

J. Lewis and H. Glennerster (1996) have completed an influential study of the community care implementation process in five local authorities which is described in *Implementing the New Community Care* (Buckingham, Open University Press). This study provides a clear account of the development of community care policy aims and a considered assessment of how far the policy aims have been achieved. G. Wistow, M. Knapp, B. Hardy, J. Forder, J. Kendall, and R. Manning (1996) give an account of detailed research into experiences of and attitudes towards community care provision in *Social Care Markets* (Buckingham, Open University Press). A. Nocon and H. Qureshi (1996) have written a comprehensive account of the impact of community care services on service users in *Outcomes of Community Care* (Buckingham, Open University Press).

CHAPTER 17

Users' Rights and
User Empowerment

- Community care and user empowerment
- Rights and resources
- Critics of a rights approach

Introduction

Rights should be seen in the words of Plant as

A way of empowering the citizen in the public sector in relation to the services provided, in response to the idea that there is a social dimension to citizenship. The idea of linking rights and entitlements to empowerment is a new one and marks a departure from the traditional approaches of both right and left. (Plant 1992: 26)

The idea of rights to social work has been a theme which has constantly emerged in this book. Market enthusiasts seek to establish the case that rights cannot match necessary budgetary constraints. Neither the 1990 NHS and Community Care Act nor associated Department of Health policy guidelines provide any concrete proposals for user empowerment. Without this it is likely that professionals will continue to dominate the processes which determine allocation of resources and the assessment of need. If anything the budget-controlling role of the care manager could further disempower the user.

This chapter will put the view that the changes within the delivery of personal social services brought about by the emergence of the internal market strengthen the arguments for a framework of service entitlements, and independent avenues of redress.

Community care and user empowerment

Empowerment is a contested concept although as Means and Smith have argued in the context of community care it is usually defined as 'Taking or being given more power over decisions affecting welfare and hence it probably involves taking at least some power away from service providers' (Means and Smith 1994: 71). Varying degrees of power are available to service users. In some situations users have the authority to take decisions. In other scenarios users have an opportunity to influence decisions. At the lower end of the ladder of empowerment users' views are sought before taking decisions. In some cases implementation information is given about decisions already taken.

Means and Smith (1994) have described three principal methods whereby empowerment can be achieved in the context of the new community care arrangements. These are referred to as the exit, voice, and rights approaches. These models will now be examined critically.

The exit model

An internal market in welfare ostensibly provides consumers with the power to exit or find another service if they are dissatisfied. The services which are continually rejected by service users will cease to exist as is the case with any market.

The exit approach is not completely synonymous with the market. It is for instance possible for consumers to be given a range of options within the public sector. The attraction of the exit approach for market enthusiasts is that it can appear as a possible way of reducing public expenditure. Such an approach was the mainstay of the White Paper published by the Conservative Party in March 1997 before their massive electoral defeat in May of the same year. It remains to be seen whether the approach taken by the Labour government is markedly different.

Such a model of exit, however, has been called into question by a number of researchers. Forecasts about the wealth and income of elderly people can now be made and indicate a significant drop in income levels at retirement. Half of all currently retired people are in receipt of social security benefits. The possibility of unlocking wealth through housing equity as suggested in the Griffiths Report also seems an impracticable suggestion given the difficulties faced by older people in simply maintaining their properties. We have previously seen that disabled people are also differentially affected by poverty (Oliver 1991).

The limitations of exit as a form of empowerment are coming to be realized. Exit says very little about the processes which define individuals as being in need of services.

The voice model

A less market-oriented model of empowerment is often associated with the voice model. Here users do not have the power to exit from a service, but can bring pressure to bear upon the manner in which services are planned and delivered. This method of empowerment relies upon processes of consultation and opportunity to voice an opinion. The methods used to enable views about services to be heard vary widely from authority to authority, and no single method of consultation is free of drawbacks. Methods of consultation currently include newsletters, road shows, leaflets, local radio phone-in surveys, questionnaires, and public meetings. The evidence seems to suggest that a wide range of conflicting views are raised which are often difficult to incorporate into a community care plan. Methods used to select people to represent the user's voice tend to be *ad hoc*. A wide range of consultation methods must be used, some tailored for particular groups of disabled people, others aimed at wider audiences (Glendinning and Bewley 1994, Thornton and Tozer 1995).

Although a number of local authorities are committed to improving communications with carer and user groups, a number of case studies confirm that local authorities are at an early stage in developing effective consultation processes. A study of six community care projects found that questions of empowerment, quality, and equal opportunities whether in relation to carers, users, voluntary, or community groups were not being adequately addressed (Nocon 1994). Although some projects have attempted to take user views into account they are still driven by professional concerns whilst resources are directly controlled by professionals.

As was the case in social services provision before the NHS and Community Care Act it would appear that certain groups are particularly disempowered. It has previously been noted that scant attention is given to the needs of black people in the 'Caring for People' document (Mizra 1991, Ahmad and Atkin 1996). More recently both the London Group on Race and Aspects of Community Care (1993) and the Institute of Race Relations (1993) have drawn attention to the lack of input of black people in the community care planning process. Black disabled people and those with sensory or learning disabilities were least likely to be involved. A further concern relating to the possible differential effects of community care policies on black people is that local authorities now have the power to recover some of the costs of community care from service users themselves. Many black elders are without pension eligibility and totally dependent on income support which makes it difficult for them to contribute towards the cost of care (Jadeja and Singh 1993). Although many local authorities proclaim that the community care plan is a way of empowering the powerless according to Glendinning and Bewley (1994) only 16 per cent of organizations involved groups representing black and disabled people in the planning process. This is despite the fact that in other areas it has proved possible to include older and disabled people in the decision-making and planning process at a number of stages (Thornton and Tozer 1995).

Section 46 of the 1990 NHS and Community Care Act placed a duty upon local authorities to produce and publish a plan of community services in their area. Publishing information is also one of the core tasks of care management as defined by the Department of Health (D.o.H. 1991a). There is a relatively unexplored relationship between formally publishing information and enabling service users to be part of a planning process. Knowledge itself is not power. There is confusion as to the purpose of advertising and public service information which presents all available options in order that those using services can make an informed choice (Deakin 1996).

Baldock and Ungerson researched thirty-two stroke patients discharged into the community and found that:

- Community care assessments are often unlikely to be understood and participated in by users in the early stages of their new dependency. Assessment must either become a more staggered, drawn out, and continuous process, or it must be updated at specific intervals.

- The content of assessment and care management must move beyond questions of information and organization. In many cases it will need to address directly the need that dependency brings to construct a new script for life in terms of daily routines and the values that inform them. 'People find it difficult to choose their own community care; they need help to learn to do so' (Baldock and Ungerson 1994: 54).

This research questions the fundamental assumption that publication enhances the quality of service delivery. The factors which prevent consumer understanding of the care system are more connected to values and culture than simply information giving as is suggested in 'Caring for People'. Lewis and Glennerster conclude that the 1990 community care legislation does not secure participation on equal terms, giving the responsibility for assessing need and deciding on service provision to the local authority. Overall their study does suggest that there has been some progress in hearing the voice of the service user (Lewis and Glennerster 1996). To what extent 'hearing the voice' constitutes an adequate response to the need for greater overall collaboration in community care delivery is still open to debate.

The rights model

The exit approach to empowerment appears to be of little use for those on low incomes, whilst the voice approach is essentially a liberal idea which fails fully to address the inequitable power relationship between purchaser/provider and service user. There are a number of reasons which have constantly appeared throughout this book which make the utilization of users' rights fundamental to the future development of social work practice.

- The changes brought about by the NHS and Community Care Act individualize care, and introduce a wider and diverse group of potential service providers. The potential for inconsistencies arising from partnerships with different private and voluntary sectors creates further potential for loss of rights within burgeoning welfare bureaucracies.

- There has been an increase in rules and procedures regulating the internal market which appear predominantly to represent the interests of agencies and staff, and work less in the interests of users despite the proliferation of users' charters and quality assurance documents.

- The scope for discretionary actions by care management staff is too extensive given the control they have over the allocation of resources.

- There is an increased tendency for welfare bureaucracies to obfuscate rather than clarify user accountability issues.

- Despite progress, the continued existence of institutional discrimination in practice through power differentials enables professional groups to devalue other less powerful groups on the basis of perceived difference. Users of services have less power than care managers or social workers. The unequal distribution of power emphasizes a double jeopardy which might be faced by particular groups differentially defined by 'race' ethnicity, age, gender, class, sexuality, or disability, who may suffer further forms of discrimination.

- The increased pressure on resources is likely to produce less rather than more equitable services.

Rights and resources

Rights to services are inextricably linked to resources. Resource starvation effectively denies the access to services which are a legal right. This point was recently illustrated by the case of Michael Barry, an 80-year-old heart attack victim from whom community services were withdrawn. Gloucestershire County Council, the providing authority, unsuccessfully argued in the courts that it had the right to withdraw services. The acting Director of Social Services for Gloucestershire is quoted as saying in relation to the judgment that:

It goes directly against the advice given to us by the Department of Health that we have been following. We regret any rationing of services is necessary, but this was forced upon us because of the increased demand for community care services and the inadequate funding made available to us. (Dyer 1996: 7)

Gloucestershire had withdrawn services to a reported 1,500 disabled people following £3 million cuts in departmental spending in December 1993.

A number of important implications for practice follow a subsequent House of Lords appeal ruling. Whilst upholding the original Gloucestershire decision, the Law Lords ruled that the availability of resources can be taken into account when deciding whether a service should be provided. Once a decision has been made to provide services, however, those services must be provided without regard to resources availability. In deciding whether to provide services, the extent of available resources is one factor amongst many which can be taken into consideration. Risk, for instance, is another salient factor which needs to be taken into account. When a decision is taken to reduce services, the council must carry out an individual reassessment of client need (Clements 1997).

This ruling effectively means that local authorities can make cuts in basic services in England and Wales. This will affect all services including ironing, cleaning, and the provision of meals. The removal of rights to services will continue to be a matter of fundamental importance as the full effects of care in the community policies are experienced by service users. Many in the disability movement advocate a rights approach based on civil rights to cash benefits and care (Campbell and Oliver 1996, Morris 1993). Following direct payment legislation recently passed through Parliament, disabled people are empowered to employ their own carers and staff whilst having a greater choice over the way in which resources are used in relation to individual requirements. Ungerson argues that direct payments could be seen as providing both procedural rights to an assessment, and contractual rights to hire and fire in the market. She goes on to identify a number of drawbacks which could cast doubt upon direct payments as a form of empowerment. Both employers and employees are likely to be on low incomes and such arrangements are likely to be insecure and unregulated. Labour supply in the long run could also be problematic (Ungerson 1997).

Ungerson has been rigorously challenged by Morris who argues that the position for disabled people in relation to cash payments is in some respects comparable with non-disabled people who pay for cleaning or child minding. Direct payments take the day-to-day allocation of resources out of the powerful hands of care managers and social workers. The state has previously failed to support direct payments to disabled people since:

People who need help in their daily lives were/are considered to be unable to 'look after themselves' in the intellectual and physical sense. Instead they were/are assumed to need a professional group, social workers, to determine what is best for them; and second, it was feared that it would be too expensive to introduce a cash payment system, thus reaffirming the social worker's key rationing role. (Morris 1997: 59)

Critics of a rights approach

The connection between rights and social work practice has been a particular thorn in the flesh of those advocating even greater dependency on the market and the gradual residualization of state social work. David Marsland quotes approvingly that 'There is little or no public support for the social orthodoxies of the 1960s which still hold sway in social work training' (*The Times*, 10 Sept. 1994). Marsland goes on to argue that there should be a decisive shift away from the current emphasis on rights, towards the education of social workers in skills which enable them to make their clients self-reliant and less dependent on the state. Notwithstanding the fact that Marsland is not clear about which aspect of the 1960s orthodoxies are being referred to, much of this argument is rhetorical.

First, the reality of social work education and training reflects, as has been argued throughout this book, not the fading gasps of ageing hippies, but the pragmatism of managers who have now come to dominate social care priorities and objectives. This point is well illustrated in the recently reworked requirements of CCETSW which Marsland acknowledges have brought about a more pragmatic approach to social work practice. Here overwhelming emphasis is placed upon the delineation and achievement of social work competencies. In the revised requirements for practice CCETSW state: 'Competence in social work is the product of knowledge, skills and values' (CCETSW 1995: 17). One of the six core competencies requires social work programmes to 'Promote opportunities for people to use their own strengths and expertise to enable them to meet responsibilities, secure rights and achieve change' (CCETSW 1995: 17).

Each student is now required by CCETSW to demonstrate a knowledge of current legislation relevant to social work, evaluate outcomes of intervention, and assemble information which is directly relevant to community care assessments. Other evidence, as has been previously mentioned, does suggest that there is widespread public support for state welfare. Moreover:

In a period of ten years, we witnessed the spectacle of the reassertion of individualism over collectivism as the dominant method of providing welfare. It has, however, been argued that this triumph is more rhetorical than real, for levels of public expenditure have remained stubbornly unchanged during the 1980s. (George and Page 1995: 1)

Even when public support for new right ideas was at its height during the mid-1980s publicly funded services were still well regarded by a large proportion of the population (Mack and Lansley 1985, 1991, Furnam and Lewis 1986). This support is differentiated, the most popular services being the NHS, education, and pensions, whilst services to disabled people are far more popular than benefits to the unemployed (Taylor-Gooby 1991).

Secondly, the purchaser/provider split is now so firmly in place that it would be impossible for the practising social worker to indulge in psychedelic radicalism. Thirdly, in his critique of social work, Marsland seems to ignore an entire literature which has developed since the 1970s into the effectiveness of social work and probation practice. It is the case that following the Seebohm Report too much attention was placed upon the process of social work with insufficient attention being given to outcome (MacDonald and Sheldon with Gillespie 1992). Sheldon argues that modifying problematic behaviour by weakening 'maladaptive emotional responses' offers clients 'more effective models of problem solving', and changes the way in which 'stimuli are recognised and interpreted in the first place' (Sheldon 1982, 1986). Other writers approaching effectiveness from a less clearly behavioural perspective have also emphasized the importance of ultimately promoting user self-reliance (Cheetham, Fuller, McIvor, and Petch 1992).

Direct work with clients can include research, whilst research findings themselves can be used to make decisions about appropriate forms of practice. Both research and practice share an essential concern with problem-solving. Fourthly, some aspects of rights particularly in the equal opportunities field have been eagerly appropriated by social work managers as examples of good-quality practice (Blakemore and Drake 1996).

Conclusion

It has been argued that some benefits might accrue under the new arrangements for welfare. The more technically competent the planning and purchasing processes the more difficult it is for government to ignore its outcomes and their own expenditure requirements. Some aspects of the internal market, e.g. direct payments, with adequate funding could offer a more responsive service if users were given more power to select and purchase their own services.

Much of the criticism which has been directed at social work from the right of British politics has been predicated upon the belief that a large proportion of service users make a conscious choice to be in the position of passive welfare recipient. The users of services, unless possibly disabled, old, or hurt in a road accident, are happy to 'scrounge' from the taxpayer indefinitely, and believe that the state has an obligation to support them in their indolent laziness. It is not difficult to see therefore why the notion of welfare recipients having rights is anathema to those who advocate the dissolution of state welfare. Their objections are based upon a heroic battle to seek out and transform a group of people many of whom find their way into social work caseloads. The 'undeserving' poor choose to be poor and live on welfare benefits which barely sustain individuals at the most basic level. This position is deeply offensive to many families whose daily lives are structured by a grinding and continuous battle against poverty. The position adopted also ignores the well-documented problem of low take-up of benefit, stigma, and the poverty trap.

Exercise

In 1985 Davies listed some basic ground rules in a book *The Essential Social Worker* (2nd edn.). Although there was not universal agreement about the content of Davies's work when it was published, since for some it presented an over-mechanistic view of social structures and institutions, it became enormously influential in social work training. It sought to express clearly the essence of professional social work.

This exercise seeks to encourage a discussion as to how social work's essentials have changed following recent developments in policy discussed throughout this book.

The essential features of good practice at the heart of professional social work were as follows:

- improve the pathways to social work service;
- work with imagination, sensitivity, and tact;
- put clients at their ease;
- be concerned with the client as a person;
- identify the client's expectations and relate these to the agency's obligations and resources;
- be active, be alert, be helpful;
- be a good counsellor;
- be honest and open about your agency's responsibilities;
- use your knowledge and experience for the benefit of the client;
- always be trustworthy and reliable (adapted from Davies 1985).

Take each one of these social work attributes and answer the following questions.

1. How relevant are these qualities to current social work practices?
2. Construct a list of essentials which characterize good social work following the development of the mixed economy of welfare.

FURTHER READING

Wilmot (1997) provides a clear and readable analysis of the general principles of ethics related to the development of community care in *The Ethics of Community Care* (London, Cassell). N. Biehal (1993) provides a specific consideration of rights with specific reference to community care in 'Changing Practice: Participation Rights and Community Care', *British Journal of Social Work*, 21: 245–57. B. Broad and D. Denney (1996) have constructed a service users' charter which although specifically related to probation has a wider application in 'Users' Rights and the Probation Service', *Howard Journal*, 35(1): 61–76.

CHAPTER 18

Problem Definitions and Solutions: Looking Back to the Future

- The welfare state as a social problem
- More unemployment, partly attributable to early retirement
- The breakdown of the nuclear and extended family which used to be a source of effective social care not chargeable to the taxpayer
- Women working: a further strain on the family?
- Increase in the number of older and disabled people
- Redefining the welfare state
- Redefining social work and the new order

Introduction

Despite the continued majority support for state welfare in public opinion studies, and the reluctance to abandon welfare across Europe, the idea of a welfare state has been under constant attack in the UK since 1979 (Timmins 1995, George and Taylor-Gooby 1996). In this chapter some of the official justifications for reducing state expenditure and changing the role of social workers will be critically examined. It will be argued that such changes create a need for practices which place the rights of service users at the forefront.

The welfare state as a social problem

Despite support the welfare state has come to be defined as problematic at a number of levels (see Chapter 4). For the new right problems tend to be presented in financial terms (see Chapter 6). Lewis and Glennerster (1996) in their detailed account of the implementation of community care in twenty-five areas argue that the reforms were driven

By the need to stop the haemorrhage in the social security budget and to do so in a way that would minimise the political outcry and not give additional resources to local authorities themselves. Most of the rest of the policy was as the Americans would say, 'for the birds'. (Lewis and Glennerster 1996: 8).

In 1996 the then Secretary of State for Health Stephen Dorrell presented the problem faced by the personal social services and health authorities as one of uncontrollable demand. Expenditure on social services provision has according to Dorrell increased in real terms. In 1971 the budget for social services provision was £900 million. In 1991 this increased to £3.5 billion and by 1995 had reached £9.2 billion (Dorrell 1996). The reasons for the uncontrollable increase in demand for social services provision were presented in the following terms:

- unemployment partly attributable to early retirement;
- labour mobility, which has increased the breakdown of the nuclear family and other informal networks of support;
- women working placing an added strain on the family;
- an increase in the numbers of older people (Dorrell 1996).

The reassessment and modernization of the welfare state advocated by New Labour appears to operate from a similar starting point. Field, who has been instrumental in constructing the 'New Labour' approach to welfare, also cites changes in the job market and increases in the number of single parents as reasons for changing the basis upon which welfare should be delivered in the future (Field with Deacon, Alcock, Green, and Phillips 1996). Policies such as 'Welfare to Work' focus attention on the importance of self-reliance. We have also seen in Chapter 10 how New Labour have emphasized the centrality of the nuclear family in their approach to social policy. We will now critically examine some basic assertions which could shape future approaches to welfare.

More unemployment, partly attributable to early retirement

Early retirement is one factor amongst many which helps to increase the rate at which people are made unemployed. Cyclical changes in the demand for labour arise from the variability of demand from customers in periods of boom and slump. Unemployment can also be brought about by technical changes or in organizational restructuring since skills simply become redundant (Spicker 1993). Other sources of unemployment include people being unwilling to work for wages which are not at the market level, and the changes resulting from a more service-based and less manufacturing-based economy. Changes in the definition of who is unemployed, so that official statistics now only include those who are entitled to benefit by reason of unemployment, serve to exclude many categories of unemployed from the statistics. High levels of unemployment in themselves encourage individuals to leave the labour force through early retirements, sick absence, or disability (Taylor-Gooby 1991).

Across Europe unemployment particularly among men is acknowledged to be a major problem. It is now widely accepted that future employment patterns will be different from those which existed in the past. Some countries will experience full employment levels for a while but they will not be providing full-time secure jobs for a lifetime. There will in the future be more part-time work of a temporary nature and more new part-time jobs for married women (George and Taylor-Gooby 1996).

The breakdown of the nuclear and extended family which used to be a source of effective social care not chargeable to the taxpayer

Murray's analysis of the developing underclass or the development of a 'new rabble' underlines the link made by right-wing commentators between the decline of the family and violent crime, growth in the rate of illegitimacy, and economic activity amongst working-age men (Murray 1994). Murray's arguments have been vigorously challenged. One of the principal criticisms is that he selectively focuses upon undeserving and essentially pathological low-income families. Increasing divorce rates for instance are accompanied by higher rates of divorced people wishing to remarry (David 1994). This possibly indicates continued support for the family.

Put crudely, for Murray we all have an equal opportunity to pull ourselves up by our bootstraps, it is all simply a question of character and individual fortitude. There is no evidence to suggest that poor people place a different value on work or family when compared with any other sector of the population (Taylor-Gooby 1991). Social workers and student social workers reading this book will undoubtedly have encountered poverty-stricken people, many of them children, who daily attempt to become independent, but fight against abject poverty, abuse, and seemingly impossible circumstances. The notion that marriage is always better than cohabitation and lone parenthood is transformed into a justification to punish the latter in order to encourage the former (Alcock 1994).

Such a position appears to be based more upon faith than social science and is perhaps more strategic than would appear on first inspection. The construction of a pathological underclass as a threat to the sanctity of family life could be seen as a diversion from a number of major economic recessions of the 1990s, the continued growth of taxation, high levels of unemployment, and growing income inequality.

Proponents of change to the welfare system emanating from the Labour government echo the concern for the breakdown of the nuclear family. Field, in his exposition of a stakeholder welfare system, is concerned about the relationship between poverty and single parenting. Field suggested before the election of the Labour government in 1997 that single parents should be offered education or training as a condition of welfare benefits (Field with Deacon, Alcock, Green, and Phillips 1996). This idea has become the basis for the 'welfare to work' approach, which will reduce benefit to those lone parents who will not take up a 'welfare to work' option. All those who seek to reduce family poverty to single parenthood fail to take into account the complexities of the relationship between family structure and family poverty. There is now a far greater extent of family poverty among families with a single earner and two parents than among lone parents. This results from a combination of low pay with a tax and benefits system which to some extent favours lone parents (Phillips 1996).

Women working: a further strain on the family?

The idea that women working is in some respects harmful to families and also concomitantly to the moral fabric is a curious idea upon which to base social policy. Such a position consigns women to the home and parenting. Further it is discriminatory in that it appears to imply that women should not be given the opportunity to have a career.

In the United States child care subsidies have been regarded as an option for increasing the market potential of single parents in order to decrease welfare dependency. Thus, as Gustafsson argues, 'Based upon the human capital theory one can argue that the opportunity cost of not working includes not only the forgone earnings of the mother but also her on the job investment in market related human capital' (Gustafsson 1994: 59).

When women do work it is still the case that they are likely to be paid less than men. In the mid-1990s the weekly average rate of pay was 71 per cent that received by men (Alcock 1996). The traditional long-term, monogamous, male-dominated, two-parent family is in decline throughout Europe. This reflects a major social structural change, and not a temporary blip or manifestation of permissiveness (George and Taylor-Gooby 1996).

As has previously been mentioned for lone parents the 'welfare to work' programme has marked a policy change which on the one hand could unlock the potential of many women, whilst introducing an element of compulsion.

Increase in the number of older and disabled people

Demographic changes have led to increases in the numbers of older people. The number of people over the age of 65 increased from 1.7 million to 8.8 million between 1901 and 1991. By the year 2021 this age group will represent 17.2 per cent of the population. On current estimates by 2041 the proportion of older people reaching the age of 75 will have exceeded 50 per cent of the population (Phillipson 1996). These groups are more likely to have needs and episodes of chronic illness, mental illness, and forms of dementia. Estimates of people suffering from forms of dementia vary although this number is expected to increase by 25 per cent over the next fifteen years (Allsop 1995). Similar increases are expected in the number of older people suffering from long-standing illnesses like osteoporosis or arthritis.

Although these trends are real the extent to which the demand will increase in relation to older people is unclear, and it is possible to give exaggerated attention to the cost of the elderly which perpetuates the notion of age creating burden. There would appear to be no immediate crisis since, according to Baldock (1997), the period 1990–2010 marks a period of reasonable stability in the numbers of people over retirement age. Although the number requiring intensive social care is growing the increase poses little more of a problem now than it did at any point during the post-war period. In the longer term there is likely to be a problem which will be exacerbated by the reduction of long-stay beds in the National Health Service. The problem is not simply understandable in terms of cost but should be viewed in the wider context of who will do the caring work and what types of care are both desirable and effective. No one model of social care has yet been shown to be particularly effective in community care. The case of Eileen and Ann (Chapter 6) illustrated some of the complexities of social care. A model of social care based upon funding problems cannot produce a solution to any impending demographic problem which is effective and universally applicable.

An over-concentration on the construction of older people as a social problem diverts attention from the cost of policies which are concerned with and used by younger people, most obviously criminal justice and education. It should also be remembered that there are significant and increasing numbers of people even amongst those who are over 85 who do not suffer from any major health problems (Phillipson 1996).

Redefining the welfare state

An underlying theme which is constantly reiterated by major political parties is that if taxes are to be kept to a minimum, the state can no longer afford to provide social care but should be regarded as a means-tested safety net. The polemic which surrounds such thinking emphasizes the undesirability and danger of a protective welfare state. It has been suggested in various parts of this book that the now familiar call for a return to the forms of social work which existed before the Beveridge Report may well be in the process of becoming reality. It has been seen in earlier chapters that the mixed economy of welfare is not being generally applied in social work related to child protection, partly as a result of the difficulties of harmonizing the purchaser/provider split with the requirements of the 1989 Children Act. This could result in a move back to pre-Seebohm specialist work with children.

We have seen throughout this book how collectivism has given way to a new market-led paradigm. The transformation from collective responsibility for social reproduction, including the precision of welfare services, towards an individualized responsibility for social reproduction can be seen across western and eastern Europe. Concern for social cohesion, which constituted a central value in the old order, has given way to the overarching need for national and international competitiveness (Ferge 1997).

Redefining social work and the new order

In Chapter 4 reference was made to the way in which social work was defined in terms of reconciliation between a caring society and the development of the interdependence of society and the individual. Social work's defining characteristic was the enhancement of the lives of individuals, families, groups, and communities (Davies 1985, Midgeley 1995). Although not completely discounting the possibility of a politics of resistance in the face of postmodern scepticism and global market capitalism, Leonard poses a poignant question: 'Can we any longer speak of the future, of the prospects for human welfare, in other than cataclysmic terms, because the party is over?' (Leonard 1997: 27).

It has been argued in previous pages that social policy, in the name of efficient management of a mixed economy, has been constructed in an attempt to redefine social work. The term 'social worker' itself is being replaced by 'care manager'. Social work is now more widely and increasingly defined in terms of social care. Whereas social work refers to the helping tasks carried out by individuals, social care is more specifically related to the system of care in which social workers operate. This is an important distinction which could serve to deprofessionalize social work. Specialist social work time can now be purchased on an hourly basis by care managers as part of a package of care in some areas. Social workers increasingly form part of multidisciplinary care management teams, working alongside those with backgrounds in other health-based disciplines, e.g. occupational therapy and nursing. Hospital-based social work is being replaced by referral systems made directly by ward staff to care managers, sometimes based outside the hospital. Assessment and evaluation is a continuous, routine, and more financially focused activity. Counselling services, once seen as an essential skill for social work, are less evident in the social work repertoire of methods. Counselling can be purchased from independent counsellors in the private sector, or regarded simply by care managers as a non-essential luxury. Attention to evaluating unit costs and effectiveness is seen almost exclusively in terms of value for money. Technical competence is judged in the context of cost-effectiveness in purchasing, rather than delivering services which are sensitive and empathetic. The overall aims of intervention are marked by the creation of 'self-reliance', flexibility, and a low-cost service.

The removal of probation training from mainstream social work education could provide increased impetus towards deprofessionalization and agency-based training in other areas of the personal services, as NVQ takes an increasing role in social work education. CCETSW as a national training organization will diversify and widen its functions, further diminishing the idea of social work as a distinctive professional activity. Labour ministers have accepted the recommendations of a review of social work training undertaken in 1997 by the Department of Health (D.o.H. 1997). Essentially the future of social work training will rest with a new independent national training organization in Northern Ireland, Scotland, Wales, and England. The function of identifying training standards and regulating professional qualifying and post-qualifying training will fall under the remit of the General Social Care Council.

The private and voluntary sectors could become principal providers of social care even though the voluntary sector is unsure as to whether it could meet greater responsibilities for providing services for older and disabled people. A recent report found that of 115 charities contacted, 69 per cent were subsidizing currently operating services from their own funds (Brindle 1997).

The 1990 NHS and Community Care Act has failed to bring about effective collaboration between health and local authority services. Lewis and Glennerster (1996) argue on the basis of research findings that the divide between NHS and local authority funding is artificial and gives rise to petty boundary conflicts. More attention needs to be given to finding: 'A saner way of bridging the divide between "free" (centrally funded) health care and means tested and locally funded social care' (Lewis and Glennerster 1996: 209). If this line of argument is followed possible solutions would include the imposition of 1 per cent on the social security contribution and using the receipts to finance community care, or tax inducements to encourage private insurance policies to cover long-term care. A separate centrally funded community care agency could be set up comprised of health and social care staff (Lewis and Glennerster 1996).

A further possibility would be to place responsibility for community care with either health or local authorities. Recent trends would seem to suggest that if this were to happen community care would become a health care rather than a social services responsibility. Local authority social services departments will in the future be acting principally as brokers within an increasingly privatized market of care, making financial assessments, setting up contracts between purchasers and providers of services, and creating packages of care.

A White Paper published by the Conservative Party some eight weeks before losing the 1997 general election described a situation in which local authorities' powers to provide residential services for older and disabled people would be severely curtailed.

Although improvements in training for child care social workers and the possible extension of direct payments to disabled people were advocated, the familiar message of individual self-reliance in adversity was reinforced. Local authorities acting as agents of local government would purchase services from the voluntary and private sectors. Local authorities would provide their own residential care only after making a vigorous attempt to purchase the services from other sources. The White Paper describes the role of the statutory social services as a support to those who are meeting social needs. Primary responsibility for care should lie with an individual's family, friends, and neighbours. Statutory social services should therefore become more targeted towards those who cannot meet their own needs through networks.

This general line of thinking does not appear to be radically different from the Labour government's approach to welfare. The result of this could be the increasing residualization of local authority care and narrower definitions of need and danger. Professional judgements will be increasingly subordinated to managerial imperatives and corporate control (Clarke 1996). In a society in which local authorities increasingly become purchasers and not providers of social services, social workers and care managers will be experts in contracting and budget control.

One view of the privatization of welfare is that it is a massive con trick imposed upon often vulnerable people in order to further a particular set of economic arrangements. It is principally designed to reduce expenditure whilst transforming belief in the intrinsic superiority of a marketized welfare into a form of common sense. The introduction of the internal market is less about needs-led assessments than it is about restructuring a welfare system to suit the needs of capitalism. From this perspective capitalism moves from a relatively organized to a disorganized, more fragmented, phase, or in other words from the centralized bureaucratic model of organization as exemplified in the generic model of social work, to more local differentiated modes of welfare provision (Lash and Urry 1987). Social work services will be de-genericized and fragmented into different types of services (e.g. child protection, family services, services for disabled people).

What appears to present itself in the next two decades and beyond is a situation in which there are ever increasing numbers of people making greater demands on community services with the same or possibly diminishing resources. Social workers will constantly work in situations in which demand outstrips available supply. Although to some extent social workers have always been forced to grapple with this essential dilemma, over the next decade and beyond this disparity will become greater.

Conclusion

Many practitioners and academics in social work now express a measured acceptance of change, preferring to pursue a middle way between overt hostility and unquestioning acceptance of policy developments which have occurred over the last two decades. Payne argues that:

Policy analysis related to practice seems to me to have two faults. It is either so critical as to be hostile to the innovation, or it derives from the government's own analysis of its policy, converted into practice and policy guidance and reinforced by selectively funded research. (Payne 1995: p. xiii)

To be helpful, Payne argues, constructive criticism must be offered. It is difficult for those more critical of recent reforms to be constructive in a political climate which appears to confer an almost sacred superiority on market principles.

It is not for some critics a question of adjusting or making the community care plan more technically competent. Jones, in a scathing attack on recent developments in social work education and training which reflect current employer requirements, has argued that: 'The national curriculum for social work is simply ridiculous. It positively endorses "anti thinking"' (Jones 1996: 208). Throughout this book it has been argued that more thinking is urgently required in social policy and social work. The case still has to be made that the most effective way of delivering social services is through privatization. It is the appropriateness and indeed the morality of infusing the welfare system with market principles in an attempt to reduce welfare costs which has yet to be resolved.

Although social work has an uncertain future it will survive within the public sector for the foreseeable future, although an extended role for the private sector is envisaged by the Labour government. Social workers provide, as Hopkins (1996) has suggested, a 'buffer between public criticism and ministerial responsibility'. At this level particularly in the areas of child care and community mental health practice it is unlikely that a minister would wish to be seen as risking public safety by removing professionals from areas of social life which are so sensitive to moral panic.

Access to personal social services sensitively and effectively delivered reflects values of care and decency which are essential in any modern democracy. The destruction of a professional culture which seeks to address the effects of human need and hardship reflects the institutionalized removal of basic rights, and will ultimately weaken society.

Exercise

Below are some statements which have been used both to support and to deprofessionalize social work. Critically discuss the arguments which emanate from the statements and add your own assessment.

Arguments against social work

- Abolition of social work will remove some of the absurdities of political correctness.

- There is a need to cut the current budget on social services spending.
- A mixed economy of welfare is more efficient and responsive to the needs of service users.
- State social work creates massive, expensive bureaucracies which drain resources.
- State welfare has not delivered efficient and effective social work services.
- Social work encourages dependency on the state.

Arguments for social work

- The abolition of social work reflects new right ideology not commitment to good care.
- Professionalism is needed in order to create an efficient service.
- Abolition of social work will create greater risks for service users.
- Social work reflects the humanitarian values of a caring society.
- The abolition of social work is merely an attempt to reduce expenditure and reduce services to people in genuine need.
- Social work is necessary to ensure the rights of service users.
- Social workers are required to be advocates for those who are oppressed in society.

Exercise

Alternative problem definitions

How far can the following be seen as alternative formulations of the problem facing social work in the future?

How are they similar and different from the problem definitions presented in current approaches to social policy?

1. Growing demand for services which outstrips supply.
2. Growing managerialism.
3. Increased emphasis prioritizing danger and cost.
4. Increasing dependency on the internal market for the delivery of social services.
5. Increasing residualization and fragmentation of state services.
6. The deprofessionalization of social work.

FURTHER READING

At the time of writing this vitally important issue has received relatively little attention in the social work literature. Midgeley's work is relevant to this topic, providing an overview of the development of social work in a changing global environment. L. Dominelli (1996) provides an account of deprofessionalization of social work in 'Deprofessionalising Social Work: Anti-

Oppressive Practice, Competencies and Postmodernism', *British Journal of Social Work*, 26: 153–75. Chapters in N. Parton (1996) (ed.), *Social Theory, Social Change and Social Work* (London, Routledge) are particularly useful in examining the debates relating to the future of social work. Chapters included deal with feminism, older people, and probation. The postmodern condition is critically examined in connection with specific issues related to social work. Peter Leonard's (1997) *Postmodern Welfare: Reconstructing an Emancipatory Project* (London, Sage) is essential reading, providing one of the most clearly articulated analyses of welfare and postmodernity to date.

BIBLIOGRAPHY

ABEL-SMITH, B., and TOWNSEND, P. (1965), *The Poor and the Poorest*, London, Bell.

ABERCROMBIE, N., HILL, S., and TURNER, B. (1980), *The Dominant Ideology Thesis*, London, Allen & Unwin.

AHMAD, W. I. U., and ATKIN, K. (1996), *'Race' and Community Care*, Buckingham, Open University Press.

ALASZEWSKI, A., and MANTHORPE, J. (1990), 'The New Right and the Professions', *British Journal of Social Work*, 20 (3): 237–51.

ALCOCK, P. (1994), 'Back to the Future: Victorian Values for the 21st Century', in C. Murray, *Underclass: The Crisis Deepens*, London, Institute of Economic Affairs/The Sunday Times.

——(1996), *Social Policy in Britain*, London, Macmillan.

ALDGATE, J. (1997), 'Family Breakdown', in M. Davies (ed.), *The Blackwell Companion to Social Work*, Oxford, Blackwell.

ALDRIDGE, M. (1994), *Making Social Work News*, London, Routledge.

ALLAN, G. (1997), 'Family', in M. Davies (ed.), *The Blackwell Companion to Social Work*, Oxford, Blackwell.

ALLSOP, J. (1995), *Health Policy and the NHS: Towards 2,000*, London, Longman.

ALTHUSSER, L. (1977), 'Ideology and the Ideological State Apparatuses', in *Lenin and Philosophy*, London, New Left Books.

AMIEL, B. (1992), 'Lady Bountiful Lethal Little Society List', *Sunday Times*, 11 Oct.

ANDERSON-FORD, D., and HALSEY, M. (1984), *Mental Health Law and Practice for Social Workers*, London, Butterworths.

ANTHIAS, F. (1992), 'Connecting Race with Ethnic Phenomena', *Sociology*, 20 (3): 421–38.

APPLEYARD, B. (1993), 'Why Paint so Black a Picture?', *Independent*, 4 Aug.

ARMSTRONG, D. (1983), *Political Anatomy of the Body: Medical Knowledge in Britain in the Twentieth Century*, Cambridge, Cambridge University Press.

ASHWORTH, A. (1984), 'Sentencing in Crown Court', Occasional Paper 10, Oxford, Centre for Criminological Research.

ASQUITH, S. (1993), *Protecting Children: Cleveland to Orkney: More Lessons to Learn*, Edinburgh, HMSO.

Association of Chief Officers of Probation (1994), 'Position Statement on Domestic Violence' (draft).

ATKINSON, A. B. (1989), *Poverty and Social Security*, Hemel Hempstead, Harvester Wheatsheaf.

Audit Commission (1986), *Making a Reality of Community Care*, London, HMSO.

——(1994), *Seen but not Heard*, London, HMSO.

BAILEY, R., and BRAKE, M. (1975), *Radical Social Work*, London, Edward Arnold.

BALDOCK, J. (1997), 'Social Care in Old Age: More than a Funding Problem', *Social Policy and Administration*, 31 (1): 73–89.

——and UNGERSON, C. (1994), *Becoming Consumers of Community Care*, York, Joseph Rowntree Foundation.

BALDWIN, S., and TWIGG, J. (1991), 'Women and Community Care: Reflections on a Debate', in M. Maclean and D. Groves (eds.), *Women's Issues in Social Policy*, London, Routledge.

BALL, C., PRESTON-SHOOT, M., ROBERTS, G., and VERNON, S. (1995), *Law for Social Workers in England and Wales*, London, CCETSW.

BALLARD, C. (1979), 'Conflict, Continuity and Change', in V. S. Khan (ed.), *Minority Families of Britain*, Oxford, Basil Blackwell.

BALLARD, R. (1992), 'New Clothes for the Emperor: The Conceptual Nakedness of the Race Relations Industry in Britain', *New Community*, 18 (3): 481–92.

BARKER, J. (1984), *Black and Asian Old People in Britain*, Mitcham, Age Concern England.

BARKER, M., and BEEZER, A. (1992), *Readings into Cultural Studies*, London, Routledge.

BARN, R. (1993), *Black Children in the Public Care System*, London, Batsford.

——SINCLAIR, R., and FERDINAND, D. (1997), *Acting on Principle: An Examination of Race and Ethnicity in Social Services Provision for Children and Families*, London, Commission for Racial Equality.

BARNES, C. (1991), *Disabled People in Britain and Discrimination*, London, Hurst.

——(1993), 'Political Correctness, Language and Rights', *Rights Not Charity*, 1 (3): 13–24.

——BOWL, R., and FISHER, M. (1990), *Sectioned: Social Services and the 1983 Mental Health Act*, London, Routledge.

BARTON, C. (1996), 'That's our Baby Now', *Guardian*, 4 June.

BARTON, L. (1993), 'Labels, Markets and Inclusive Education', in J. Visser and G. Upton, *Special Education in Britain after Warnock*, London, David Fulton.

BEAN, P. (1986), *Mental Disorder and Legal Control*, Cambridge, Cambridge University Press.

——and MOUSER, P. (1993), *Discharged from Psychiatric Hospitals*, London, Macmillan/Mind.

BELL, D. (1960), *The End of Ideology*, Glencoe, Ill., Freer Press.

BERRIDGE, D., and BRODIE, I. (1996), 'Residential Child Care in England and Wales: The Inquiries and After', in M. Hill and J. Aldgate (eds.), *Child Welfare Services: Developments in Law, Policy, Practice and Research*, London, Jessica Kingsley.

BIEHAL, N. (1993), 'Changing Practice: Participation Rights and Community Care', *British Journal of Social Work*, 21: 245–57.

BIESTEK, K. (1961), *The Casework Relationship*, London, Allen & Unwin.

BINNEY, V., HARKELL, G., and NIXON, J. (1988), *Leaving Violent Men: A Study of Refuges and Housing for Battered Women*, Leeds, Women's Aid Federation.

BLAKEMORE, K., and DRAKE, R. (1996), *Understanding Equal Opportunity Policies*, Hemel Hempstead, Harvester Wheatsheaf.

BLOOM-COOPER, L. (1985), *A Child in Trust*, London, Brent Council.

BODLOVIC, M. (1992), 'Disability: Responses of Probation Areas to a Survey by Sub-group on Disability', *NAPO News*, 36: 4–5.

BOLGER, S., CORRIGAN, P., DOCKING, J., and FROST, N. (1981), *Towards Socialist Welfare Work*, London, Macmillan.

BOOTH, T. (1997), 'Learning Difficulties', in M. Davies (ed.), *The Blackwell Companion to Social Work*, Oxford, Blackwell.

BORSAY, A. (1986), *Disabled People in the Community*, London, Bedford Square Press.

BOSANQUET, N., and PROPPER, C. (1991), 'Charting the Grey Economy in the 1990s', *Policy and Politics*, 19 (4): 269–82.

BOSWELL, G. (1989), *Holding the Balance between Court and Client*, Social Work Monographs, Norwich, University of East Anglia.

Bibliography

BOURNE, J., and SIVANANDAN, A. (1980), 'Cheerleaders and Ombudsmen', *Race and Class*, 21 (1): 331–52.

BRADLEY, M., and ALDGATE, J. (1994), 'Short Term Family Based Care for Children in Need', *Adoption and Fostering*, 18 (4): 24–9.

BRADSHAW, J. (1972), 'A Taxonomy of Social Need', *New Society*, 496: 640–3.

BRAKE, M., and HALE, C. (1992), *Public Order and Private Lives*, London, Routledge.

BRAYE, S., and PRESTON-SHOOT, M. (1995), *Empowering Practice in Social Care*, Buckingham, Open University Press.

BREMNER, J., and HILLIN, A. (1994), *Sexuality, Young People and Care*, London, Russell House Press/Central Council for Education and Training in Social Work.

BREWER, C., and LAIT, J. (1980), *Can Social Work Survive*, London, Maurice Temple Smith.

BRIGGS, A. (1961), 'The Welfare State in Historical Perspective', *European Journal of Sociology*, 228.

BRINDLE, D. (1996a), 'Alarm over Suicide Rates', *Guardian*, Tuesday, 16 Jan.

——(1996b), 'Hospital Beds "Blocked" by Social Care Patients', *Guardian*, 28 Dec.

——(1997) 'Government Puts its Faith in Charity', *Guardian*, 13 Mar.

BROAD, B., and DENNEY, D. (1996), 'Users' Rights and the Probation Service: Some Opportunities and Obstacles', *Howard Journal*, 35 (1): 61–76.

BROWN, M. (1985), *Introduction to Social Administration* (6th edn.), London, Hutchinson.

BRUEGAL, I. (1983), 'Women's Employment, Legislation and the Labour Market', in J. Lewis (ed.), *Women's Welfare, Women's Rights*, Beckenham, Croom Helm.

BURROWS, R., PLEACE, N., and QUILGARS, D. (1997) (eds.), *Homelessness and Social Policy*, London, Routledge.

BUSFIELD, J. (1986), *Managing Madness: Changing Ideas and Practice*, London, Unwin Hyman.

BUTLER-SLOSS, L. J. (1988), *Report of the Inquiry into Child Abuse in Cleveland*, London, HMSO.

CAHILL, M. (1994), *The New Social Policy*, Oxford, Blackwell.

CAMBRIDGE, P. (1992), 'Case Management in Community Services: Organisational Responses', *British Journal of Social Work*, 22 (5): 495–517.

——HAYES, L., and KNAPP, K., with GOULD, E., and FENYO, A. (1994), *Care in the Community: Five Years on*, Canterbury, PSSRU, University of Kent, Arena.

CAMPBELL, J. (1996), 'Competence in Mental Health Social Work', in K. O'Hagan (ed.), *Competence in Social Work: A Practical Guide for Professionals*, London, Jessica Kingsley.

——and OLIVER, M. (1996), *Disability Politics: Understanding our Past, Changing our Future*, London, Routledge.

CARABINE, J. (1992), 'Constructing Women: Women's Sexuality and Social Policy', *Critical Social Policy*, 34 (12): 23–38.

CAREW, R. (1979), 'The Place of Knowledge in Social Work Activity', *British Journal of Social Work*, 9 (3): 349–64.

CARTER, P., EVERITT, A., and HUDSON, A. (1992), 'Malestream Training? Women, Feminism and Social Work Education', in M. Langan and L. Day (eds.), *Women, Oppression and Social Work*, London, Routledge.

CASHMORE, E., and TROYNA, B. (1983), *Introduction to Race Relations*, London, Routledge & Kegan Paul.

——(1990), *Introduction to Race Relations* (2nd edn.), Basingstoke, Falmer Press.

CASSAM, E., and GUPTA, H. (1992), *Quality Assurance for Social Care Agencies*, London, Longman.

CAVADINO, M., and DIGNAN, J. (1992), *The Penal System*, London, Sage.

CCETSW (1976), *Values in Social Work* (Paper 13) London, Central Council for Education and Training in Social Work.

—— (1991*a*), *Rules and Requirements for the Diploma in Social Work* (Paper 30) (2nd edn.), London, Central Council for Education and Training in Social Work.

—— (1991*b*), *One Small Step towards Racial Justice*, London, Central Council for Education and Training in Social Work.

—— (1994*a*), *Second Report on Applications via the Social Work Admissions System: 1994 Entry*, London, Central Council for Education and Training in Social Work.

—— (1994*b*), *The Mental Health Dimension in Social Work: Guidance for DipSW Programmes*, Improving Social Work Education series 16, London, Central Council for Education and Training in Social Work.

—— (1995), *Rules and Requirements for the Diploma in Social Work* (Paper 30), London, Central Council for Education and Training in Social Work.

CHALLIS, D., and DAVIES, B. (1986), *Case Management in the Community: An Evaluated Experiment in the Home Care of the Elderly*, Aldershot, Gower.

—— —— and TRASKE, K. (1994), *Community Care: New Agendas and Challenges from the UK and Overseas*, Aldershot, British Society of Gerontology and PSSRU, Ashgate.

CHAPPEL, A. (1992), 'Towards a Sociological Critique of the Normalisation Principle', *Disability, Handicap and Society*, 7 (1): 33–53.

—— (1994), 'Disability, Discrimination and the Criminal Justice System', *Critical Social Policy*, 42: 19–33.

CHECKLAND, S. G., and CHECKLAND, E. (1974), *The Poor Law Report, 1834*, Harmondsworth, Penguin.

CHEETHAM, J. (1972), *Social Work and Immigrants*, London, Routledge & Kegan Paul.

—— FULLER, J., MCIVOR, G., and PETCH, A. (1992), *Evaluating Social Work Effectiveness*, Buckingham, Open University Press.

CLARK, D. (1987), *The New Loving Someone Gay*, Berkeley, Celestial Arts.

CLARKE, J. (1993) (ed.), *A Crisis in Care*, London, Sage.

—— (1996), 'After Social Work?', in N. Parton (ed.), *Social Theory, Social Change and Social Work*, London, Routledge.

—— COCHRANE, A., and MCLAUGHLIN, E. (1994) (eds.), *Managing Social Policy*, London, Sage.

—— —— and SMART, C. (1987), *Ideologies of Welfare*, London, Hutchinson.

CLARKE, K., CRAIG, G., and GLENDINNING, C. (1996), *Small Change: The Impact of the Child Support Act on Lone Mothers and Children*, London, Family Policy Studies Centre.

CLAYTON, S. (1983), 'Social Need Revisited', *Journal of Social Policy*, 12 (2): 215–34.

CLEMENTS, K. (1997), 'Rule of Law', *Community Care*, Apr.: 24–5.

Cm. 62 (1987), *The Law Relating to Child Care and Family Services*, London, HMSO.

Cm. 412 (1988), *Report of the Inquiry into Child Abuse in Cleveland, 1987*, London, HMSO.

CNAAN, R. (1994), 'The New American Social Work Gospel: Case Management of the Chronically Mentally Ill', *British Journal of Social Work*, 24 (5): 533–59.

COATES, K., and SILBURN, R. (1970), *Poverty, the Forgotten Englishman*, Harmondsworth, Penguin.

COHEN, R. (1992), *Hardship Britain*, London, Child Poverty Action Group.

COHN, A. H. (1983), 'The Prevention of Child Abuse: What do we Know about What Works?', in J. E. Leavitt (ed.), *Child Abuse and Neglect: Research and Innovation*, Leiden, Martinus Nijhoff.

Bibliography

COMMON, R., and FLYNN, N. (1992), *Contracting for Care*, York, Joseph Rowntree.

CONNELLY, N. (1990), *Between Apathy and Outrage: Voluntary Organisations in Multi Racial Britain*, London, Policy Studies Institute.

COOPER, P., and COOPER, J. (1994), 'Enforcing Instructions against Oppression', *Probation Journal*, 41 (1): 14–18.

COOTE, A. (1992) (ed.), *The Welfare of Citizens*, London, Oram Press.

——and GILL, T. (1979), *Battered Women and the New Law*, London, Interaction Imprint/National Council for Civil Liberties.

CORRIGAN, P., and LEONARD, P. (1978), *Social Work Practice Under Capitalism: A Marxist Approach*, London, Macmillan.

COSIS-BROWN, H. (1993), 'Lesbians, the State and Social Work Practice', in M. Langan and L. Day (eds.), *Women, Oppression and Social Work*, London, Routledge.

CRAIG, G. (1992), *Cash or Care: A Question of Choice?*, York, Social Policy Research Unit, University of York.

CREPAZ-KEAY, D., BINNS, C., and WILSON, E. (1997), *Dancing with Angels*, London, CCETSW.

CROOK, F. (1993), 'Discrimination in the Criminal Justice System', in P. Senior and B. Williams (eds.), *Values, Gender and Offending*, Sheffield, Pavic.

CROW, J. (1993), 'Awareness and Recognition', in *Good Practice in Child Protection*, Edinburgh, HMSO.

DALE, J., and FOSTER, P. (1986), *Feminists and State Welfare*, London, Routledge.

Dartington Research Unit (1995), *Child Protection and Child Abuse: Messages from Research*, London, HMSO.

DAVID, M. (1994), 'Fundamentally Flawed', in C. Murray, *Underclass*, London, Institute of Economic Affairs/Sunday Times.

DAVIDSON, R., and HUNTER S. (1994) (eds.), *Community Care in Practice*, London, Batsford.

DAVIES, B., BEBBINGTON, A., and CHARNLEY, H. (1990), *Resources, Needs and Outcomes in Community Care*, Aldershot, Ashgate.

DAVIES, D., and NEAL, C. (1996), *Pink Therapy*, Buckingham, Open University Press.

DAVIES, M. (1985), *The Essential Social Worker*, Aldershot, Gower.

——(1991) (ed.), *The Sociology of Social Work*, London, Routledge.

——CROALL, H., and TYRER, J. (1995), *Criminal Justice: An Introduction to the Criminal Justice System in England and Wales*, London, Longman.

DAVIS, K. (1993), 'On the Movement', in J. Swain, V. Finkelstein, S. French, and M. Oliver (eds.), *Disabling Barriers: Enabling Environments*, London, Sage.

DEACON, A. (1995), 'Spending More to Achieve Less: Social Security since 1945', in D. Gladstone (ed.), *British Social Welfare: Past, Present, Future*, London, UCL.

DEAKIN, N. (1987), *The Politics of Welfare*, London, Methuen.

——(1996), 'What does Contracting do to Users?', in D. Billis and M. Harris (eds.), *Voluntary Agencies: Challenges of Organisation and Management*, Basingstoke, Macmillan.

——and WRIGHT, A. (1995), 'Tawney', in V. George and R. Page (eds.), *Modern Thinkers on Welfare*, London, Harvester Wheatsheaf.

DENNEY, D. (1983), 'Some Dominant Perspectives in the Literature Relating to Multi Racial Society', *British Journal of Social Work*, 13 (2): 149–74.

——(1985), 'Race and Crisis Management', in N. Manning (ed.), *Social Problems and Welfare Ideology*, Aldershot, Gower.

——(1992), *Racism and Antiracism in Probation*, London, Routledge.

Department of Health (1976), *The Court Report*, London, HMSO.

——(1985), *Social Work Decisions in Child Care*, London, HMSO.

——(1989*a*), *Griffiths Report*, London, HMSO.

——(1989*b*), *An Introduction to the Children Act 1989*, London, HMSO.

——(1989*c*), *Community Care in the Next Decade and Beyond*, London, HMSO.

——(1991*a*) *Implementing Community Care: Purchaser, Commissioner, and Provider Rules*, London, HMSO.

——(1991*b*), *The Children Act 1989: Guidance and Regulations*, London, HMSO.

——(1993), *Code of Practice: Mental Health Act 1983*, London, HMSO.

——(1995), *The Challenge of Partnership in Child Protection*, London, HMSO.

——(1996), 'John Bowis: Comments on Inquiry into Homicides and Suicides by Mentally Ill People', press release, 15 Jan.

——(1997*a*), *Social Services: Achievement and Challenge*, London, HMSO.

——(1997*b*), *Review of the Functions of the Central Council for Education and Training in Social Work*, Report to sponsoring ministers, London, Department of Health.

——Social Services Inspectorate (1997), *Services for Mentally Disordered Offenders in the Community: An Inspection Report*, London, HMSO.

Department of Health and Social Security (1980), *The Black Report*, London, HMSO.

Department of Social Security (1997), *Family Resources Survey: Great Britain 1995–1996*, London, The Stationery Office.

DIMBLEBY, R., and BURTON, G. (1985), *More than Words: An Introduction to Communication*, London, Methuen.

DINGWALL, R. (1989), 'Some Problems about Predicting Child Abuse and Neglect', in O. Stevenson (ed.), *Child Abuse: Public Policy and Professional Practice*, London, Wheatsheaf.

——EEKELAAR, J. M., and MURRAY, T. (1983), *The Protection of Children: State Intervention and Family Life*, Oxford, Basil Blackwell.

DOBASH, R. E., and DOBASH, R. P. (1980), *Violence against Wives: A Case against Patriarchy*, London, Open Books.

DOBASH, R. P., and DOBASH, R. E. (1992), *Women, Violence and Social Change*, London, Routledge.

DODD, C. (1981), 'The Legal Problems of Homosexuals', in J. Hart and D. Richardson (eds.), *The Theory and Practice of Homosexuality*, London, Routledge & Kegan Paul.

DOMINELLI, L. (1979), 'The Challenge to Social Work Education', *Social Work Today*, 10 (25): 27–9.

——(1988), *Antiracist Social Work*, Basingstoke, Macmillan (2nd edn., 1997).

——(1990), *Women across Continents*, Brighton, Harvester Wheatsheaf.

——(1991*a*), *Gender, Sex Offenders and Probation Practice*, Norwich, Novata.

——(1991*b*), '"What's in a Name?" A comment on "Puritans and Paradigms"', *Social Work and Social Sciences Review*, 2 (3): 231–5.

——(1996), 'Deprofessionalising Social Work: Anti-oppressive Practice, Competencies and Postmodernism', *British Journal of Social Work*, 26 (2): 153–75.

——and MCCLEOD, E. (1989), *Feminist Social Work*, Basingstoke, Macmillan.

DOMINY, N., and RADFORD, L. (1996), *Domestic Violence in Surrey: Towards an Effective Inter-agency Response*, London, Surrey County Council/Roehampton Institute.

DONNAN, C. (1991), *Domestic Violence and the Law*, Belfast Conference held at the Law Society

Bibliography

House, quoted in K. O'Hagan and K. Dillenburger (1995), *The Abuse of Women within Childcare Work*, Buckingham, Open University Press.

DORRELL, S. (1996), 'Local Authority Social Services: Twenty Five Years On', lecture to Politeia, the Royal Society, 9 July.

DOYAL, L., and GOUGH, I. (1991), *A Theory of Human Needs*, Basingstoke, Macmillan.

DOYLE, N., and HARDING, T. (1992), 'Community Care: Applying Procedural Fairness', in A. Coote (ed.), *The Welfare of Citizens*, London, Institute for Policy Research/Oram.

DUNCAN, S., and EDWARDS, R. (1997), *Single Mothers in an International Context*, London, University College Press.

DYER, C. (1996), 'Councils' Cuts in Home Care Services "Illegal"', *Guardian*, 28 June.

EATON, M. (1986), *Justice for Women?*, Milton Keynes, Open University Press.

EDWARDS, J. (1990), 'What Purpose Does Equal Opportunity Serve?', *New Community*, 17 (1): 19–35.

EDWARDS, S. (1989), *Policing Domestic Violence*, London, Sage.

EEKELAAR, J. (1991), 'Parental Responsibility: State of Nature or Nature of the State', *Journal of Social Welfare and Family Law*, 37–50.

ELY, P., and DENNEY, D. (1987), *Social Work in a Multi Racial Society*, Aldershot, Gower.

EVANS, E. J. (1978), *Social Policy 1830–1914: Individualism, Collectivism and the Origins of the Welfare State*, London, Routledge & Kegan Paul.

FARRINGTON, D. (1984), 'England and Wales', in M. Klein (ed.), *Western Systems of Juvenile Justice*, Beverly Hills, Sage.

FERGE, Z. (1997), 'The Changed Welfare Paradigm: The Individualisation of the Social', *Social Policy and Administration*, 31 (1): 20–45.

FEVRE, R. (1984), *Cheap Labour and Racial Discrimination*, Aldershot, Gower.

FIELD, F., with DEACON, A., ALCOCK, P., GREEN, D., and PHILLIPS, M. (1996), *Stakeholder Welfare*, London, Institute of Economic Affairs.

FIELDING, N. (1984), *Probation Practice, Client Support and Social Control*, Aldershot, Gower.

FINKELSTEIN, V. (1980), *Attitudes and Disabled People*, New York, World Rehabilitation Fund.

FISHER, M., NEWTON, C., and SAINSBURY, E. (1984), *Mental Health Social Work Observed*, London, National Institute of Social Work.

FITZGERALD, M., and SIM, J. (1982), *British Prisons*, Oxford, Basil Blackwell.

FITZHERBERT, K. (1967), *West Indian Children in London*, London, Bell.

FLETCHMAN-SMITH, B. (1984), 'Effects of Race on Adoption and Fostering', *International Journal of Social Psychiatry*, 30 (1): 121–8.

FORD, R., and ROBINSON, N. (1993), 'Gay Men: Discrimination within the Criminal Law and Sex Offender Programmes', in C. McCaughey and K. Buckley (eds.), *Sexuality, Youth Work and Probation Practice*, Sheffield, Pavic Publications.

FOUCAULT, M. (1972), *The Archaeology of Knowledge*, London, Routledge.

FOX-HARDING, L. (1991), *Perspectives in Child Care Policy*, London, Longman.

FRANCIS, E. (1991), 'Racism and Mental Health: Some Concerns for Social Work', in *Setting the Context for Change*, London, Central Council for Education and Training in Social Work.

FRASER, D. (1984), *The Evolution of the British Welfare State*, 2nd edn., London, Macmillan.

FRENCH, M. (1993), *War against Women*, New York, Dunnitt Books.

FRIEDMAN, M. (1962), *Capitalism and Freedom*, Chicago, University of Chicago Press.

FUKUYAMA, F. (1992), *The End of History and the Last Man*, New York, Basic Books.

FULLER, R. C., and MYERS, R. R. (1941), 'The Natural History of a Social Problem', *American Sociological Review*, 6 (4): 320–9.

FURNAM, A., and LEWIS, A. (1986), *The Economic Mind*, Brighton, Wheatsheaf.

GALTUNG, S., and RUDGE, R. H. (1965), 'The Structure of Foreign News', *Journal of Peace Research*, 1: 64–89.

GARLAND, D. (1985), *Punishment and Welfare: A History of Penal Strategies*, Aldershot, Gower.

GELSTHORPE, L., and MORRIS, A. (1994), 'Juvenile Justice 1945–1992', in M. Maguire, R. Morgan, and R. Reiner (eds.), *The Oxford Handbook of Criminology*, Oxford, Clarendon.

GENDERS, E., and PLAYER, E. (1989), *Race Relations in Prisons*, Oxford, Oxford University Press.

GEORGE, V., and PAGE, R. (1995) (eds.), *Modern Thinkers on Welfare*, London, Harvester Wheatsheaf.

——and TAYLOR-GOOBY, P. (1996), *European Welfare Policy: Squaring the Welfare Circle*, Basingstoke, Macmillan.

——and WILDING, P. (1976), *Ideology and State Welfare*, London, Routledge.

————(1984), *The Impact of Social Policy*, London, Routledge.

————(1985), *Ideology and Social Welfare*, London, Routledge & Kegan Paul.

————(1995), *Welfare and Ideology*, Hemel Hempstead, Harvester Wheatsheaf.

GILL, O., and JACKSON, B. (1983), *Adoption and Race*, London, Batsford.

GILLESPIE-SELLS, K., and CAMPBELL, J. (1991), *Disability Equality Training Guide*, London, CCETSW/London Boroughs Disability Resource Team.

GILROY, P. (1987), *There Ain't no Black in the Union Jack*, London, Hutchinson.

——(1990), 'The End of Antiracism', *New Community*, 17 (1): 71–83.

——and SIM, J. (1985), 'Law, Order and the State of the Nation', *Capital and Class*, 25: 15–51.

GIOVANNONI, J. M. (1982), 'Prevention of Child Abuse and Neglect: Research and Policy Issues', *Social Work Research Abstracts*, 18 (3): 22–31.

GLADSTONE, D. (1995*a*), *British Social Welfare*, London, University College London Press.

——(1995*b*), 'The Welfare State and the State of Welfare', in D. Gladstone (ed.), *British Social Welfare*, London, University College London Press.

GLENDINNING, C., and BEWLEY, C. (1994), 'Involving Disabled People in Community Care Planning: The First Steps', Manchester, Manchester University, Department of Social Policy and Social Work.

——and MILLAR, J. (1992), *Women and Poverty in Britain* (2nd edn.), Brighton, Wheatsheaf.

GLENNERSTER, H. (1983) (ed.), *The Future of the Welfare State*, London, Heinemann.

——(1995), *British Social Policy since 1945*, Oxford, Blackwell.

——MATSAGANIS, M., and OWENS, P. (1994), *Implementing GP Fundholding*, Buckingham, Open University Press.

GOODWIN, S. (1997), *Comparative Mental Health Policy*, London, Sage.

GOSS, S., and MILLER, C. (1995), *From Margin to Mainstream: Developing User and Carer Centred Community Care*, York, Joseph Rowntree Community.

GOUGH, I. (1979), *The Political Economy of the Welfare State*, London, Macmillan.

GREEN, A. E. (1994), *The Geography of Poverty and Wealth: Evidence on the Changing Spatial Distribution and Segregation of Poverty and Wealth from the Census of Population 1991 and 1981*, Warwick, Institute for Employment Research.

GRIMSHAW, R., and BERRIDGE, D. (1994), *Educating Disruptive Children*, London, National Children's Bureau.

Bibliography

GUSTAFSSON, S. (1994), 'Childcare and Types of Welfare States', in D. Sainsbury (ed.), *Gendering Welfare States*, London, Sage.

HADLEY, R., and HATCH, S. (1981), *Social Welfare and the Failure of the State*, London, Allen & Unwin.

HAGUE, G., and MALOS, E. (1995), 'Domestic Violence, Social Policy and Housing', *Critical Social Policy*, 42 (1): 112–25.

HALLETT, C. (1991), 'The Children Act 1989 and Community Care: Comparisons and Contrasts', *Policy and Politics*, 198 (4): 283–91.

HALL, S. (1979), *Drifting into a Law and Order Society*, London, Cobden Trust.

——CLARKE, J., CRITCHER, C., JEFFERSON, T., and ROBERTS, B. (1978), *Policing the Crisis*, London, Macmillan.

HANMER, J., and STATHAM, D. (1988), *Women and Social Work: Towards a Women Centred Practice*, London, Macmillan.

HARDIKER, P. (1996), 'The Legal and Social Construction of Significant Harm', in M. Hill and J. Aldgate (eds.), *Child Welfare Services: Developments in Law and Policy Practice and Research*, London, Jessica Kingsley.

HARDING, T. (1992), *Great Expectations and Spending on Social Services*, London, National Institute of Social Work.

HART, J., and RICHARDSON, D. (1981), *The Theory and Practice of Homosexuality*, London, Routledge & Kegan Paul.

HAVAS, E. (1995), 'The Family as Ideology', *Social Policy and Administration*, 29 (1): 1–9.

HAYEK, F. (1949) *Individualism and Economic Order*, London, Routledge & Kegan Paul.

HEDDERMAN, C., and HOUGH, M. (1994), *Does the Criminal Justice System Treat Men and Women Differently?*, Home Office Research and Statistics Department, 10, London, HMSO.

HEIDENSOHN, F. (1994), 'Gender and Crime', in M. Maguire, R. Morgan, and R. Reiner (eds.), *The Oxford Handbook of Criminology*, Oxford, Clarendon.

HENDRICK, H. (1994), *Child Welfare in England 1872–1989*, London, Routledge.

HEPPLE, B. (1987), 'The Race Relations Act and the Process of Change', *New Community*, 14: 1–2.

HERAUD, B. (1970), *Sociology and Social Work*, London, Open Books.

HILL, M., and ALDGATE, J. (1996), 'The Children Act 1989 and Recent Developments in Research in England and Wales', in M. Hill and J. Aldgate (eds.), *Child Welfare Services: Developments in Law, Policy, Practice and Research*, London, Jessica Kingsley.

HILLS, J. (1993), *The Future of Welfare: A Guide to the Debate*, York, Joseph Rowntree Foundation.

——(1995), *Joseph Rowntree Inquiry into Income and Wealth*, vol. ii, York, Joseph Rowntree.

——(1996), *New Inequalities*, Cambridge, Cambridge University Press.

HINDNESS, B. (1987), *Freedom, Equality and the Market*, London, Tavistock.

HM Prison Service (1993), *Equal Opportunities: Annual Progress Report*, London, Home Office.

HOBSBAWM, E. (1969), *Industry and Empire*, Harmondsworth, Penguin.

HOLLIS, F. (1964), *Casework: A Psychosocial Therapy*, New York, Random House.

Home Office (1990*a*), *Crime, Justice and Protecting the Public*, Cmnd. 965, London, HMSO.

——(1990*b*), *Supervision and Punishment in the Community*, Cmnd. 966, London, HMSO.

——(1990*c*), *Victims' Charter: A Statement of Rights for Victims*, London, Home Office.

——(1991*a*), 'Discussion Document: Towards National Standards for Pre-sentence Reports', Nov., unpublished.

——(1991*b*), *Organising, Supervision and Punishment in the Community: A Decision Document*, London, HMSO.

——(1992*a*), 'Quality of Service and the Citizens Charter', discussion document, unpublished.

——(1992*b*), *The Probation Service: Three Year Plan for the Probation Service, 1993–1996*, London, HMSO.

——(1992c), *Race and the Criminal Justice System*, London, HMSO.

——(1994), *Equal Opportunities: Annual Progress Report 1992/1993*, London, Home Office.

——(1995), *Young People and Crime*, Research Study 145, London, HMSO.

——(1997), *Tackling Youth Crime: A Consultation Paper*, London, Home Office.

HOPKINS, J. (1996), 'Social Work through the Looking Glass', in N. Parton (ed.), *Social Theory, Social Change and Social Work*, London, Routledge.

HOUGH, M., and MAYHEW, P. (1983), *The British Crime Survey*, Home Office Research Study 76, London, Home Office.

HOWE, D. (1986), *Social Workers and their Practice in Welfare Bureaucracies*, Aldershot, Gower.

——(1988), 'Review', *Issues in Social Work Practice*, 8 (1): 65–6.

——(1994), 'Modernity, Postmodernity and Social Work', *British Journal of Social Work*, 24 (5): 513–32.

——(1996), 'Surface and Depth in Social Work Practice', in N. Parton (ed.), *Social Theory, Social Change and Social Work*, London, Routledge.

HOYES, L., and LART, R. (1992), 'Taking Care', *Community Care*, 20 Aug.: 14.

——and MEANS, R. (1993), 'Markets, Contracts and Social Care Services: Prospects and Problems', in J. Bornat, C. Pereira, D. Pilgrim, and F. Williams (eds.), *Community Care: A Reader*, London, Macmillan.

HUDSON, B. L. (1982), *Social Work with Psychiatric Patients*, London, Macmillan.

——(1989), 'Discrimination and Disparity: The Influence of Race on Sentencing', *New Community*, 16 (1): 21–32.

——(1992), 'Community Care Planning: Incrementalism to Rationalism?', *Social Policy and Administration*, 26 (3): 185–200.

——CULLEN, R., and ROBERTS, C. (1993), *Training for Work with Mentally Disordered Offenders*, London, CCETSW.

HUDSON, R., and WILLIAMS, A. (1995), *Divided Britain* (2nd edn.), Chichester, Wiley.

HUGHES, B. (1995), *Older People and Community Care*, Buckingham, Open University Press.

HUGMAN, B. (1991), *Power and the Caring Professions*, Basingstoke, Macmillan.

HUXLEY, P. (1993), 'Case Management and Care Management in Community Care', *British Journal of Social Work*, 23 (4): 365–81.

——(1997), 'Mental Illness', in M. Davies (ed.), *The Blackwell Companion to Social Work*, Oxford, Blackwell.

Institute of Race Relations (1993), *Community Care: The Black Experience*, London, Institute of Race Relations.

JACKSON, V. (1996), *Racism and Child Protection: The Black Experience of Child Abuse*, London, Cassell.

JADEJA, S., and SINGH, J. (1993), 'Life in a Cold Climate', *Community Care*, 22 Apr.: 12–13.

JENNES, V. (1995), 'Social Movement Growth, Domain Expansion, and Framing Processes: The Gay Lesbian Movement and Violence against Gays and Lesbians as a Social Problem', *Social Problems*, 42 (1): 143–70.

JESSOP, B., BONNET, K., BROMLEY, S., and LONG, T. (1984), 'Authoritarian Populism: Two Nations and Thatcherism', *New Left Review*, 147: 32–64.

Bibliography

JONES, C. (1996), 'Anti-intellectualism and the Peculiarities of British Social Work Education', in N. Parton (ed.), *Social Theory, Social Change and Social Work*, London, Routledge.

——(1997), 'Poverty', in M. Davies (ed.), *The Blackwell Companion to Social Work*, Oxford, Blackwell.

JONES, K. (1960), *Mental Health and Social Policy 1845–1959*, London, Routledge & Kegan Paul.

——(1988), *Experience in Mental Health Community Care and Social Policy*, London, Sage.

——(1991), *The Making of Social Policy in Britain 1830–1990*, London, Athlone.

——and FOWLES, A. J. (1984), *Ideas and Institutions*, London, Routledge & Kegan Paul.

Joseph Rowntree Foundation (1995), *Inquiry into Income and Wealth*, vol. i, York, Joseph Rowntree Foundation.

JOWELL, T. (1991), *Community Care: A Prospectus for the Task*, York, Joseph Rowntree.

KAGANAS, F., KING, M., and PIPER, C. (1995), *Legislating for Harmony: Partnership under the Children Act 1989*, London, Jessica Kingsley.

KARN, V. (1984), 'Race and Housing in Britain: The Role of the Major Institutions', in N. Glazer and K. Young (eds.), *Ethnic Pluralism and Public Policy*, London: Heinemann.

KEEBLE, U. (1979), *Aids and Adaptations*, London, Bedford Square Press.

——and PINKERTON, J. (1996), 'The Children (Northern Ireland) Order', in M. Hill and J. Aldgate (eds.), *Child Welfare Services*, London, Jessica Kingsley.

KELLY, G. (1996), 'Competence in Risk Analysis', in K. O'Hagan (ed.), *Competence in Social Work Practice*, London, Jessica Kingsley.

KESTENBAUM, A. (1992), *Cash for Care*, Nottingham, Independent Living Fund.

KING, M. (1981), *The Framework of Criminal Justice*, London, Croom Helm.

KNAPP, M. (1996), 'Are Voluntary Agencies Really More Effective?', in D. Billis and M. Harris (eds.), *Voluntary Agencies: Challenges of Organisation and Management*, London, Macmillan.

LAING, R. D. (1967), *The Politics of Experience*, Harmondsworth, Penguin.

LAND, H. (1991), 'Time to Care', in M. Maclean and D. Groves (eds.), *Women's Issues in Social Policy*, London, Routledge.

LANGAN, M. (1990), 'Community Care in the 1990s', *Critical Social Policy*, 29: 58–70.

——and DAY, L. (1992) (eds.), *Women, Oppression and Social Work*, London, Routledge.

——and LEE, P. (1989) (eds.), *Radical Social Work Today*, London, Unwin Hyman.

LASH, S., and URRY, J. (1987), *The End of Organised Capitalism*, London, Verso.

LEA, J., and YOUNG, J. (1984), *What is to be Done about Law and Order?*, Harmondsworth, Penguin.

LE GRAND, J. (1982), *The Strategy of Equality*, London, Allen & Unwin.

——(1991), 'Quasi Markets and Social Policy', *Economic Journal*, 101: 1256–67.

——and BARTLETT, W. (1993) (eds.), *Quasi Markets and Social Policy*, London, Macmillan.

LEONARD, P. (1966), *Sociology and Social Work*, London, Routledge & Kegan Paul.

——(1997), *Postmodern Welfare: Reconstructing an Emancipatory Project*, London, Sage.

LEVY, A., and KAHAN, B. (1991), *The Pindown Experience and the Protection of Children: The Report of the Staffordshire Child Care Inquiry*, Stafford, Staffordshire County Council.

LEWIS, J. (1995), *The Voluntary Sector: The State and Social Work in Britain*, London, Edward Elgar.

——and GLENNERSTER, H. (1996), *Implementing the New Community Care*, Buckingham, Open University Press.

——and PIAUCHAUD, D. (1987), 'Women and Poverty in the Twentieth Century', in C. Glendinning and J. Millar (eds.), *Women and Poverty in Britain*, Brighton, Wheatsheaf.

LEWIS, O. (1966), 'The Culture of Poverty', *Scientific American*, 214 (1): 19–25.

LLOYD, M. (1993), 'Lesbian and Gay Clients and Residential Work', in C. McCaughey and K. Buckley (eds.), *Sexuality, Youth Work and Probation Practice*, Sheffield, Pavic Publications/Sheffield Hallam University.

London Group on Race and Aspects of Community Care (1993), *Black Communities—Who Cares? Incorporating Race Equality Principles into Community Care*, London, HMSO.

LONEY, M., BOSWELL, D., and CLARKE, J. (1983), *Social Policy and Social Welfare*, Milton Keynes, Open University Press.

LONSDALE, S. (1990), *Women and Disability: The Experiences of Physical Disability among Women*, London, Macmillan.

LOWE, R. (1993), *The Welfare State in Britain since 1945*, London, Macmillan.

LUTHRA, M. (1997), *Britain's Black Population*, Aldershot, Arena.

McCAUGHEY, C., and BUCKLEY, K. (1993) (eds.), *Sexuality, Youth Work and Probation Practice*, Sheffield, Pavic Publications.

McCONVILLE, F. H., and BALDWIN, J. (1982), 'The Influence of Race on Sentencing in England', *Criminal Law Review*, 652–8.

Mc CORMACK, J., and PHILO, C. (1995), 'Where is Poverty? The Hidden Geography of Poverty in the United Kingdom', in J. Mc Cormack and C. Philo (eds.), *Off the Map: The Social Geography of Poverty in the UK*, London, Child Poverty Action Group.

McCULLOCH, A. (1996), 'Care in the Community is Massively Underfunded', *Guardian*, 18 May.

MacDONALD, G. (1994), 'Developing Empirically Based Practice in Probation', *British Journal of Social Work*, 24: 405–27.

——SHELDON, B., with GILLESPIE, J. (1992), 'Contemporary Studies of the Effectiveness of Social Work', *British Journal of Social Work*, 22 (6): 615–43.

MACEY, M., and MOXON, E. (1996), 'Antiracist and Anti-oppressive Theory', *British Journal of Social Work*, 26 (3): 297–314.

MACK, J., and LANSLEY, S. (1985), *Poor Britain*, London, Allen & Unwin.

———— (1991), *Breadline Britain*, London, Unwin Hyman.

MacLACHLAN, G. (1972) (ed.), *Problems and Progress in Medical Care*, Oxford, Oxford University Press.

MACLEAN, M., and GROVES, D. (1991) (eds.), *Women's Issues and Social Policy*, London, Routledge.

McQUAIL, D. (1987), *Mass Communications Theory* (2nd edn.), London, Sage.

McWILLIAMS, M., and McKIERNAN, J. (1993), *Bringing it Out in the Open: Domestic Violence*, London, Whiting & Birch.

MADOC-JONES, B., and COATES, J. (1996) (eds.), *An Introduction to Women's Studies*, Oxford, Blackwell.

MAGUIRE, M. (1994), 'Crime Statistics, Patterns and Trends', in M. Maguire, M. Morgan, and R. Reiner, *The Oxford Handbook of Criminology*, Oxford, Clarendon.

——MORGAN, R., and REINER, R. (1994), *The Oxford Handbook of Criminology*, Oxford, Clarendon.

MAGURA, S., and MOSES, B. S. (1984), 'Clients as Evaluators in Child Protective Services', *Child Welfare*, 53 (2): 99–112.

MAIR, G. (1989), 'Ethnic Minorities and Magistrates Courts', *British Journal of Criminology*, 26 (2): 147–55.

MAJOR, J. (1996), speech to Conservative Party Conference, Oct.

Bibliography

MALIN, N. (1994) (ed.), *Services for People with Learning Disabilities*, London, Routledge.

MANNING, N. (1985) (ed.), *Social Problems and Welfare Ideology*, Aldershot, Gower.

——and PAGE, R. (1992), *Social Policy Review*, Canterbury, Social Policy Association.

MARSH, A., FORD, R., and FINLAYSON, L. (1997), *Lone Parents, Work and Benefits*, London, HMSO.

MARSLAND, D. (1996*a*), *Welfare or Welfare State*, London, Macmillan.

——(1996*b*), 'The Obsession with Social Justice: A Threat to Progress', *Right Now.* 12.

MARTIN, L., and GASTER, L. (1993), 'Community Care Planning in Wolverhampton Involving the Voluntary Sector and Black and Ethnic Minority Groups', in R. Smith, L. Gaster, L. Harrison, L. Martin, R. Means, and P. Thistlethwaite, *Working Together for Better Community Care*, Bristol, School for Advanced Urban Studies, University of Bristol.

MAY, T. (1991), *Probation: Politics, Policy and Practice*, Milton Keynes, Open University.

——and VASS, T. (1996), *Working with Offenders*, London, Sage.

MAYHO, P. (1996), *Positive Carers*, London, Cassell.

MEANS, R., and SMITH, R. (1994), *Community Care: Policy and Practice*, London, Macmillan.

MEETHAN, K., and THOMPSON, C. (1993), *In their own Homes: Incorporating Carers' and Users' Views in Care Management*, York, Social Policy Research Unit.

MIDGELEY, J. (1995), *Social Development*, London, Sage.

MILLER, G., and HOLSTEIN, J. (1993), *Issues in Social Problems Theory*, New York, Aldine de Gruyter.

MILLS, C. W. (1956), *The Power Elite*, Oxford, Oxford University Press.

MISHRA, R. (1990), *The Welfare State in Capitalist Society*, Hemel Hempstead, Harvester Wheatsheaf.

MIZRA, K. (1991), 'Waiting for Guidance', in *One Small Step towards Racial Justice*, London, CCETSW.

MOHAN, J. (1995), *A National Health Service*, London, Macmillan.

MORGAN, R. (1994), 'Imprisonment', in M. Maguire, M. Morgan, and R. Reiner, *The Oxford Handbook of Criminology*, Oxford, Clarendon.

MORRIS, A., and GILLER, H. (1987), *Understanding Juvenile Justice*, Beckenham, Croom Helm.

MORRIS, J. (1993), *Independent Lives: Community Care and Disabled People*, Basingstoke, Macmillan.

——(1997), 'Care or Empowerment? A Disability Rights Perspective', *Social Policy and Administration*, 31 (1): 54–61.

MOXON, D. (1988), *Sentencing Practice in the Crown Court*, Home Office Research Study 103, London, HMSO.

MULLEN, P. M. (1992), 'Is there a Future for Planning Teams?', *Health Services Management Research*, 5 (3): 186–97.

MURRAY, C. (1990), *The Emerging British Underclass*, London, Institute of Economic Affairs.

——(1994), *Underclass: The Crisis Deepens*, London, Institute of Economic Affairs.

NACRO (1988), 'The Electronic Monitoring of Offenders', NACRO briefing, London: National Association for the Care and Resettlement of Offenders.

——(1991), 'Race and Criminal Justice', briefing, London, National Association for the Care and Rehabilitation of Offenders.

NAIK, D. (1991), 'An Examination of Social Work Education within an Antiracist Framework', in *National Curriculum Development Project: Setting the Context for Change*, Antiracist Social Work Education, London, CCETSW.

NAPO (1989), 'Black Probation Staff' (news item), *NAPO News*, Sept., London National Association of Probation Officers: 5.

——(1990a), *The Response of the National Association of Probation Officers to the White Paper 'Crime, Justice and Protecting the Public' Cmnd. 965*, London, National Association of Probation Officers.

——(1990b), *The Response of the National Association of Probation Officers to the Green Paper 'Supervision and Punishment in the Community'*, London, National Association of Probation Officers.

——(1993a), 'Speech Made by Chair of NAPO to the TUC on Lesbian and Gay Rights', *NAPO News* (London, National Association of Probation Officers), 46 (Jan.): 11.

——(1993b), *Disability Pack 27–93*, London, National Association of Probation Officers.

NCVO (1992), *The Charities Act 1992: A Guide for Charities and Other Voluntary Organisations*, London, National Council for Voluntary Organisations.

NELLIS, M. (1996), 'Probation Training: The Links with Social Work', in T. May and A. A. Vass, *Working with Offenders*, London, Sage.

NEWBURN, T. (1995), *Crime and Criminal Justice Policy*, London, Longman.

NEWMAN, J., and CLARKE, J. (1992), 'Going about our Business? The Managerialisation of Public Services', in J. Clarke, A. Cochrane, and E. McLaughlin (eds.), *Managing Social Policy*, London, Sage.

NOCON, A. (1994), *Collaboration in Community Care*, Sunderland, Business Education Publishers.

——and QURESHI, H. (1996), *Outcomes of Community Care for Users and Carers*, Buckingham, Open University Press.

NORMAN, A. (1985), *Triple Jeopardy: Growing Old in a Second Homeland*, London, Centre for Policy on Ageing.

Northern Curriculum Development Project (1991), *Improving Practice in the Criminal Justice System*, Leeds, Central Council for Education and Training in Social Work.

O'HAGAN, K. (1996) (ed.), *Competence in Social Work Practice*, London, Jessica Kingsley.

——and DILLENBURGER, K. (1995), *The Abuse of Women within Childcare Work*, Buckingham, Open University Press.

OLIVER, J. P. J., and MOHAMAD, H. (1992), 'The Quality of Life of the Chronically Mentally Ill: A Comparison of Public, Private, and Voluntary Residential Provisions', *British Journal of Social Work*, 22 (4): 391–404.

OLIVER, M. (1990), *The Politics of Disablement*, London, Macmillan.

——(1991), 'Disability and Participation in the Labour Market', in P. Brown and R. Scase (eds.), *Poor Work*, Milton Keynes, Open University Press.

——(1993), *Disabling Barriers: Enabling Environments*, London, Sage.

——(1994), 'Does Special Education have a Role to Play in the Twenty First Century?', address to the Irish Association of Teachers in Special Education, Sixth Annual Conference, 9–11 June.

——(1996), *Understanding Disability: From Theory to Practice*, London, Macmillan.

——and ZARB, G. (1992), 'Personal Assistance Schemes: An Evaluation', Greenwich, Association of Disabled People.

OLSEN, R. (1984) (ed.), *Social Work and Mental Health: A Guide for the Approved Social Worker*, London, Tavistock.

OPPENHEIM, C., and HARKER, L. (1996), *Poverty: The Facts*, London, Child Poverty Action Group.

Bibliography

PACKMAN, J., and JORDAN, B. (1991), 'The Children Act: Looking Forward, Looking Back', *British Journal of Social Work*, 21 (3): 315–27.

PAHL, J. (1982), 'Police Response to Battered Women', *Journal of Social Welfare Law*, Nov.: 337–43.

——(1985), 'Violence against Women', in N. Manning (ed.), *Social Problems and Welfare Ideology*, Aldershot, Gower.

PARKER, G., and LAWTON, D. (1994), 'Different Types of Care, Different Types of Carer', in *Evidence from the General Household Survey*, London, HMSO.

PARKER, R. (1995), 'Child Care and the Personal Social Services', in D. Gladstone (ed.), *British Social Welfare*, London, University College Press.

PARRY, G., and LIGHTBOWN, J. (1981), 'Presenting Problems of Gay People Seeking Help', in J. Hart and D. Richardson (eds.), *The Theory and Practice of Homosexuality*, London, Routledge & Kegan Paul.

PARTON, N. (1989), 'Child Abuse', in B. Kahan (ed.), *Child Care Research: Policy and Practice*, London, Hodder & Stoughton.

——(1991), *Governing the Family: Child Care, Child Protection, and the State*, London, Macmillan.

——(1996) (ed.), *Social Theory, Social Change and Social Work*, London, Routledge.

PASCALL, G. (1986), *Social Policy: A Feminist Analysis*, London, Routledge.

——(1997), *Social Policy: A New Feminist Analysis*, London, Routledge.

PATEMAN, C. (1988), 'The Patriarchal Welfare State', in A. Gutman (ed.), *Democracy and the Welfare State*, Princeton, Princeton University Press.

PAYNE, M. (1991), *Modern Social Work Theory: A Critical Introduction*, London, Macmillan.

——(1995), *Social Work and Community Care*, London, Macmillan.

——(1997), *Modern Social Work Theory* (2nd edn.), London, Macmillan.

PERCY-SMITH, J. (1996), *Needs Assessments in Public Policy*, Buckingham, Open University Press.

PERKIN, H. (1969), *The Origins of Modern English Society*, London, Routledge & Kegan Paul.

PETCH, A. (1992), *At Home in the Community*, London, Avebury.

PETERSILIA, J., and TURNER, S. (1992), 'An Evaluation of Intensive Probation in California', *Journal of Criminal Law and Criminology*, 82 (2): 610–58.

PHILLIPS, M. (1993), 'Antiracist Zealots Drive away Recruits', *Observer*, 1 Aug.

——(1996), 'Welfare and the Common Good', in F. Field with P. Alcock, A. Deacon, D. Green, and M. Phillips, *Stakeholder Welfare*, London, Institute of Economic Affairs.

PHILLIPSON, C. (1996), 'The Frailty of Old Age', in M. Davies (ed.), *The Blackwell Companion to Social Work*, Oxford, Blackwell.

PILGRIM, D. (1993), 'Mental Health Services in the Twenty First Century: The User–Professional Divide', in J. Bornat, C. Pereira, D. Pilgrim, and F. Williams, *Community Care: A Reader*, Milton Keynes, Open University Press.

——and ROGERS, A. (1993), *A Sociology of Mental Health and Illness*, Buckingham, Open University Press.

PINCHBECK, I., and HEDWITT, M. (1973), *Children in English Society*, London, Routledge & Kegan Paul.

PINCUS, A., and MINAHAN, A. (1973), *Social Work Practice: Model and Method*, Itasca, Ill., Peacock.

PINKER, R. (1971), *Social Theory and Social Policy*, London, Heinemann.

——(1979), *The Idea of Welfare*, London, Heinemann.

PINKERTON, J., and HOUSTON, S. (1996), 'Competence and the Children Act', in K. O'Hagan (ed.), *Competence in the Social Work Process*, London, Sage.

PITTS, J. (1988), *The Politics of Juvenile Justice*, London, Sage.

PIZZEY, E. (1974), *Scream Quietly or the Neighbours Will Hear*, London, Penguin.

PLANT, R. (1992), 'Citizenship Rights and Welfare', in A. Coote (ed.), *The Welfare of Citizens*, London, Oram.

PLATT, A. (1978), *The Child Savers*, Chicago, Chicago University Press.

POLLITT, C. (1993), *Managerialism and the Public Services* (2nd edn.), Oxford, Blackwell.

POULANTZAS, N. (1975), *Political Power and Social Classes*, London, New Left Books.

PRESTON-SHOOT, M., and WILLIAMS, J. (1987), 'Evaluating the Effectiveness of Practice', *Practice*, 1 (4); 393–406.

PRIOR, P. (1992), 'The Approved Social Worker: Reflections on its Origins', *British Journal of Social Work*, 22 (2): 105–19.

QUINNEY, R. (1977), *Class, State and Crime*, London, Longman.

QURESHI, H., and WALKER, A. (1989), *The Caring Relationship*, London, Macmillan.

RAMAZANOGLU, C. (1989), *Feminism and the Contradictions of Oppression*, London, Routledge.

RAMON, S. (1991), 'Principles and Conceptual Knowledge', in S. Ramon (ed.), *Reassessing Community Care: Normalisation and Integration Work*, London, Macmillan.

——(1992) (ed.), *Psychiatric Hospital Closure: Myths and Realities*, London, Chapman Hall.

RASHID, S., and BALL, C. (1984), *Mental Health—Disability—Homelessness—Race Relations*, University of East Anglia, Social Work Monographs.

RAYNOR, P. (1996), 'Evaluating Probation: The Rehabilitation of Effectiveness', in T. May and A. A. Vass (eds.), *Working with Offenders*, London, Sage.

——SMITH, D., and VANSTONE, M. (1994), *Effective Probation Practice*, Basingstoke, Macmillan.

REED, J. (1992), *Review of Health and Social Services for Mentally Disordered Offenders and Others Requiring Similar Services: A Report of the Staffing and Training Advisory Group*, London, Department of Health and Home Office.

REID, W., and EPSTEIN, L. (1977) (eds.), *Task Centred Practice*, New York, Columbia University Press.

REID, W. J., and HANRAHAN, P. (1981), 'The Effectiveness of Social Work: Recent Evidence', in E. M. Goldberg and N. Connelly (eds.), *Evaluative Research in Social Care*, London, Heinemann.

REINER, R. (1989), 'Race and Criminal Justice', *New Community*, 19 (1): 5–21.

RICHARDSON, D., and HART, J. (1981), 'Married and Isolated Homosexuals', in J. Hart and D. Richardson (eds.), *The Theory and Practice of Homosexuality*, London, Routledge & Kegan Paul.

ROBERTSON, T. (1993), 'Probation and Sexuality: A Study of Attitudes to Sexuality in Hereford and Worcester Service', unpublished M.Sc. thesis, University of Oxford.

RODGER, J. J. (1991), 'Discourse Analysis and Social Relationships in Social Work', *British Journal of Social Work*, 21 (1): 63–79.

ROGERS, A., and PILGRIM, D. (1996), *Mental Health Policy in Britain*, London, Longman.

————and LACEY, R. (1993), *Experiencing Psychiatry: Users' Views of Services*, Basingstoke, Macmillan/Mind.

ROJEK, C., and COLLINS, S. (1988), 'Contract or Con Trick Revisited: Comments on the Reply by Corden and Preston-Shoot', *British Journal of Social Work*, 18: 611–22.

——PEACOCK, S., and COLLINS, S. (1988), *Social Work and Received Ideas*, London, Routledge.

Bibliography

ROSE, M. E. (1970), 'The Anti Poor Law Agitation', in J. T. Ward (ed.), *Popular Movements c.1830–1850*, London, Macmillan.

ROWE, J., and LAMBERT, L. (1973), *Children who Wait*, London, Association of British Adoption Agencies.

RUMGAY, J. (1989), 'Talking Tough: Empty Threats in Probation', *Howard Journal*, 28 (3): 177–86.

RUSHTON, A. (1990), 'Community Based versus Hospital Based Care for Acutely Mentally Ill People', *British Journal of Social Work*, 20 (3): 373–83.

RYBURN, M. (1996), 'Adoption in England and Wales: Current Issues and Future Trends', in M. Hill and J. Aldgate (eds.), *Child Welfare Services*, London, Jessica Kingsley.

SAFILIOS-ROTHSCHILD, C. (1970), *The Sociology and Social Psychology of Disability and Rehabilitation*, New York, Random House.

SAINSBURY, D. (1994) (ed.), *Gendering Welfare Services*, London, Sage.

SAINSBURY, E. (1977), *The Personal Social Services*, London, Pitman.

SAINSBURY, S. (1995) 'Disabled People and the Personal Social services', in D. Gladstone (ed.), *British Social Welfare: Past, Present, Future*, London, UCL Press.

SALTER, B., and SALTER, C. (1993), 'Theatre of the Absurd', *Health Service Journal*, 11 Nov.: 30–1.

Sane (1996), 'The Boyd Report on Homicide and Suicide: Sane's Statement', press release, 16 Jan., London, Sane.

SAUSSURE, F. de (1974), *Course in General Linguistics*, London, Fontana.

SCHLESINGER, P., TUMBER, H., and MURDOCK, G. (1991), 'The Media Politics of Crime and Criminal Justice', *British Journal of Sociology*, 42 (3): 397–420.

SCHOFIELD, H. (1994), 'Revision of National Standards', *NAPO News*, Apr.: 59.

Scottish Office (1991), *The Justice Charter*, Edinburgh, Scottish Courts Administration.

SEED, P., and KAYE, G. (1994), *Handbook for Assessing and Managing Care in the Community*, London, Jessica Kingsley.

SELDEN, R. (1989), *A Readers' Guide to Contemporary Literary Theory*, London, Harvester.

SELLICK, C. (1992), *Supporting Short Term Foster Carers*, Aldershot, Avebury.

SENIOR, P. (1992), 'Gender Conscious Service Delivery: Implications for Staff Development', in P. Senior and P. Woodhill (eds.), *Gender, Crime and Probation Practice*, Sheffield, Pavic.

SHAKESPEARE, T. (1993), 'Allies, Advocates and Obstacles', *Coalition* (Oct.).

SHARKEY, P. (1995), *Introducing Community Care*, London, Collins.

SHEARER, A. (1981), *Disability: Whose Handicap*, Oxford, Blackwell.

SHELDON, B. (1982), *Behaviour Modification*, London, Tavistock.

——(1986), 'Social Work Effectiveness and Experiments: Review and Implications', *British Journal of Social Work*, 16 (2): 223–42.

SHEPPARD, M. (1990), *Mental Health: The Role of the Approved Social Worker*, Sheffield, JUSSR.

SIBEON, R. (1991), *Towards a New Sociology of Social Work*, Aldershot, Avebury.

SIEGEL, D. H. (1984), 'Defining Empirically Based Practice', *Social Work*, 29 (4): 325–31.

SILBURN, R. (1995), 'Beveridge', in V. George and R. Page (eds.), *Modern Thinkers on Welfare*, London, Harvester Wheatsheaf.

SIMKIN, M. (1982), 'Review', *Critical Social Policy*, 1 (3): 92–4.

——(1989), 'Radical Social Work: Lessons for the 1990s', in P. Carter, T. Jeffs, and M. Smith (eds.), *Social Work and Social Welfare Yearbook*, Milton Keynes, Open University Press.

SINGH, G. (1992), *Race and Social Work: From Black Pathology to Black Perspectives*, Bradford, Department of Social and Economic Studies, University of Bradford.

SIVANANDAN, A. (1991), 'Black Struggles against Racism', in *Setting the Context for Change*: *Northern Curriculum Development Project*, Leeds, CCETSW.

SMALL, J. W. (1984), 'The Crisis in Adoption', *International Journal of Social Psychiatry*, 30 (1): 129–42.

SMART, C. (1989), *Feminism and the Power of Law*, London, Routledge.

SMITH, D. J. (1994), 'Race, Crime and Criminal Justice', in M. Maguire, R. Morgan, and R. Reiner (eds.), *The Oxford Handbook of Criminology*, Oxford, Clarendon.

SMITH, G., and CANTLEY, C. (1985), *Assessing Health Care: A Study in Organisational Understanding*, Milton Keynes, Open University Press.

SOLOMOS, J. (1993), *Race and Racism* (2nd edn.), London, Macmillan.

——and BACK, L. (1996), *Racism and Society*, London, Routledge.

SPEED, M., and SEDDON, T. (1995), *Child Support Agency National Satisfaction Survey 1994*, Department of Social Security Research Project 39, London, HMSO.

SPICKER, P. (1988), *Principles of Welfare*, London, Routledge.

——(1993), *Poverty and Social Security*, London, Routledge.

——(1995), *Social Policy: Themes and Perspectives*, London, Harvester Wheatsheaf.

STANLEY, S. (1991), 'Studying Talk in Probation Interviews', in M. Davies, *The Sociology of Social Work*, London, Routledge.

STEINBERG, R. M., and CARTER, G. W. (1983), 'Case Management and the Elderly', in M. Payne, *Social Work and Community Care*, London, Macmillan.

STENSON, K. (1993), 'Social Work Discourse and the Social Work Interview', *Economy and Society*, 22 (1): 42–76.

STEVENS, A. (1991), *Disability Issues: Developing Antidiscriminatory Practice*, London, CCETSW.

STEVENS, P., and WILLIS, C. (1979), *Race Crime and Arrests*, Home Office Research Study 58, London, HMSO.

SULLIVAN, M. (1987), *Sociology and Social Welfare*, London, Allen & Unwin.

Sunday Times (1997), 'Tories to Privatise Social Services', 19 Jan.

SWANN, A. (1993), 'Recognition of Abuse', in H. Owen and J. Pritchard (eds.), *Good Practice in Child Protection*, London, Jessica Kingsley.

SWANN, W. (1997), *Gay, Lesbian Transgender Public Policy Issues*, New York, Harrington Park Press.

SZASZ, T. (1974), *The Myth of Mental Illness*, New York, Harper & Rowe.

TARGETT, S. (1995), 'Setback for Social Work', *THES* 6 Oct.: 11.

TATCHELL, P. (1991), 'Speech to Fringe Meeting at the National Association of Probation Officers', *NAPO News* (London, National Association of Probation Officers), 27 (Jan.): 7.

TAVANYA, J. (1992), *The Terence Higgins Trust HIV/Aids Book*, London, Thorsons.

TAYLOR, P., and BALDWIN, M. (1989), 'Travelling Hopefully: Antiracist Practice and Practice Learning Opportunities' *Social Work Education*, 10 (3): 5–32.

TAYLOR-GOOBY, P. (1991), *Social Change, Social Welfare and Social Science*, Hemel Hempstead, Harvester.

——(1994), 'Postmodernism and Social Policy: A Great Leap Backwards?', *Journal of Social Policy*, 23 (3): 385–404.

THANE, P. (1982), *The Foundations of the Welfare State*, London, Longman.

——(1984), 'The Working Class and State Welfare in Britain 1800–1914', *History Journal*, 27 (4).

THATCHER, M. (1993), *The Downing Street Years*, London, HarperCollins.

Bibliography

THOMPSON, E. P. (1968), *The Making of the English Working Class*, Harmondsworth, Penguin.

THORBURN, J. (1997), 'The Community Child Care Team', in M. Davies (ed.), *The Blackwell Guide to Social Work*, Oxford, Blackwell.

——LEWIS, A., and SHEMMINGS, D. (1995), *Paternalism or Partnership? Family Involvement in the Child Protection Process*, London, HMSO.

THORNTON, P., and LUNT, N. (1995), *Employment for Disabled People: Social Obligation or Individual Responsibility*, York, Social Policy Research Unit, University of York.

——and TOZER, R. (1995), *Having a Say in Change: Older People and Community Care*, York, Joseph Rowntree.

TIDSALL, K. (1996), 'From the Social Work Scotland Act 1968 to the Children Scotland Act 1995', in M. Hill and J. Aldgate (eds.), *Child Welfare Services*, London, Jessica Kingsley.

TILBURY, D. (1993), *Working with Mental Illness: A Community Based Approach*, London, Macmillan.

TIMMINS, N. (1995), *The Five Giants: A Biography of the Welfare State*, London, HarperCollins.

TINKER, A. (1994), 'Working with a Variety of Agencies', in C. McCreadie (ed.), *Ageing Update Conference Proceedings*, London, Age Concern, Institute of Gerontology.

TITMUS, R. (1958), *Essays on the Welfare State*, London, Allen & Unwin.

——(1968), *Commitment to Welfare*, London, Allen & Unwin.

TITMUS, R. (1970), *The Gift Relationship*, Harmondsworth, Penguin.

TOMLINSON, D. (1991), *Utopia, Community Care and the Retreat from the Asylums*, Buckingham, Open University Press.

——and CARRIER, J. (1996) (eds.), *Asylum in the Community*, London, Routledge.

TOMLINSON, S. (1982), *A Sociology of Special Education*, London, Routledge & Kegan Paul.

TOWNSEND, P. (1976), 'Seebohm and Family Welfare', in P. Townsend (ed.), *Sociology and Social Policy*, Harmondsworth, Penguin.

——(1983), 'A Theory of Poverty and the Role of Social Policy', in M. Loney, D. Boswell, and J. Clarke (eds.), *Social Policy and Social Welfare*, Milton Keynes, Open University Press.

——(1984), *Why are the many poor?*, London, Fabian Society Trust.

——(1996), *A Poor Future*, London, Lemos & Crane.

TRAVIS, A. (1996), 'Victims Get a Say in Trial of Criminals', *Guardian*, Wednesday, 19 June: 6.

Treasury (1992), 'Competing for Quality', June, London, HMSO.

TRISELIOTIS, J. (1991), 'Adoption Outcomes: A Review', in E. Hibbs (ed.), *Adoption: International Perspectives*, Madison, International Universities Press.

TWIGG, J., and ATKIN, K. (1994), *Carers Perceived: Policy and Practice in Informal Care*, Buckingham, Open University Press.

UNGERSON, C. (1997), 'Give them Money: Is Cash a Route to Empowerment?', *Social Policy and Administration*, 31 (1): 45–54.

United Nations (1982), *The Tokyo Rules: Standard Minimum Rules for Non-custodial Measures*, New York, United Nations.

UTTING, W. (1994), *Creating Community Care*, London, Mental Health Foundation.

VASS, A. A. (1996), 'Community Penalties: The Politics of Punishment', in T. May and A. A. Vass (eds.), *Working with Offenders*, London, Sage.

VON HIRSH, A. (1990), 'The Ethics of Community Based Sanctions', *Crime and Delinquency*, 36: 162–73.

Wagner Report (1988), *Residential Care: A Positive Choice*, London, HMSO.

WALKER, A. (1984), *Social Planning: A Strategy for Socialist Welfare*, Oxford, Basil Blackwell.

——(1993), 'Community Care Policy, from Consensus to Conflict', in J. Bornat, C. Pereira, D. Pilgrim, and F. Williams (eds.), *Community Care: A Reader*, Milton Keynes, Open University Press.

——and WALKER, C. (1996), *Britain Divided: The Growth of Social Exclusion in the 1980s and 1990s*, London, Child Poverty Action Group.

WALKER, M. (1988), 'The Court Disposal of Young Males by Race in London, 1983', *British Journal of Criminology*, 28(4): 281–93.

WALMSLEY, J. (1991), 'Talking to Top People: Some Issues Relating to the Citizenship of People with Learning Disabilities', *Disability, Handicap and Society*, 6 (1).

WARD, J. T. (1970), *Popular Movements 1830–1850*, London, Macmillan/St Martin's Press.

WATERHOUSE, L. (1997), 'Child Abuse', in M. Davies (ed.), *The Blackwell Companion to Social Work*, Oxford, Blackwell.

——and McGHEE, J. (1996), 'Families, Social Workers and Police Perspectives on Child Abuse Investigations', in M. Hill and J. Aldgate (eds.), *Child Welfare Services Developments in Law, Policy, Practice, and Research*, London, Jessica Kingsley.

WATTERS, C. (1996), 'Representations and Realities: Black People, Community Care and Mental Illness', in W. Ahmad and K. Atkin (eds.), *Race and Community Care*, Buckingham, Open University Press.

WEBB, A., and WISTOW, G. (1987), *Social Work, Social Care and Social Planning: The Personal Social Services after Seebohm*, London, Longman.

WEBB, D. (1991), 'Puritans and Paradigms: A Speculation on the Form of New Moralities in Social Work', *Social Work and Social Sciences Review*, 2 (2): 146–59.

WEBER, M. (1949), *The Methodology of the Social Sciences*, trans. E. Shils and A. M. Henderson, Glencoe, Ill., Free Press.

WEEKS, J. (1986), *Sexuality*, London, Routledge.

WENGER, C. (1994), *Understanding Support Networks and Community Care: Network Assessment for Elderly People*, Aldershot, Avebury.

WEIL, M. (1985), 'Key Components in Providing Efficient and Effective Services', in M. Weil and M. James, *Case Management in Human Service Practice: A Systematic Approach to Mobilising Resources for Clients*, San Francisco, Jossey Bass.

WHITE, M. (1995), 'Tory Disabled Bill Faces Competitor', *Guardian*, 25 Jan.

WHITEHEAD, S. (1992), 'The Social Origins of Normalisation', in H. Brown and H. Smith (eds.), *Normalisation: A Reader for the Nineties*, London, Routledge.

WILDING, P. (1994), 'Maintaining Quality in Human Services', *Social Policy and Administration*, 28 (1): 57–72.

WILKIN, D., and HUGHES, B. (1987), 'Residential Care of Elderly People: The Consumers' Views', *Ageing and Society*, 7: 507–26.

WILLIAMS, C. (1995), *Invisible Victims*, London, Jessica Kingsley.

WILLIAMS, F. (1989), *Social Policy: A Critical Introduction*, London, Polity.

——(1996a), 'Race Welfare and Community Care: An Historical Perspective', in W. Ahmad and K. Atkin (eds.), *'Race' and Community Care*, Buckingham, Open University Press.

——(1996b), 'Post Modernism, Feminism and the Question of Difference', in N. Parton (ed.), *Social Theory, Social Change and Social Work*, London, Routledge.

WILLIAMS, R. H. (1995), 'Contracting the Public Good: Social Movements and Cultural Resources', *Social Problems*, 42 (1): 124–44.

WILMOT, S. (1997), *The Ethics of Community Care*, London, Cassell.

Bibliography

WILSON, A. (1970), 'Chartism', in J. T. Ward (ed.), *Popular Movements 1830–1850*, London, Macmillan.

WISTOW, G., and HARDY, B. (1987), 'Transferring Care: Can Financial Incentives Work?', in A. Harrison and J. Gretton (eds.), *Health Care UK: An Economic, Social and Policy Audit*, Hemel Hempstead, Policy Journal.

————(1994), 'Community Care Planning', in N. Malin (ed.), *Implementing Community Care*, Buckingham, Open University Press.

————and LEEDHAM, I. (1993), 'Where do we Go from Here?', *Community Care*, 21 Jan.: 20–1.

——KNAPP, M., HARDY, B., and ALLEN, C. (1994), *Social Care in a Mixed Economy*, Buckingham, Open University Press.

————————FORDER, J., KENDALL, J., and MANNING, R. (1996), *Social Care Markets: Progress and Prospects*, Buckingham, Open University Press.

WITCHER, S. (1996), 'Benefit Guides Published with Warning of Cuts to Service for 20 Million Claimants', press release, London, Child Poverty Action Group.

WOLFENSBERGER, W., and THOMAS, S. (1983), 'Program, Analysis of Service Systems' Implementations of Normalisation Goals (PASSING): A Method of Evaluation in the Quality of Human Services According to the Principles of Normalisation Criteria and Ratings Manual' (2nd edn., Toronto, National Institute on Mental Retardation), in R. Means and R. Smith, *Community Care: Policy and Practice*, London, Macmillan.

WOOD, P., and BADLEY, N. (1978), 'An Epidemiological Appraisal of Disablement', in A. Bennet (ed.), *Recent Advances in Community Medicine*, London, Heinemann.

WOODHOUSE, S. (1995), 'Child Protection and Working in Partnership with Parents', in F. Kaganas, M. King, and C. Piper (eds.), *Legislating for Harmony: Partnership under the Children Act 1989*, London, Jessica Kingsley.

WOODROOFE, K. (1971), *From Charity to Social Work in England and the United States*, London, Routledge & Kegan Paul.

WORRAL, A. (1990), *Offending Women*, London, Routledge.

——(1993), 'The Contribution to Practice of Gender Perspectives in Criminology', in P. Senior and B. Williams, *Values: Gender and Offending*, Sheffield, Pavic.

YELLOLY, M. (1987), 'Why the Theory Couldn't Become Practice', *Community Care*, 29 Jan.: 18–19.

YOUNG, J. (1986), 'The Failure of Criminology: The Need for a Radical Realism', in R. Matthews and J. Young (eds.), *Confronting Crime*, London, Sage.

——(1994), 'Incessant Chatter: Recent Paradigms in Criminology', in M. Maguire, M. Morgan, and R. Reiner (eds.), *The Oxford Handbook of Criminology*, Oxford, Clarendon.

ZEDNER, L. (1994), 'Victims', in M. Maguire, R. Morgan, and R. Reiner (eds.), *The Oxford Handbook of Criminology*, Oxford, Clarendon.

INDEX

to *Social Policy and Social Work*
by David Denney

Index

Index

Index

Index

Pizzey, Erin, and domestic violence 130
place of safety orders 146
Plant, R. on users' rights 220
police,
  and black people 105
  and domestic violence 131
Police and Criminal Evidence Act (1984) 105
Police and Magistrates Courts Act (1994) 190
Police Complaints Authority 105
political correctness 54, 55, 56
Pollitt, C. on managerialism 181
Poor Law 6–7, 80, 162, 163
Poor Law Amendment Act (1834) 6–7, 10, 84–5
Poor Law Commission (1832) 6–7
Poor Law Commission (1905) 85, 142
populism 189
postmodernity, and social work 26–7, 65, 69–71, 73–4
postmodernism and women 118
Potter, Dennis, on community care 167–8
Poulantzas, N. on effects of ideology 27
poverty,
  absolute 45
  deserving and undeserving forms of 10, 46, 85
  and families 126–30, 232
  and Poor Law 6–7, 80, 162, 163
  and social policy 45–6
  and 'trickle down' effect 47
Powell, Enoch, and hospital bed closures 164–5
Powers of Criminal Courts Act (1973) 188
pressure groups,
  for child poverty 128
  for Child Support Agency 129
  for disabled 81–2
  for empowerment 91
  for the family 151–2
  for mentally ill 172, 174
Preston-Shoot, M. and Williams, J. new left
    interventionism 68
Prior, P. social worker and mental health 180
prison riots 105–6
prisons,
  and black offenders 106
  and social work practice 191
  and women offenders 122
Prisons Act (1877) 186
private sector care, for disabled people 83
Probation of Offenders Act (1907) 11, 12, 18
probation service,
  and black people 104–5
  centralized role of 189
  and disabled people 97–8
  and legislation 12, 18–19
  market effectiveness of 192–4
  and rehabilitation of offenders 188
  and training policy 19–20, 56, 235

  and victim's views 191
Property Acts (1860–1880) 115
prostitution 115
psychopharmacology 163
publication of social services information 223
'punitive bifurcation', and sentencing 189
purchaser/provider split 226, 234

Race Relations Act (1976) 52
racial discrimination; *see* discrimination
RADAR (Royal Association for Disability and
    Rehabilitation) 82
Radzinowicz Committee, on long-term prisoners 187
Ramazanoglu, C. and oppression of women 53
Ramon, S. on risk-taking in mental health cases 171
Raynor, P. on probation service 194
reductionism, in social work theory, on 25–6
Reed Committee, mentally ill offenders 175
Registered Homes Act (1984) 17
Registration of Homes Act (1984) 83
rehabilitation of offenders 188, 195
Reiner, R. on criminal justice system 104
residential care,
  for children 148–9
  comparative study of 174
  Wagner Committee (1988) on 16, 17
residential segregation 103
resources,
  and the internal market 212
  and rights to services 224–5
Review of Child Care Law 146
rights,
  of children 145
  of disabled people 80, 90
  of prisoners 188
  of psychiatric service users 174
  of victims 191–2
rights model, of empowerment 223–7
risk assessment, in mental health 171
RNIB (Royal National Institute for the Blind) 82
Rodger, J. J. social work discourse 178
Rogers, A. and Pilgrim, D.
  and concept of dangerousness 170
  and rights of psychiatric service users 174
Rojek, C. and Collins, S. and professional discourse
    26–7
Rowe, J. and Lambert, L. and child care 145
Rowntree Trust, study of income inequality 128
Royal Commission of the Poor Laws and the Relief
    of the Distressed (1905) 80–1
Runciman Commission, on suspects with learning
    difficulty 88
Ryburn, M. and adoption 155–6

Sainsbury, S. and disabled people 80, 81

Salt, Charlene, child abuse victim 147, 154
SANE 172
Scarman Report, on community and police 105
schizophrenia 177, 179
Schlesinger, P., Tumber, H. and Murdoch, G. on
 media attention 43
Seebohm Report (1968) 11
 criticisms of 13–17
 and probation training 19
 and social workers training 152, 164, 226
Seed, P. and Kaye, G. needs-led assessments 207
self-help groups 82; *see also* pressure groups
sentencing,
 alternatives to 188
 and black people 104
 suspended 187
 and twin-track strategy 189
 and women 122
service brokerage 201
severe disability allowances 84
Sex Discrimination Act (1975) 117
sex offenders 123
Sexual Offences Act (1967) 136
sexuality, and social work 135–40
Sheldon, B.
 and problem solving 226–7
 and research studies 49
 and social work evaluation 15
Short Committee, on children's rights 145–6
'short, sharp, shock' regime 25, 187, 189, 193
Sibeon, R.
 and gender of social work managers 121–2
 and reductionism 25–6
sickle cell anaemia, in black community 103
Silcock, Ben, mental health service user 170–1
single parents; *see* lone parents
Sivanandan, A. and black social workers 109
Smart, C. on nineteenth-century women's policies
 114–15
Smith, C. ideology and social work 62
Smith, D. J. on criminal justice system 104
social administration,
 definition of 30–1
 and Fabianism 31–2
 and Green issues 33–4
 and political ideology 32–3
 and social development approach 34
 and social partnership model 34
 and social policy 30–3
 and social science 36–8
social development approach 34
social oppression 91, 96, 114–15
social partnership model 34
social policy,
 and adoption 155

and black people 102–6, 110
and children 146, 148, 151–2, 152–3
and community care; *see* community care
and control theories of crime 195
and disabled 84–6, 94
and families 126–7, 131–2
and Green issues 33–4
and homosexuals 137–8
and housing 128–9
ideology and 22–7
major landmarks in 11
and mental health 161–84
and offenders 192, 193, 194
and social administration 30–3
and social development approach to 34
and social problems 35–8
and social work practice 180–1
and women 120–2, 123
social problems 35–8
social science, and social work 36–7
Social Security Act (1986) 126
Social Security (Person from Abroad) Miscellaneous
 Amendments 102
Social Services Domestic Violence Policy guidelines
 133
social work,
 and anti-racism 54–7, 107–11
 and black people 106–7
 care managers and 206–7
 and children 145, 147–50
 competency approach to 171, 176
 and disabled people 88–90
 and discourse 92–3, 177–80
 effectiveness of 118–20
 and families 131–2
 and feminism 48
 good practice in 228
 media presentation of 154–5
 and medical model ideology 175–7
 and needs-led assessment 46–7, 202, 207
 in prisons 191
 redefined 234–7
 and sexuality 138–9
social workers,
 black 107
 and black children 156–7
 and compulsory admissions 164, 166
 and disability action plan 94–5
 and men 131–2
 and mentally ill 180–1
 women 120
Speenhamland System (1795) 6
Spicker, P.
 defending Beveridge Report 121
 and human needs 42

Index